# GETTING BETTER

# GETTING BETTER

## INSIDE ALCOHOLICS ANONYMOUS

Nan Robertson

# M
MACMILLAN LONDON

First published in the United States of America 1988 by
William Morrow and Company, Inc., New York

First published in the United Kingdom 1989 by
MACMILLAN LONDON LIMITED
4 Little Essex Street London WC2R 3LF
and Basingstoke

Associated companies in Auckland, Delhi, Dublin, Gaborone,
Hamburg, Harare, Hong Kong, Johannesburg, Kuala Lumpur,
Lagos, Manzini, Melbourne, Mexico City, Nairobi, New York,
Singapore and Tokyo

ISBN 0-333-49604-3

A CIP catalogue record for this book is available
from the British Library

Designed by Richard Oriolo

Printed in Great Britain by Richard Clay Ltd, Bungay, Suffolk

Grateful acknowledgment is made for permission to reprint lines from the following:

THE ENCYCLOPEDIA OF ALCOHOLISM by Robert O'Brien and Morris Chafetz, M.D. © 1982. Reprinted with permission of Facts on File, Inc., New York.

From FIRST STEPS, LOIS REMEMBERS, AL-ANON FACES ALCOHOLISM, ONE DAY AT A TIME IN AL-ANON, used by permission. Copyright © 1965, 1968, 1979, 1986 by the Al-Anon Family Group Headquarters, Inc.

Material from the radio program series *We the People* is used with the permission of CBS, Inc., and the estate of Gabriel Heatter.

From WHAT ARE THE SIGNS OF ALCOHOLISM? THE NCA SELF TEST. Reprinted by permission of the National Council on Alcoholism, Inc.

From the American Medical Association MANUAL ON ALCOHOLISM, used by permission of the American Medical Association. Copyright © 1968, 1977.

From DRINKING IN AMERICA: A HISTORY by Mark Edward Lender and James Kirby Martin. Copyright © 1982 by The Free Press. Used by permission of the Macmillan Publishing Company.

From Ann Landers used by permission of the Los Angeles Times-Creators Syndicate.

From MARTY MANN'S NEW PRIMER ON ALCOHOLISM: HOW PEOPLE DRINK, HOW TO RECOGNIZE ALCOHOLICS, AND WHAT TO DO ABOUT THEM by Marty Mann. Copyright © 1958. Used by permission.

From THE A. A. EXPERIENCE: A CLOSE-UP VIEW FOR PROFESSIONALS by Milton A. Maxell. Copyright © 1984 by McGraw-Hill Book Company. Used by permission.

From THE DISEASE CONCEPT OF ALCOHOLISM by Sheila B. Blume, M.D. Copyright © 1983. Used by permission of the Johnson Institute. All rights reserved.

TO THE ANONYMOUS ALCOHOLICS
WHO SAVED MY LIFE

AUTHOR'S NOTE

This book is not an authorized book about Alcoholics
Anonymous. By tradition A.A. and the Al-Anon Family
Groups neither endorse nor oppose any outside opinions,
causes or books. They publish their own literature. But
I wish to thank the hundreds of anonymous individuals
who cooperated in many places and with unfailing generosity in this effort. Their anonymity is protected in these
pages. To ensure absolute privacy, the first names and
certain identifying characteristics of many current members have been changed, but their quotations and personal stories, which are specific to their lives, remain
intact.

# CONTENTS

## PART ONE

1. The Journey     15
2. Two Men     29
3. The Early Christians     56
4. A.A. Today     86
5. How A.A. Works     109
6. The God Part     138

## PART TWO

7. The Families     155
8. The Disease     183
9. The Drunk Tanks     210
10. Nan's Story     226
Afterword: Who Is an Alcoholic?     255

## APPENDICES

Where to Find Help     271
Notes and Sources     275
Acknowledgments     281

Index     285

# PART
# ONE

# 1

## THE JOURNEY

In the winter of 1987, I went back to the elegant drunk tank in Manhattan where I had gotten sober for good. This time I was a visitor and an observer, and what I saw was the woman I had been eleven years before. I saw, truly and for the first time, what alcohol had made of me. I saw what I had done to myself. It was the patients, fresh from the bottle, who held the mirror up to me in what they said and did and how they looked. I remembered Nan, the Nan of November 1975.

I had come there with some shine and sparkle left on the surface. Inside I was empty: a self-deluding, frightened, successful, charming, pathetic fraud. In that place—the Rehabilitation Unit of the Smithers Alcoholism Center—I began the search for the Nan that I hoped would still be there, somewhere in the void, and for something better. It took years to find me. It will take all the time I have left. But Smithers began the process, and Alcoholics Anonymous continued it and is continuing it to this day.

In Smithers, I began by telling my mother the truth. Sort of. But let me tell you what happened.

I was expected to spend Thanksgiving of 1975 with her at home in Illinois, as I had often done before. But I would not complete my twenty-eight-day treatment inside Smithers until early December. I had planned to lie to her, to tell her that I was being sent on an assignment elsewhere in the country over the Thanksgiving weekend. It is easy to make such social excuses if you are a newspaper reporter. But my counselor and my therapy group of Smithers patients were adamant. You are finally getting honest with yourself and others, they said. You cannot lie to your mother.

"But she is eighty-three years old!" I pleaded. "She was born in Victorian times. She'll never understand. I can't say I am an alcoholic. This will kill her!"

"For Chrissakes," said a longshoreman in the group. "So don't tell her you're an alcoholic. Tell her you're a problem drinker."

I went sweating with apprehension into the patients' telephone booth and called Mother. I told her I could not come home for Thanksgiving. Oozing counterfeit charm, I went on, "Oh, Mother, I am in the most *wonderful* place with the most *wonderful* people. There are stockbrokers here from Yale, and welfare mothers, and accountants like yourself and . . ."

My mother came back like a shot: "Is that a place for alcoholics?"

"Wellll, Mother," I said, "Wellll, yes, there are some problem drinkers among us, and . . ."

"Oh, Nan darling," my mother said, "you've made me so happy. I've worried about your drinking for years."

Tears came to my eyes. I have never loved my mother more.

Time passed. Life passed. I got better, one day at a time, first at Smithers, then in Alcoholics Anonymous. Sometimes I got worse. I kept going to A.A. meetings. I saw wrecks turning back into human beings and rejoiced in their recovery and mine.

And then one day in 1983, with eight years in A.A. and more than a thousand meetings behind me across the United States and abroad, I went to see Lois Wilson.

Lois, then in her early nineties, was the living link to the co-founder of Alcoholics Anonymous, her husband, Bill Wilson. She had seen A.A. grow from two men in 1935 to almost two million men and women around the world in the 1980's. She herself was the co-founder of the Al-Anon movement for the families of alcoholics, which had begun as a closed society—an auxiliary only for the wives of men sober in A.A.—and had grown to an international organization of half a million members.

Lois sat on a chintz-covered sofa in the sun-drenched living room of the Wilson home in rolling, wooded Bedford Hills, New York, a tiny husk of a woman with snapping brown eyes and an aureole of wispy white hair. Near her at the side of the huge stone fireplace hung an oil painting of her husband copied from a photograph. Under it was a table with a candle and a slender vase of red carnations. Out of the little body came a voice that was surprisingly deep and strong. She welcomed me, and I began to tell her why I had come.

"I want to write a book that gives an inside view of Alcoholics Anonymous," I blurted out. "I want to demystify it." I told her I'd read all the A.A. literature, but I'd never found anything quite like this. I wanted to pull it all together, I said, to write about not just the lives of Bill and Dr. Bob—Dr. Robert Holbrook Smith, the other founder—and the early years in A.A., but what it's like today, in all its enormous scope and diversity, and how the membership has changed, and how A.A. works and perhaps why it works, if I could. "Nobody," I said, "has really told outsiders before what part religion plays and does not play in A.A., which I think is the biggest misconception people have about us—some people think we're a bunch of religious nuts."

By this time Lois was nodding her head. I rushed on. I told her I wanted to bring readers inside A.A. meetings to show them what goes on there, to try to portray the foxhole humor as well as the drama that knits members together. "That's a good idea," Lois said. "Nobody seems to understand the fun we have. People think alcoholics without drinks have to be gloomy. What else?"

And then, I said, there should be one chapter on Al-Anon and the families of alcoholics, and maybe another on the disease of alcoholism and perhaps one on the intensive alcoholism rehabs, because so many new members were coming from them into A.A. I was beginning to run out of steam.

Lois looked at me sharply. "Are you going to write this book under your full name?"

I said yes.

"Are you going to say that you're a member of A.A.?," she asked. "Remember, this is an anonymous program."

I blushed and said, "I don't know. I'm a reporter as well as an alcoholic; I don't think I should cheat the reader by not being completely honest." I told her that I thought the book would be much more authentic and believable if I revealed that I was in A.A. I said that everybody else in A.A. I wrote about would be protected. I added, "I think the disclosure of my own affiliation should be a matter between me and my own conscience."

Lois frowned. She reminded me that the eleventh A.A. Tradition warns against breaking even one's own anonymity at the public level, in print or broadcasts. No wonder she remembered. Her husband wrote it.

We fell into an uncomfortable silence. Then Lois smiled. She said, "It's high time for such a book."

With that conversation, my journey began.

For the next three and a half years I crisscrossed the United States, where half of all the members of Alcoholics Anonymous live. There was a detour to Mexico, which has the biggest A.A. contingent outside the U.S. I went back to A.A.'s roots in Akron, Ohio, the city where Bill Wilson met Dr. Bob. I talked to A.A. old-timers everywhere who remembered what it was like in the

1930's, when A.A. was a secret little band of shakily sobered-up drunks who didn't even have a name for their new club and who, on their knees, had surrendered to God and their powerlessness over alcohol.

I saw the A.A. of today: the 3,000 recovered alcoholics, festively dressed, who attended the annual Bill W. banquet at the New York Hilton, dancing and table-hopping and having an uproarious time on nothing stronger than Coca-Cola, coffee or club soda. I saw the 44,000 members who streamed into Montreal from all over the world in July 1985 to celebrate the fiftieth birthday of Alcoholics Anonymous. It was the biggest convention the city had ever seen, and the best-behaved, and the Montrealers were stunned by the tons of ice cream those people put away.

I traveled empty stretches of the American West, where members had to cope with the fact that the closest town and A.A. meeting were a two hours' drive away. At four o'clock one morning I sat in an isolated ranch house as a woman put on tape cassettes to hear alcoholics tell their stories at meetings in far-off places. "It's a comfort to me when I can't sleep," she said. She subscribed to one of the underground tape services that specializes in recording A.A. meetings all over the country: Members exchange favorite tapes ("Wait till you hear this one!") with a relish that recalls little kids swapping comic books. We heard Dan O., a stellar speaker, Irish, from the South Bronx, now a judge, describing his first beer at the age of fourteen: "I loved the look of it. I loved the smell of it and the taste of it. I loved the bar and the fights and the bullshit." We heard Jim, a California doctor: "My wife and I lived in Anaheim and we went to meetings down in Laguna Beach, about forty-five miles away. We had to go down so we wouldn't run into anybody we knew. We went there; got hooked on the meetings down there; went there long enough until I ran into everybody that goes to Laguna Beach so they won't run into anybody they know." He told how he resisted the meetings at first: "I was making a list of reasons why I wasn't really, really, really, *really* an alcoholic. And I had a list of things that you had done that I hadn't done and how I was different from you. And then some guy raised his hand and said of himself, 'I was judging me by my intentions, and the world was judging me by my actions.' And I was sorry he said that." Laughter rolled off these tapes, the laughter of people who knew every delusion and every dodge. It is a sound that echoes throughout A.A.—understanding laughter.

Snapshots from my journey:

**Nocona, Texas.** Population 2,992. On the northern edge of the state. Heat and dust. One could see forever across those limitless plains. In Nocona, the nosier inhabitants' favorite amusement was to drive by the church Monday nights to see whose cars were parked outside the A.A. meeting. Here lived "Young Bob," the only son of Dr. Robert Holbrook Smith, the co-founder of Alcoholics Anonymous. Young Bob was in his sixties, a large, friendly man, a retired oil producer. He was seventeen years old that Sunday in May 1935 when he drove with his father and his mother, Anne, up to Henrietta Seiberling's little gatehouse on the Seiberling estate in Akron, Ohio. Young Bob is one of only two people still alive who were in that house that day, the day Dr. Bob met Bill Wilson, a self-styled "rum hound" from New York who had found a way to stay sober. Their six-hour conversation, alone in Mrs. Seiberling's library, led to the founding of Alcoholics Anonymous and a friendship between the two men that deepened and endured until Dr. Bob's death in 1950.

Young Bob remembered the early gatherings of alcoholics in Akron, in the Smith house on Ardmore Avenue during the Great Depression. Everybody was so poor that for the alcoholic men and their long-suffering wives the main dish at supper was often potato salad or bread and milk. Anne Smith, the first mother of A.A., a heavy, shy woman, gathered guests in her arms, made them feel at home, served them endless pots of Eight O'Clock Coffee, moved her children out of their beds to put the drunks in, read the Bible with them mornings, and was once chased around her own kitchen by a knife-wielding boarder when he fell off the wagon. "And Sue, my adopted sister, and I were the first Alateens," said Young Bob, "the first children of alcoholics in A.A., even though there wasn't any Alateen then."

Today, pictures of Young Bob's lantern-jawed father and Bill Wilson hang in hundreds of thousands of A.A. meeting rooms around the world. Some revere these two men as saints. This is not surprising when you consider the lives, directly and indirectly, they have saved.

**Akron, Ohio.** Rubber tire capital of the world. Two great American fortunes were amassed in this city, those of the Firestones and of the Seiberlings. To me it had the look of yesterday, of early auto-age prosperity gone to seed. If Alcoholics Anonymous has a Holy Ground, it is here.

I toured all the shrines, known only to the initiated in A.A.: the Mayflower Hotel, where Bill Wilson, struggling to overcome a rage to drink, telephoned Henrietta Seiberling on a May weekend in 1935. The gabled Tudor gatehouse on the fringes of the Seiberling estate, where Henrietta introduced Bill Wilson to Dr. Bob Smith and the two founders of A.A. had their first, and historic, conversation. The Smith home with its roomy porch at 855 Ardmore Avenue, where Dr. Bob hid his liquor supply in the coal bin and later sat up long nights in the kitchen with his new friend, Bill, smoking cigarettes, drinking coffee and figuring out how to sober up other drunks. City Hospital, where Bob smuggled raving alcoholics into private rooms (in those days, no general hospital in America accepted alcoholics, and what they suffered and died from was not diagnosed as a disease but branded as a weakness and a disgrace).

There was the house once owned by Clarace and T. Henry Williams, among the earliest nonalcoholic friends of A.A., where the first Akron meetings were held. The wives waited downstairs while the men (there were only men in A.A. then and for years thereafter) stood over the recruit kneeling in the bedroom, hearing his litany of drunken sins and his plea for redemption. The red-brick King School, the first public building to house an A.A. meeting, still stood. And there was the grave. The plain granite stone over the bodies of Robert Holbrook Smith and Anne Robinson Ripley Smith in Mount Peace Cemetery was inscribed only with their names and dates of birth and death.

The June I went to Akron for the annual Founders' Day weekend, thousands of tourists from around the United States and abroad were visiting the Smiths' grave and trundling in awed busloads past the other A.A. shrines. Meetings were held almost nonstop around the campus of the University of Akron, and there was a brisk business in meeting tapes and A.A. souvenirs. A.A. slogans—ONE DAY AT A TIME; KEEP IT SIMPLE—festooned bumpers and dormitory windows. At a big meeting in a gymnasium the crowds gave standing ovations to the most famous A.A. family in Ohio: five brothers and a father who all found sobriety in A.A. One by one the brothers had come in. The father had been the last to join.

The local headquarters puts out a pamphlet listing highlights of the A.A. historic tour. It includes a photograph of an icon of sorts, a homey, comforting object; underneath the photo is a caption that reads: "Anne Smith's coffeepot."

**The Flatiron Building, Fifth Avenue, New York.** A wedge-shaped antique skyscraper, an architectural curiosity that points north at Madison Square and Twenty-third Street. In Room 219 is the office of New York Intergroup. This is the A.A. nerve center for the entire New York area, open from 9 A.M. to 10 P.M., six days a week, from noon on Sundays. The recovered alcoholics at the phones are ready to direct a caller to the nearest A.A. meeting or promptly find another A.A. member who will see or telephone an alcoholic in need. For many, Intergroup is their first contact with A.A. Intergroups, simply listed as "Alcoholics Anonymous," can be found in the telephone books of every big city in the United States and Canada and many cities overseas.

The day I worked at Intergroup, Chuck was in charge of the office. It was a long, narrow, somewhat seedy room in institutional tan with windows along two walls, rows of desks and the ever-present A.A. coffee urn in a corner. One man was stationed at the Hospital Desk, which deals with seriously ill alcoholics who need to go to a hospital for detoxification—medically supervised withdrawal from alcohol. On the walls at the back were huge maps of the five boroughs of New York and all the surrounding counties;

hundreds of little paper flags on pins with the names of A.A. groups on them were stuck at their appropriate sites all over the maps. Manhattan had the most meetings—almost 1,000 every week.

Chuck gave me and Lenny, the other neophyte at Intergroup that day, a briefing about some possible situations: If a man called about his mother, we were to suggest that he phone Al-Anon, which is for the families of alcoholics, since the caller himself was not the alcoholic but kin. Legally, we could not do anything to help the alcoholic herself, the man's mother, unless she asked for it. Chuck said many wives called for help for their alcoholic husbands—again, they had to be referred to Al-Anon—but few husbands phoned about their alcoholic wives. "Men think there's something sissy about asking for help," he said, and shrugged. He told how, the Saturday before, eight callers in a row would not give even their first names or telephone numbers so that a Twelve-Stepper could call back and follow up. (A Twelve-Stepper is an A.A. member who responds to an emergency cry from an active alcoholic and takes that person to a nearby meeting as soon as possible.) We leafed through thick books that gave up-to-date information on what meetings were where and included the names and phone numbers of all current officers and members in each group who were willing to give emergency counseling to alcoholics.

My heart was pounding and I was trembling slightly as Chuck spoke about all the vituperative, impatient drunks who call Intergroup. He allayed my nervousness by saying that if we didn't succeed in giving an alcoholic a phone contact and getting him or her to a meeting, we shouldn't blame ourselves. "Don't despair," he said, "and don't take this home with you."

My first call. It was Claire. A burly man at another desk had switched her over to me because that day I was the only woman at the office. I answered as I had been instructed: "Good afternoon, this is A.A., may I help you?" Claire was slurring her words. She told me she had been in A.A. for twelve or fourteen months—she couldn't remember which—and I thought she was saying she was at a subway station at West 126th Street. She said she had had a quart to drink the night before and another quart that morning.

"Claire, I can't talk to you while you're drunk in a subway station," I told her. "Go home, get some sleep, call us tomorrow when you're sober."

"I got to see somebody!" she shouted. "You send some fuckin' body over right away to talk to me!"

I told her it was no good now, I was just talking to the bottle, not her. The man at the next desk nodded approvingly. The coin dropped in Claire's pay phone.

"I'm not in a subway station!" she shrieked. "I'm in a fuckin' *sobering-up* station at West 126th! I'm in a hospital! Get me outta here!" A man came on the phone. He was Fred, at the Central Harlem Sobering Up Station. "Now Claire," he told her gently, "I got the A.A. number right here. You call tomorrow, when your head has cleared up some and you can talk better." I thanked Fred and hung up, drenched with sweat.

This place was the knife edge of desperation.

**Mexico City.** It was Christmastime. Pinwheels, stars, candles and FELIZ NAVIDAD! signs flashed red, blue, green and yellow from the ancient arcaded buildings, and the brilliance stabbed into the night. Streams of cars zoomed around the Zócalo, the gargantuan central square. Filling the north end was the cathedral, encrusted with the accumulated stone decorations of centuries. Beggars and peddlers accosted passersby.

Inside, a wedding mass being celebrated. A young bride and her groom knelt at the altar; in the drafty cavern, her long tulle veil had drifted like a snowfall across his shoulders. I had been told that an A.A. meeting was held here every Wednesday evening. I tried every side door, looking in vain for an A.A. sign on the doorknobs, the walls. I went out and around to the back, stumbling over rough pavement in darkness the blazing Zócalo did not penetrate. Above me there was one lighted window, illuminating a tiny, hand-painted placard that said "A.A." Through the unlocked door underneath was the priests' robing room, stacked with surplices and gleaming holy vessels. The high altar could be glimpsed at the right through an open door. The mass went on.

Ahead was another open door, where the Cathedral Group of

A.A. met. I was early, and there was only Francisco to greet me. I responded in my primitive Spanish, saying that I was an alcoholic from New York. Pictures of Bill Wilson and Dr. Bob hung on the wall. There were A.A. slogans in Spanish and another welcoming sign:

HERE WE LOVE EACH OTHER, BELIEVE IN EACH
OTHER, HOPE FOR EACH OTHER.

People wandered in, said "*Hola!*" with hugs and thumps on the back. The atmosphere was noisy, merry, like a cantina bar. "*Mi nombre es Nan, soy de Nueva York, y soy alcohólica!*" I said, and they embraced me and pressed my hands with both of theirs. One young man filled Styrofoam cups with coffee and passed them around on a tray with hard candies. Organ music came faintly through the door, and whiffs of incense. There was the tinkle of a bell as, only yards away, the priest raised the Host.

The meeting began. I realized I was the only woman in a roomful of dark, vivid, callous-palmed men—the evidence in flesh of the statistics that Alcohólicos Anónimos in Mexico, with 250,000 members, is overwhelmingly male and working-class. Each man stepped to the lectern and told his story. Each told of the terrible things he had done in his drinking life to his wife, his sainted mother, his daughters. Each spoke of the beauty of today. Each gazed at me as he spoke. I felt like the Virgin of Guadalupe.

**Rancho Mirage, California.** Driving to the top of a wrinkled mountain range, purple in the morning light. Below lay Palm Springs, Palm Desert, Rancho Mirage: fountains, bright flowers, lawns like putting greens in the midst of a hostile desert. Bob Hope Drive crossed streets named after Frank Sinatra and Dinah Shore. A.A. groups outnumbered the golf courses two to one: fifty of them, meeting weekly. They were named Early Birds, Candlelight Beginners, There Is a Solution. Dolls of the Valley, a popular women's group, gathered every Wednesday at Hope Lutheran Church's Fellowship Hall.

I sat with Betty Ford, the wife of the thirty-eighth President of the United States, a recovering pill addict and alcoholic, in the soothing beige and pink interior of the intensive rehabilitation center named after her. She is a vital part of that center, informing and inspiring patients by her own example of steadfastness and honesty. "I was in a little euphoria of my own once," she said, "functioning but less than aware."

Just before her sixtieth birthday, in April 1978, her children and her husband, Gerald Ford, only fourteen months out of the White House, confronted her. With them was Dr. Joseph Pursch, then head of the Long Beach Naval Hospital's Alcohol and Drug Rehabilitation Service. He had carefully rehearsed the family, all its members armed with written lists detailing specific instances of Mrs. Ford's drugged, drunk behavior as each had experienced it.

The President recalled times she had fallen asleep in a chair, her blurry speech, her memory lapses. Her son Mike and his wife told her why they hadn't wanted to have a child—because they didn't want it to have a grandmother who was not there for the baby. Another son, Steve, remembered bringing a new girlfriend home and cooking dinner for his mother while Mrs. Ford slipped into a haze in front of the TV with one drink, two drinks, three. "You hurt me," Steve said.

Mrs. Ford collapsed in a storm of weeping and shock. But, she said, she had enough sense left to realize her family was doing this because they loved her and wanted to help. She entered the Long Beach hospital for treatment and issued a statement to a stunned nation. She confessed to "overmedicating" herself: "It's an insidious thing, and I mean to rid myself of the damaging effects." But she resisted any suggestion that liquor was also a major problem. Dr. Pursch ordered her to read the basic text that Bill Wilson had written for A.A., known informally as the Big Book. Just substitute "chemically dependent" for the word "alcoholic," he told her. Mrs. Ford comforted herself with the thought that she never needed to take a drink in the morning to stop the shakes. She found people who knocked back Bloody Marys well before lunch "pathetic." She could admit to the pills, prescribed for arthritis, a pinched nerve, muscle spasms in her neck. After all, the doctors had done it to her. She could not face the alcoholism—because that meant she had done it to herself.

Finally, after further treatment at Long Beach, with her husband's assurance that it would not embarrass him, she issued another statement: "I have found that I am not only addicted to the medications I have been taking for my arthritis but also to alcohol. I expect this treatment and fellowship to be a solution for my problem, and I embrace it not only for me but for all the others who are here to participate." I said to Mrs. Ford that it was hard enough for ordinary people to confess they are drunks and then set about to rebuild their lives. "I think it was my bravest act," I told her. "What it must have been like for a President's wife?"

She replied, "Granted, I had the advantage of being the wife of a former President, which put me, in the eyes of others, in a special place. But I never could have found recovery if I thought myself to be in a special place. I am just another recovering woman."

**Kent, Connecticut.** New Year's Eve. A faded, peeling sign pointed up a steep hill four miles north of Kent, a New England village on Connecticut's western edge. HIGH WATCH, the sign said. A plain, eighteenth-century farmhouse, painted white. A scattering of red clapboard outbuildings. In the old days, said Tom S., the manager, a recovered alcoholic like everyone on the staff, "They used to trundle the drunks with the D.T.'s in a wheelbarrow to the farthermost shack. We called it the Leper Colony."

This was High Watch Farm, the oldest retreat and rest house based on A.A. principles. High Watch was a continent and a world away from glamorous Rancho Mirage, its press releases, its "Serenity Room" with the artificial waterfall that alcoholics and addicts could contemplate from a pink-carpeted amphitheater, its state-of-the-art recovery programs and its heated swimming pool. At High Watch, the most vigorous sports were shoveling snow in the winter and playing croquet and horseshoes in the summer.

There, alcoholics who were seventy-two hours or twenty-five years away from their last drink had to go to daily A.A. meetings and 11 A.M. chapel, a "spiritual but not religious" half hour held in one of the cozy, low-beamed rooms. These were the only rules. Everybody pitched in: to vacuum the hooked rugs, clear and set tables, wash dishes, stack chairs.

High Watch was founded in 1939, the year Bill Wilson wrote the Big Book and Alcoholics Anonymous got its name. It was also the year of his first visit there. It was called Joy Farm then. A rich woman named Mrs. Ethelred Helling ran it as a shelter for homeless men; a lantern was lighted every night to guide travelers to its door. Early members of A.A. came to that place. They saw it as a kind of halfway house, somewhere to spend time healing and talking to others like themselves before entering the world again and once more confronting temptation beckoning from every bar. Mrs. Helling was interested in religion and the supernatural. She renounced her money and her name and tried to emulate the life of Saint Francis of Assisi by giving her all to the poor. She called herself Sister Francis.

"Bill Wilson came with Marty Mann," Tom, the manager, said, referring to the first woman to get permanently sober in A.A., "and they sat down with Sister Francis in 1939 and found they had something in common. Sister Francis was able to embrace the notion that alcoholism was a disease. Her grandparents would have rolled over in their graves at the idea of giving over the farm to a bunch of alcoholics. To them and to most people even in 1939, drunkenness was a sin."

Bill and Marty persuaded Sister Francis to turn her farm into a nonprofit corporation called the Ministry of High Watch. It is not owned by A.A., for A.A. owns no property, runs no business, accepts no money from any outsider and refuses all large gifts and bequests even from its members.

"Bill came here many times," Tom said. "He talked about A.A. He sat in that chair. It sends chills up my spine."

I spent New Year's Eve and New Year's Day and the second day of 1987 at High Watch with my own kind: alcoholics, all of us. It seemed the best place to be quiet, to think back on a long journey, to thank God, as I do every day, for my life.

# 2

## TWO MEN

"It was there—in our house—where the spark was ignited that led to A.A."

—Dorothy Seiberling, daughter of the woman who brought A.A.'s founders together

Bill Wilson told the story of his drunkenness and his salvation thousands of times to other alcoholics, always leading his listeners on to the key moments in Akron, Ohio, that changed his life forever. It was a Saturday in May 1935. He was dying for a drink. As he walked agitatedly back and forth across the lobby of the Mayflower Hotel in Akron, he was gripped by a frenzy of longing, away from his home and his wife in New York, alone at the tail end of yet another doomed business venture. Wilson was a Wall Street hustler, a margin trader with grand dreams who had failed at every job he ever had. He was thirty-nine years old. He was a recently sobered-up drunk. Only months before, he had been panhandling on the streets, stealing from his wife's purse, falling down stairs, lying in his own vomit, accosting strangers in the New York subway to tell them that religion was "pious shit." His wife, Lois, the steady breadwinner during seventeen years of marriage, had been reaching the end of her patience as he entered the drying-out hospital in Manhattan for the fourth time. He had been discharged in December of 1934. For five months he had managed to stay sober by helping other drunks and attending meetings of the Oxford Group, an international movement that preached a return to the simple faith of the early Christians.

There was little for a stranger to do in Akron on a Saturday except go to the movies; Ginger Rogers and Fred Astaire were playing in *Roberta* at the nearby Rialto, but sitting solitarily in the dark with celluloid companions was not Wilson's idea of fun. He told of how he heard bursts of laughter and chatter from the bar at one end of the Mayflower lobby. He thought: Why not sit there with a bottle of ginger ale? He had been sober for months. Or perhaps he could handle three drinks—no more. Then he thought: "God, I am going to get drunk." For the first time as a sober man, he panicked.

Bill's recounting of this scene and all the events of the crucial weeks that followed form part of the oral history and shared legend of Alcoholics Anonymous. It is like A.A.'s own Christmas story, familiar and loved, which never palls in the retelling. As Bill did, all of us in A.A. have told our own stories repeatedly over the years in meetings and to those outside still drinking whom we wish to help and comfort. Two people are left alive who saw and heard directly or were told by their parents—the protagonists of the drama—much of what happened that weekend in Akron. Both were teenagers then. Their detailed memories, evoked in long interviews with this author, reinforced and expanded Bill's tale.

Wilson knew there where only two ways for a drunk to go in

the America of the 1930's if the family wouldn't take care of him or he couldn't afford a "drink cure" in a fancy sanitarium—to the drunk tank in jail or to the insane asylum. In those days and for years thereafter, alcoholics who wound up in the loony bin were locked in wards with criminal psychopaths, terminal syphilitics and those afflicted with senile dementia. Nobody knew what else to do with them. Besides, people believed, it was their own fault, these weak-willed lushes. Many members of the clergy, unlike those working in the Oxford Groups, thought drunkenness was a sin. But Wilson had been told by the doctor who ran the drying-out hospital where he had at last gotten sober—his bills paid by his brother-in-law—that alcoholism was an "allergy," a sickness over which alcoholics had no control.

In the hospital one day, Wilson experienced an overwhelming religious exaltation that might have been the result of hallucinations during his withdrawal from alcohol. Whatever it was, he came out of it believing in God for the first time in his life and thinking that there was hope for his condition. He soon became obsessed with helping other drunks. Working with them during the months that followed his last hospital stay convinced him that what he needed to do to keep from drinking was to talk to another drunk. Now, a stranger in Akron, he fled the sound of laughter from the hotel bar and went to the church directory posted at the other end of the lobby, seeking a clergyman who might be in the Oxford Group. He picked up the telephone and made his first call—to an Episcopal minister he chose at random. Wilson was amused by the name: Walter Tunks. Tunks, it turned out, was not in the Oxford Group. But he did have many friends who were members. He gave Bill the names and numbers of about ten of them. But when he phoned them, all had other plans. Wilson was becoming frantic. The last man, explaining he was going out of town that night, suggested Wilson call Henrietta Seiberling. His first words to here were: "I'm from the Oxford Group, and I'm a rum hound from New York."

Henrietta Seiberling was not an alcoholic, but she was an enthusiastic member of the Oxford Group, from which many alcoholics were beginning to derive strength and hope. She was a well-bred Kentuckian, a Vassar graduate, a lifelong seeker after the things of the spirit. She had married a son of Frank A. Seiberling, the founder and first president of the Goodyear Tire and Rubber Company, but her husband had abandoned her and their three adolescent children. She was forty-seven years old. Snubbed and condescended to by her rich and socially prominent relatives, she had found solace in Oxford meetings; they gave her an outlet for her spiritual yearnings and her wish to serve others, and a new direction, away from her marital and money problems. At a meeting two years before, she had met Dr. Robert Holbrook Smith and his wife, Anne. She had grown to love them. But she was worried sick about Dr. Smith's drinking, his slipping medical practice, the snickers behind his back. He was a proctologist and rectal surgeon, and now his colleagues at City Hospital were saying, "When you go to Dr. Smith, you *really* bet your ass!"

Henrietta was bent on saving her drunken doctor friend. But she never drank much herself and did not understand his compulsion. He had already confessed his drinking problem to the Oxford Group and had had long private conversations with the sympathetic "Henri" about it. But nothing—not the advice and support he received in Oxford meetings in private homes, or the churchgoing, or the Bible readings, or his own desire to stop, or a series of "cures" in sanitariums—was helping him. So on Saturday, May 11, 1935, when Henrietta got the telephone call from the New Yorker who said he needed to talk to another drunk in order to preserve his own shaky sobriety, her first thought was: "This is like manna from heaven." Acting on an inspired hunch, she told the stranger to come right away to her house. Her next thought was to bring Bill Wilson and Bob Smith together.

Henrietta was a handsome woman with captivating ways and a magnolia skin who put a brave face on her struggles to survive and raise three children. She was also a bit of a snob. Despite her estrangement from her husband, the Seiberling family had allowed her to stay on in the gatehouse of their great estate, called Stan Hywet. To this day, the little brick and half-timbered Tudor house with its tiny-paned windows, snuggled under a steeply pitched roof of mock thatch, looks as if it had popped out from under a toadstool in the Cotswolds. When the tall, awkward Wilson slouched over her doorstep that Saturday and proceeded to make himself much too readily at home, Henrietta was appalled. She found him both vulgar and servile, with a smarmy grin; he was loud and garrulous. She disliked him on sight. Years later she described Wilson as he was then: "Bill stood hunched over, and was dressed in ill-fitting and unmatched clothes. He laughed too loudly, and showed too many teeth even when talking. He had this mannerism of rubbing his hands together and a simpering smile—a regular Uriah Heep."

Her youngest child, Dorothy, then thirteen, was there. "I remember when he phoned and how ecstatic Mother was," Dorothy said. "Bill came in the middle of the afternoon and stayed right through for dinner. He was this big, tall, lanky person, with huge feet. I remember his stretching out on a chair, that great long creature."

Nonetheless, Henrietta saw in this lout the savior of Dr. Smith. Nobody else in his right mind would have thought those two men would hit it off. Dr. Smith was an intimidating man, commandingly tall and erect, who struck new acquaintances as gruff, formal and taciturn. He was then fifty-five years old, sixteen years older than Wilson. "He had a very stern look to begin with," his son, Bob, said. "He had icy blue eyes that could just look right through you." The doctor's daughter, now Suzanne Smith Windows, compared those eyes, when her father was displeased, to "a couple of ice cubes."

But Henrietta was a strong-willed person. She was also mystically inclined, with a faith that comes through powerfully in the diaries and marked-up meditation books Dorothy Seiberling kept. Her mother, despite her initial distaste for Wilson, did not swerve from the conviction that Divine Providence had somehow sent the stranger to help her friend Bob. That afternoon she got on the phone to invite the Smiths to dinner to meet him. "It was the day before Mother's Day and I had come home plastered, carrying a big potted plant which I had set down on the table," the doctor later wrote, "and forthwith went upstairs and passed out." A mortified Anne apologized to her friend.

Henrietta called the Smiths again the next day, Sunday, with a second dinner invitation. Dr. Smith was suffering from a shattering hangover and was reluctant to go. "Wishing to be polite, though I felt very badly, I said, 'Let's make the call,' " Dr. Smith remembered. Then he extracted a promise from his wife: "A promise that we would not stay over fifteen minutes." They drove to the Seiberling gatehouse in their old Cadillac with their son, Bob, then seventeen. They arrived at 5 P.M.

Describing his meeting with Dr. Smith, Bill Wilson told how Smith was "shaking badly" and obviously ill at ease. Wilson was nervous too. What could he tell this medical doctor about drinking, or staying away from it? "Though embarrassed, he brightened a little when I said I thought he needed a drink," Wilson recalled. After dinner, which the doctor picked at, Henrietta put the two men into her library for a little talk. Wilson and Smith talked there until 11:15 P.M. They had spent six hours together, most of it alone. No one will ever know exactly what they said to each other. But each told the gist of it later, in countless conversations with other alcoholics. It is clear that the dialogue between the two men who became the founders of Alcoholics Anonymous set a pattern that has been followed since by millions of drunks all over the world, desperate to be well.

There could not have been just one founder of A.A. There had to be two, because the essence of the process is one person telling his story to another as honestly as he knows how. Bob Smith, never the talker or writer that Bill Wilson was, nonetheless was the one who seemed to understand that meeting best. Years later he wrote:

The question which might naturally come into your mind would be: "What did the man do or say that was different from what others had done or said?" It must be remembered that I had read a great deal and talked to everyone who knew, or thought they knew, anything about the subject of alcoholism.

This man was a man who had experienced many years of frightful drinking, who had had most all the drunkard's experiences known to man, but who had been cured by the very means I had been trying to employ, that is to say, the spiritual approach. He gave me information about the subject of alcoholism which was undoubtedly helpful.

The doctor italicized the following sentences: *"Of far more importance was the fact that he was the first living human with whom I had ever talked, who knew what he was talking about in regard to alcoholism from actual experience. In other words, he talked my language."* Dr. Smith went on, "He knew all the answers, and certainly not because he had picked them up in his reading."

Despite their personality differences, the two men had some things in common. Both of them rawboned and about six feet two inches tall, they had been attractive in youth and were impressive in middle age. They were Anglo-Saxon Protestants, middle-class to the core, and political and economic conservatives. In his drunken years, Wilson wrote angry letters to the man he loathed in the White House, Franklin Delano Roosevelt; sober, he stopped the hate mail but remained convinced that Roosevelt was a menace, and Dr. Smith agreed. Both were compassionate men, generous in sharing what they had. But their special bond was one of identical, remembered suffering. In addition, Wilson had saved Smith's life on that day in May 1935. Men in war—indeed, anyone who has lived through a particularly intense and frightening experience with others—can understand this bond of memory and gratitude. It is perpetuated endlessly in A.A.

Bill Wilson and Bob Smith were dramatically different, however, in many ways. Wilson was a name-dropper who sought out friends among the rich and super-achieving and was fascinated by success, money and power—quite an irony for the founder of an organization that shuns all three. A promoter and a dreamer with intellectual pretensions who had never been able to complete his formal education, he indulged in overstatement and fantasy. He was uncomfortable with the unadorned truth and felt compelled to embroider it. He became the idea man of Alcoholics Anonymous. A great talker, he could dominate conversations. His moods could swing violently, from extreme optimism to despair. Beginning at the age of seventeen, he suffered crippling bouts of depression. The final and most prolonged, which came on a decade after he had become sober, went on for eleven years, until 1955.

Wilson's marriage to Lois Burnham in 1918 lasted until his death at the age of seventy-five in 1971. She believed in him fiercely and tended his flame. Yet, particularly during his sober decades in A.A. in the forties, fifties and sixties, Bill Wilson was a compulsive womanizer. His flirtations and his adulterous behavior filled him with guilt, according to old-timers close to him, but he continued to stray off the reservation. His last and most serious love affair, with a woman at A.A. headquarters in New York, began when he was in his sixties. She was important to him until the end of his life, and was remembered in a financial agreement with A.A. This affair, and experiments in spiritualism, LSD and megavitamin therapy, scandalized A.A. trustees and other veterans in the home office. Some felt Wilson was not upholding the high ideals of the organization and was muddying its singleness of purpose and peddling crackpot ideas to a membership that worshiped him. But his qualities of generosity, openness to change and humility about his own shortcomings were particularly endearing. "I never heard him bitch about anybody," said a man who joined A.A. in the 1940's and was one of its first homosexual members. "It wouldn't have mattered if I was a cannibal. He was delighted by eccentricities. His attitude was, 'Here's one of the camels that wandered into our tent! Aren't people wonderful?' "

Another said, "As a failed human I couldn't stand it if I thought Bill hadn't failed. I couldn't live up to a perfect example."

Dr. Bob, as he has always been called by A.A. members, is a more shadowy figure than Bill Wilson, partly because he died when A.A. was only fifteen years old, in 1950. Understated, unflappable, a man of few words, he avoided the limelight; it was said of him that he never led an A.A. meeting—that is, performed the function of being the meeting's principal speaker and guide. He was a dignified man, gallant to women, yet had a slangy way of speaking about them. He called women "frails," or "skirts," or, if he really liked one, simply "Woman." He relished a dirty joke in the company of men. He was the steady hand that held the cord of Bill Wilson's high-flying, erratic kite. While Bill was impulsive, Dr. Bob was deliberate and cautious. He was the soul of common sense. A graduate of Dartmouth College and Rush Medical College in Chicago, he was for years the best-educated man and only doctor in A.A. Bill both loved him and at times was in awe of him. Conventional and sometimes dogmatic, Dr. Bob opposed the admission of women alcoholics into the initially all-male A.A. In those days, "nice" women were not supposed to be drunks. Perhaps because of his professional standing, his dominating presence and steady convictions, he was far more effective with active alcoholics in private conversation than was Bill. He treated almost five thousand alcoholics without charge, most of them at Akron's St. Thomas's Hospital. Hundreds he had worked with wound up in A.A.

One of Dr. Bob's rare public speeches, and his last, was at A.A.'s first international conference in Cleveland in 1950. Three thousand members attended; by then there were an estimated 100,000 in A.A. across the nation. He was dying of cancer, and he apologized for being so brief. What he told the delegates is typical of the man's thinking and style. "There are two or three things that flashed into my mind on which it would be fitting to lay a little emphasis," he said. "One is the *simplicity* of our program. Let's not louse it all up with Freudian complexes and things that are interesting to the scientific mind but have very little to do with our actual A.A. work. Our Twelve Steps, when simmered down to the last, resolve themselves into the words 'love' and 'service.' "

When he died on November 16, 1950, at the age of seventy-one, his obituary in *The New York Times*, the nation's newspaper of record, identified him as a co-founder of Alcoholics Anonymous, but the item was only six inches long and ran on an inside page without a picture. Twenty years and two months later, Bill Wilson's obituary ran with a full-face photograph across three columns of the front page of *The Times*, continuing inside for three columns.

Wilson was considered to be more important in the eyes of the world and the membership of A.A. not just because he had lived twenty years longer than Dr. Bob, or even because at the time of his death in 1971 A.A. had almost five times the membership it had in 1950—475,000 men and women in the United States and eighty-eight other countries. It was also because the man, an instinctive promoter of A.A. and himself, had put together the thoughts and the philosophy, the words and the means to action, that the movement lived by. Unlike Dr. Bob, whose personal influence remains strong but restricted to the Akron and Cleveland areas where he lived and recruited members, Bill traveled widely and spoke often, not just to A.A. groups but to an enormous variety of interested parties outside, from doctors, clergymen, professors and philanthropists to committees of Congress. He wrote the Twelve Steps and the Twelve Traditions, the uniquely effective system of recovery from alcoholism and approach to a life of quality. His four books, beginning in 1939 with *Alcoholics Anonymous,* which gave the movement its name and is called the Big Book by members, preserved his ideas and the experiences common to many alcoholics. They have been printed in the millions by A.A.'s own publishing empire. In addition, he wrote hundreds of articles, most of them for the *A.A. Grapevine,* a monthly magazine.

The only world in which Wilson succeeded was the world of Alcoholics Anonymous. That was more than enough. Both bright and foolish, imaginative and even visionary, he was the driving force behind the only mass movement that has ever given hundreds of thousands of people a way to arrest the disease of alcoholism for good and reconstruct their lives. It has continued to grow with ever greater velocity after his death, and the members have followed his teachings, despite great diversity in their backgrounds and even cultures. There have been many other group attempts through history to deal with alcohol, one of mankind's most seductive friends and most intractable enemies. None has worked for as long or involved so many people as Alcoholics Anonymous.

William Griffith Wilson, the man who shaped A.A., was born in East Dorset, a small town in southwestern Vermont, on November 26, 1895. His father, Gilman Wilson, was an easygoing, likable man, the foreman at a nearby marble quarry. Bill remembered him, according to Lois Wilson, as an "irresistible storyteller" and singer at home with his family. He was also a heavy drinker. Bill's mother, Emily Griffith, was an intelligent, determined, positive woman. There was one younger sister, Dorothy.

When Bill was about nine, his parents were divorced, which Bill believed had come about because of his father's drinking. "Gilly" left Vermont, eventually settled in western Canada and remarried. Emily went to Boston to study osteopathy, leaving Bill and Dorothy in the full-time care of her own parents in East Dorset. The Griffith grandparents who raised the two children were prosperous, loving and warm. Bill was considered privileged, with his motorcycle, wireless set and saddle horse, and a violin he taught himself to play. He played it badly, but music was to prove a solace for the rest of his life.

When he was almost fourteen, he was enrolled at Burr and Burton Seminary, a boarding school in Manchester, Vermont. A boy named Ebby, son of a prominent Albany family, who later played a critical role in Bill's life, was a classmate there briefly. Bill's years at Burr and Burton were happy and successful. At sixteen, he fell in love with a beautiful, popular girl, the daughter of a local Episcopal minister. She died just before Bill's seventeenth birthday in 1912. The loss precipitated a three-year-long depression, the first of many. All who were close to Bill were familiar with his swings from almost manic elation to the gloomiest depths.

Bill entered Norwich University, a Vermont military academy. While he was a freshman, the fantasies he lived in began to separate almost entirely from reality. A "nobody" by his own account who "couldn't even begin to compete in athletics, in music, or even for popularity," Bill did not get a bid to a single one of four fraternities. He nonetheless wrote his mother that he had received bids from three but had refused and "can't seem to get away from being popular."

In mid-1914, when he was eighteen, Bill began to court Lois Burnham, the daughter of a respected Brooklyn doctor whose family spent their summer vacations in Vermont. Lois was twenty-two, the eldest of six children, already a young lady who had completed school at Brooklyn's Packer Collegiate Institute and was working at the YWCA. The four-year gap in their ages seemed to matter little at the time, but much later Bill was often to complain to close friends about it. "He deeply resented her mothering," said one. "He came out to our home and talked all through dinner about her 'momism,' trying to persuade me it was all right to leave her for another woman. I told him, 'I can't argue with you about what the reaction of the movement will be, but I can tell you that unless we individuals live up to what we're supposed to, you're going to hurt somebody.' I think it was all part of his mood swings at the time." In 1971, flying back home with Bill's body, Lois burst out in a storm of tears, sobbing to a confidante: "I was possessive —*I was, I was,* possessive!"

They became engaged in 1915. From the time of their marriage in 1918, through Bill's catastrophic drinking years in the late 1920's and early 1930's and beyond into sobriety, Lois was her husband's confidante and nurse, his decision-maker and financial support. If she knew of Bill's infidelities, it did not seem to affect her devotion. "She never mentioned his philandering," said one of Lois's oldest friends. "She wouldn't share such a thing. It would have offended her sense of dignity, of the rightness, the appropriateness, of things." She added, "I think he never would have left her. He was grateful to her. He was tolerant of her temper outbursts and feistiness."

Bill took the first drink of his life in 1917, as a newly commissioned second lieutenant at Fort Rodman in New Bedford, Massachusetts. America had recently entered World War I. Bill was twenty-one years old. Society families were throwing frequent parties for officers. Until that time he had been afraid of liquor. Lois wrote in her memoirs: "Bill had been warned since childhood not to touch alcohol. His mother had divorced his father largely because of drink, he thought."

He was an excessive drinker from the start. He rarely held his liquor well, unlike many alcoholics who can be moderate social drinkers for years, gradually increasing their intake before slipping over that invisible line into problem drinking. They were married just before he was shipped with his unit to Europe, far from the front. When he returned to his bride in New York in 1919, without a college degree and untrained for any trade or profession, he had trouble finding a job. He clerked, did manual labor, quitting a job on the docks rather than join the union, went backpacking with Lois in Vermont, started studying law at night in Brooklyn. Lois became pregnant in 1922. It was the first of three ectopic pregnancies, in which the egg developed outside the uterus in the Fallopian tubes. The Wilsons realized they would never have the children they deeply wanted. Their attempts to adopt came to nothing. The Wilsons always believed it was because of Bill's increasing bouts of drunkenness and bad public behavior.

Bill had been taking business courses during the stock market's dizzying upward spiral. "The inviting maelstrom of Wall Street had me in its grip," he said. He decided that investors could choose stocks more wisely if they knew more about the factories and managements the stocks represented, a novel idea in 1925. So the new "securities investigator," then almost thirty, and his wife, thirty-four, took off on their Harley-Davidson motorcycle for a year of camping out, analyzing the solidity and prospects of companies from New York to Florida. The motorcycle and its sidecar were heaped with clothes, a fold tent, cooking equipment and a set of manuals, from Moody's Investors Service, which were financial reference books. They loved camping and Lois had an additional secret motive. "I was so concerned about Bill's drinking," she said, "that I wanted to get him away from New York and its bars." The husband of Lois's best friend, a millionaire Wall Street speculator, began to pay Bill handsomely for his reports from the field and then hired him.

After that year on the road, which was marred only by several bad drinking bouts, Bill became a margin trader on Wall Street. He described his success in the somewhat overheated prose that was always his style:

> For the next few years fortune threw money and applause my way. I had arrived. My judgment and ideas were followed by

many to the tune of paper millions. The great boom of the late twenties was seething and swelling. Drink was taking an important and exhilarating part in my life. There was loud talk in the jazz places uptown. Everyone spent in thousands and chattered in millions. Scoffers could scoff and be damned. I made a host of fair-weather friends.

His drinking assumed more serious proportions, continuing all day and almost every night. "The remonstrances of my friends terminated in a row and I became a lone wolf," he wrote of those times. There were ugly scenes at home with Lois. He kept writing promises to his wife such as: "There will be no booze in 1927." At the end of 1927, he was so depressed by his own behavior that he told her, "I'm halfway to hell now and going strong."

Two years later, the stock market crashed. "Abruptly in October 1929 hell broke loose on the New York stock exchange," Bill recalled. "After one of those days of inferno, I wobbled from a hotel bar to a brokerage office. It was eight o'clock—five hours after the market closed. The ticker still clattered. I was staring at an inch of the tape which bore the inscription XYZ-32. It had been 52 that morning. I was finished and so were many friends. The papers reported men jumping to death from the towers of High Finance. That disgusted me. I would not jump. I went back to the bar. My friends had dropped several million since ten o'clock—so what? Tomorrow was another day. As I drank, the old fierce determination to win came back."

Pleasant and courteous when sober, he would become overbearing and loud when drunk. As the nation plunged into the Great Depression, Bill and Lois moved in with her father, Dr. Clark Burnham, on Clinton Street in Brooklyn Heights. (Bill had been too drunk to attend his mother-in-law's funeral in 1930.) Lois got a selling job at Macy's for nineteen dollars a week. Bill would lie in bed and drink, or make the rounds of the brokerage houses to give the appearance of working.

His hangovers and hallucinations were becoming more frequent. He panhandled and stole from his wife's purse. He would ride the subways for hours after buying a bottle of bootleg gin, talking gibberish to frightened strangers. He threw a sewing machine at Lois and stormed around their house in Brooklyn kicking out door panels. She called him a "drunken sot." He would be sober for days and weeks and then settle into bottomless bingeing. He barely ate. He was forty pounds underweight. His dark, withdrawn periods alternated with delusions of grandeur. Once he told Lois that "men of genius" conceived their best projects when drunk. Another night, at the house of Dorothy and Leonard Strong, his sister and brother-in-law, Bill did not show up for supper. The Strongs played three-handed bridge with Lois, then went to bed. Lois was sleepless. At 4 A.M. the doorbell rang. On the doorstep was her husband, cold and shivering, without shoes or pants.

Only the Strongs stood by Bill. Like Bill's mother, Strong was an osteopath. By late 1933, realizing that Bill was a physical and psychological rubble heap, Dr. Strong arranged for his brother-in-law's first admission to the Charles B. Towns Hospital on Central Park West in Manhattan and paid the fees. Prohibition was about to be repealed. The fourteen-year-long "noble experiment" to curb drunkenness by outlawing liquor had been flaunted in speakeasies the nation over; respectable people made bathtub gin at home; gangsters amassed fortunes on bootlegging and smuggling. In many circles it was chic to drink and get drunk and outwit the Feds. Nonetheless, chronic alcoholism was considered to be a moral weakness, or a sin. Seemingly hopeless alcoholics like Bill Wilson received little understanding and compassion. Towns Hospital had been a fashionable and expensive place for treating alcoholics during the twenties. Basically, patients were "purged and puked" there, according to someone who remembered Towns. The treatment consisted of frequent, vigorous doses of various narcotics and cathartics such as belladonna and castor oil. The neurologist who had run the hospital since 1930 was Dr. William Duncan Silkworth, a kindly man who believed alcoholism was due not to a moral defect or a lack of willpower but a physical "allergy" to liquor and an overpowering compulsion to drink. Despite Bill's relief at Dr. Silkworth's insistence that alcoholism was an illness,

a concept that would help many thousands of alcoholics to overcome their shame, he left the hospital for more bingeing. He rarely
went out now except to replenish his liquor supply. There were
periods of blackouts, drunken rages with Lois as the object, falls
and head injuries. He was treated at Towns twice more without
lasting results.

One day in the late fall of 1934, Lois came home to find Ebby,
Bill's old classmate at Burr and Burton, talking earnestly with her
husband in the kitchen. The two had often gone on drinking jags
since their boyhood days. This time, Bill said, when he pushed a
drink across the table, his old friend refused it. "Come, what's
this all about?" Bill asked. Ebby looked at him with a smile. "I've
got religion," he said. Bill was aghast—"last summer an alcoholic
crackpot; now, I suspected, a little cracked about religion." Ebby
had, Bill said, "that starry-eyed look." Then he thought, "But bless
his heart, let him rant! Besides, my gin would last longer than his
preaching." Despite himself, however, Bill became absorbed in
what Ebby had to tell him about the Oxford Group and their
simple program for a better and more spiritual life.

On December 11, 1934, Bill admitted himself to Towns Hospital
for the fourth time. Dr. Silkworth sedated him and began the
belladonna treatment. Ebby visited him. He repeated the Oxford
Group's formula that had released him from drinking. First, Ebby
said, he surrendered his life to God, having recognized that he
couldn't run it himself. Then he tried to be honest with himself,
making amends when possible to people he had hurt. He tried to
give himself to others without asking any return. And finally, although he hadn't believed in prayer, he found to his surprise that
it had worked. Ebby lifted Bill's spirits. Soon after he left, however,
Bill's mood turned rebellious, depressed and desperate. At last he
began praying for help.

In describing what happened next—first to Dr. Silkworth, then
to his wife and for decades afterward to any alcoholic listening to
his story—Bill said he thought, "I'll do anything, anything for
release."

"The effect was 'electric,' he wrote in the Big Book. "There was a sense of victory, followed by such a peace and serenity as I had never known. There was utter confidence. I felt lifted up, as though the great clean wind of a mountain top blew through and through. God comes to most men gradually, but His impact on me was sudden and profound." He cried out, "If there be a God, let Him show Himself!" He told Lois how the room blazed with light, how he was filled with a "joy beyond description."

He became alarmed and asked Dr. Silkworth if he was going crazy. "Something has happened to you I don't understand," the doctor said. "But you had better hang on to it. Anything is better than the way you were."

In years to come, Wilson, who never joined any church but took Roman Catholic instruction in the 1940's and had close friends in the clergy, continued to seek a dramatic spiritual transformation. His most controversial searches revolved around seances and the hallucinogen LSD. In recent years physicians and pharmacists have analyzed the drugs involved in the Towns treatment of alcoholics and theorized that Wilson's visual and auditory experiences in the hospital room in 1934 were delirium precipitated by toxic psychosis. Later in his life, Bill himself usually referred ironically to the episode as his "hot flash." Whatever it was, that day was a watershed in his life. After his release from Towns on December 18, 1934, Bill Wilson never took another drink.

Lois and Bill began attending Oxford Group meetings and were attracted by the warmth they found there. The atmosphere reminded Lois of a Quaker meeting, where the members sat quietly together and listened for the "guidance of God" for each one. To the precepts of surrender, confession, restitution, prayer and assistance to others were added what the group called the "Four Absolutes"—absolute honesty, absolute purity, absolute unselfishness and absolute love.

Bill was full of plans to save every alcoholic in sight. Lois said his attitude was, "Since a miracle had happened to him and Ebby, why couldn't it happen to . . . all the drunks in the world perhaps? I went along with the idea enthusiastically."

He found no jobs on Wall Street in the winter of 1934–35, and

Lois went on supporting them both with her job at a Brooklyn department store. "I was not too well at the time, and was plagued by waves of self-pity and resentment," Bill wrote later. "This sometimes nearly drove me back to drink. I soon found that when all other measures failed, work with another alcoholic would save the day." Many times, he said, he would proselytize the drunks in the beds at Towns Hospital. "On talking to a man there, I would be amazingly lifted up and set on my feet. It is a design for living that works in rough going." The problem was, he gained no converts. Dr. Silkworth told him to lay off the religious stuff and start telling these desperate souls that they were ill—that they would go insane or die if they didn't stop drinking altogether and seek to rebuild their lives.

Although Bill's high-pressure evangelism had not worked on other drunks, he found that he had kept himself sober for the longest period in eighteen years through the sheer vigor of his efforts to help them. He could once again also think about working, even though nothing was left of his once bright career. Then, in April of 1935, he learned about a proxy fight for control of a small machine-tool company in Akron, Ohio. He spent several weeks there with some associates, trying to persuade disgruntled stockholders of the National Rubber Machinery Company to support his group's bid for control. He had fantasies that he would win, rebuild his shattered career and restore his standing on Wall Street. As he had since his return from World War I, he talked to his wife about becoming the head of "vast enterprises," which he would "manage with utmost assurance." The fight soon appeared hopeless. Wilson's colleagues went back to New York.

They left on a Friday. Bitterly disappointed and resentful, Bill faced a weekend alone in Akron. On Saturday, May 11, 1935, he was in the lobby of the Mayflower Hotel wrestling with an overwhelming desire to have just one drink. Instead he made the phone call that led him to Dr. Bob Smith.

Robert Holbrook Smith was born August 8, 1879, in St. Johnsbury, Vermont, about a hundred miles northeast of Bill Wilson's birthplace in East Dorset. His father was a judge of the county probate court, a former state's attorney, a member of the Vermont legislature, a director and president of local banks and a super-intendent of schools. He taught Sunday school in St. Johnsbury for forty years. His mother was also very active in the little town's religious and social doings. There was a foster daughter, so much older than Bob that in effect he was raised as an only child. In some ways his boyhood was idyllic, with his free time spent hunting in the hills, fishing, swimming and picnicking. His father was understanding, even indulgent, under a rather forbidding manner. But there was one part of Bob's life that he grew to loathe. "From childhood through high school," he recalled, "I was more or less forced to go to church, Sunday school and evening service, Monday-night Christian Endeavor, and sometimes to Wednesday evening prayer meeting. This had the effect of making me resolve that when I was free of parental domination, I would never again darken the doors of a church. This resolution I kept steadfastly for the next FORTY years, except when circumstances made it seem unwise to absent myself."

In 1894, at the age of fifteen, he entered St. Johnsbury Academy, which had been established for the "intellectual, moral and religious training of boys and girls in northeastern Vermont." One of its alumni was Calvin Coolidge, the thirtieth President of the United States. Bob met his future wife, Anne Robinson Ripley of Oak Park, Illinois, then a scholarship student at Wellesley College, at an dance in 1898. He was nineteen. She was eighteen months younger, plain and shy.

At Dartmouth College in Hanover, New Hampshire, Bob took to alcohol in heroic doses. The college was then called "the drinkingest of the Ivy League schools," and its students were known to the townfolk as "the Dartmouth animals." "Drinking seemed to be a major extracurricular activity," Bob said. "Almost everyone seemed to do it. I did it more and more, and had lots of fun without much grief. . . . I seemed to be able to snap back the next morning better than most of my fellow drinkers, who were cursed (or perhaps blessed) with a great deal of morning-after nausea. . . . I was graduated with 'summa cum laude' in the eyes of the drinking fraternity, but not in the eyes of the Dean."

He was tall, lanky and good-looking, with broad shoulders, a penetrating eye and a frank and unpretentious manner. He never lost his flat-voweled, twangy Vermont accent despite forty years in Ohio. He rarely cracked a book but got creditable grades. He played cards like a demon, then and all his life: bridge, gin rummy, poker. He could chugalug a bottle of beer without any apparent movement of his Adam's apple.

He was graduated from Dartmouth in 1902. There followed three years of drifting, selling heavy hardware in Boston, Chicago and Montreal. In 1905, at the age of twenty-six, he entered the University of Michigan as a premedical student. He joined a drinking society and began to binge, dropped out of school, returned, was asked to leave and finally, after taking makeup exams, was allowed to transfer in his junior year to Rush Medical College in Chicago. His drinking worsened. He began to get the shakes. During final exams he turned in three completely blank booklets. The medical school dean told him that if he wished to graduate, he had to come back for two more quarters and remain absolutely dry. He did so. In 1910, at the age of thirty-one, he received his medical degree and got a two-year internship at City Hospital in Akron, Ohio.

In 1915, in Chicago, Smith married Anne at last. They were both in their mid-thirties; their courtship had lasted for seventeen years. There are only theories about why they waited so long. Among them are Bob's early heavy drinking and the length of time it took him, despite his obvious intelligence, to finish his schooling and medical training. He brought his bride back to the comfortable frame house in Akron, at 855 Ardmore Avenue, which he had bought for $4,000 and in which they lived for the rest of their lives. Dr. Bob's son, Young Bob, said much later it reminded him of Archie Bunker's house (a reference to the prototype of a blue-collar boob who captivated television watchers beginning in the 1970's), although it was then in a fashionable neighborhood. Young Bob was born in 1918. In 1923, when Anne was told she could have no more children—she was then forty-two—the Smiths adopted a five-year-old girl named Suzanne, just a couple of months younger than her new brother.

Prohibition was in full swing, but the government allowed physicians virtually unlimited quantities of grain alcohol for medicinal purposes. Often, during those dry years, Dr. Bob would pick a name at random from the phone book and then fill out a prescription that would get him alcohol. He was developing two deep phobias: the fear of not sleeping and the fear of not having enough liquor.

"I knew that if I did not stay sober enough to earn money, I would run out of liquor," he said. "Most of the time, therefore, I did not take the morning drink which I craved so badly, but instead would fill up on large doses of sedatives to quiet the jitters, which distressed me terribly. Occasionally I would yield to the morning craving, but if I did, it would be only a few hours before I would be quite unfit for work. . . . During the subsequent fifteen years I had sense enough never to go to the hospital if I had been drinking, and very seldom did I receive patients." At times he would not go to his office in downtown Akron; Anne would telephone his nurses to say he was "sick."

Typically, the rather inhibited Dr. Bob was never the kind of mean or flamboyant drunk that Bill Wilson became. His drinking was secret and he hid his liquor. "If my wife were planning to go out in the afternoon," he later recalled, "I would get a large supply of liquor and smuggle it home and hide it in the coal bin, the clothes chute, over doorjambs, over beams in the cellar and in cracks in the cellar tile. I also made use of old trunks and chests, the old can container and even the ash container. The water tank on the toilet I never used because that looked too easy. I found out later that my wife inspected it frequently. "I used to put eight- or twelve-ounce bottles of alcohol in a fur-lined glove and toss it onto the back airing porch when winter days got dark enough. My bootlegger had hidden alcohol at the back steps where I could get it at my convenience."

Sometimes he would bring it home in his pockets, "but they were inspected" by the suspicious Anne and "that became too risky." He retaliated, with the cunning common to all drunks, by putting liquor up in four-ounce bottles, sticking several in his stocking tops. "This worked nicely," he recalled, "until my wife and I went to see Wallace Beery in 'Tugboat Annie.'" In that movie the character used the same stratagem, "after which the pant-leg and stocking racket were out," Bob recalled.

Often he would tie one on at the City Club in Akron, or, in order to drink in privacy, he would register in a hotel under an assumed name. ("Who would believe 'Robert Smith'?" he would later tell alcoholics delightedly listening to his story.) "The boys at the central garage" frequently had to drive him home. When Smitty, as Young Bob was called, and his sister, Sue, were about high school age, they became aware of their father's problem. "I could kind of sense the tension," Sue remembered. "Mother was very upset. I'd catch her crying, and then of course she'd say that nothing was the matter."

The children, of course, saw everything. When the doctor came home reeling and almost unconscious, Smitty, Sue and their mother would drag the tall, heavy man upstairs to bed, where he would pass out. As Bill Wilson did with his wife, Dr. Bob would repeatedly promise Anne, who did not drink, never to touch another drop. He swore off the booze to his two children, to friends. Those were promises "which seldom kept me sober even through the day," he said, "though I was very sincere when I made them." The Smiths' friends began to ostracize them. They were rarely invited out anymore, and when they were, Anne was loath to accept invitations for fear of what her husband would do. According to his son, only Franklin D. Roosevelt's moratorium on mortgage foreclosures saved the house from being taken.

For many years, Dr. Bob's life was a surreal circle. As he described it, it consisted of "earning money, getting liquor, smuggling it home, getting drunk, morning jitters, taking large doses of sedatives to make it possible for me to earn more money, and so on *ad nauseam*." His daughter, Sue, said, "I remember once he asked me to get his bottle for him. I wouldn't do it, and he offered me money. He finally got to ten dollars, and I still wouldn't do it. That was when I realized how much he wanted it."

Prohibition was repealed in 1933. Dr. Bob decided to try "the beer experiment." The story is familiar to anyone who has tried to control drinking by switching from hard liquor to beer or wine. "It was harmless; nobody ever got drunk on beer," the doctor rationalized. "So I filled the cellar full, with the permission of my good wife. It was not long before I was drinking at least a case and a half a day." He put thirty pounds on his big-boned frame within two months, "looked like a pig" and began suffering from shortness of breath. "It then occurred to me that after one was all smelled up with beer nobody could tell what had been drunk, so I began to fortify my beer with straight alcohol."

At about the same time, Anne persuaded her husband to go with her to meetings of the Oxford Group in Akron. Two groups had formed there under the impetus of Harvey Firestone, Sr., the rubber tycoon, whose son Russell had once had a serious drinking problem. With the aid of Oxford Groups in England, he had been able to dry out. Harvey senior brought sixty Oxford Group leaders and members to Akron for a ten-day "house party" similar to the religious and spiritual retreats of today. It culminated in a dinner for 400 prominent citizens of the city and the formation of local groups. Henrietta Seiberling was one of the earliest and most ardent participants.

The Oxford Group came along when Henrietta's marriage to J. Frederick Seiberling was crumbling. "It gave her a new focus," her daughter Dorothy said. "It helped her to see there was more to life than marital problems." Bob and Anne Smith were equally impressed with the Oxford Groupers "because of their seeming poise, health and happiness," the doctor said. "These people spoke with great freedom from embarrassment, which I could never do, and they seemed very much at ease on all occasions and appeared very healthy. More than these attributes, they seemed to be happy. I was self-conscious and ill at ease most of the time, my health was at the breaking point, and I was thoroughly miserable. I sensed they might have something I did not have, from which I might readily profit. I learned that it was something of a spiritual nature, which did not appeal to me very much, but I thought it could do no harm. I gave the matter much time and study for the next two and a half years, but still got tight every night. . . ."

He didn't like their habit of praying for God's guidance for each other's problems. He did approve of the fact that they met not in churches but at the Mayflower Hotel and in each other's homes. For quite a long time he did not connect what they did at their Thursday meetings with his drinking problem. He knew only that he was unhappy and that his life was spinning out of control. Still, in the years before Bill Wilson's fateful trip to Akron, the Smiths were faithful in their attendance at Oxford Group meetings.

Bob read everything the members recommended. He threw off his boyhood vow of never darkening the doors of a church and joined the local Presbyterians. He read the Bible again. Sometimes he even prayed, although that was the most difficult of all. He was running out of money. His family was eating potato soup, bread and milk for dinner. He could not figure out what was wrong. His wife, children and the nurses at City Hospital noticed his bloodshot eyes, his shaking hands. His frequent absences from work were noted. The hospital put him on warning and he was close to dismissal. His surgical practice was dwindling; he began taking on general as well as proctological patients to supplement his income. But he was a skilled doctor, well liked by the other doctors and nurses, who covered up for him. Finally, there was (and to some extent still is) a tacit denial in the medical profession that alcoholism is a serious problem among physicians.

Meantime, Henrietta Seiberling was growing closer to the Smiths. She and Anne called each other every day, talking endlessly about their troubles and the comfort they both received in the Oxford Group. Sue remembered that, when she tried to get her mother's attention, Anne would often reply, "Just a moment, I'm talking to Henrietta." Bob's disintegrating life was the central topic of conversation.

"Everybody knew he had a drinking problem," Dorothy Seiberling said. "Everybody whispered about it, or came right out and said it. Mother finally planned to lead Bob to a confession in an Oxford Group meeting. We were all involved. Mother used to take me, my sister Mary and my brother John to all the meetings. It was the center of her life, and she thought we children could learn something from the group." In the spring of 1935, Dorothy recalled, "it was Mother's turn to lead a meeting. I was there. The Smiths were not. Mother said, 'The only way we're going to get Bob to admit it or for us to be of help is if we bare our souls—tell something that is costly to us.'" Only then, Henrietta felt, would the doctor feel that he, too, had to "share."

Her technique worked. Soon thereafter, Dr. Bob admitted shame-facedly to the Oxford Groupers the "secret" that many in Akron knew. Henrietta had set it off by saying, "Tonight, we are going to share something costly." Bob ended his confession with, "I'd like you to pray for me."

"From then on," said Dorothy, "that was a major concern—how to help him. Nobody knew anything about the problem." Henrietta—whom the doctor called "Hen" or "Henri"—prayed mightily for guidance. One day she telephoned Bob to say, "I've had some guidance for you." She meant, of course, divine guidance. Bob asked what her solution might be. "You must never touch another drop," said Henrietta. The doctor was crushed. It wasn't, he said, that simple. But the fact that Henrietta knew and deeply cared strengthened their bond of friendship.

This was the situation when Bill Wilson, the "rum hound from New York," telephoned Mrs. Seiberling to set off what her daughter called the "spark that ignited A.A."

Henrietta found temporary housing for Bill. In early June, 1935, he moved into the Smiths' house for the summer. He later said it was because Anne Smith had decided that someone needed to be around to protect her husband's newfound sobriety. The invitation came at a perfect time: Bill was almost broke. He wrote to Lois back in New York that he was "working to change" a new friend, and that he was living with them so that each man could keep an eye on the other. Then Dr. Bob went on his last, long binge—at the American Medical Association convention in Atlantic City.

The doctor described it:

I drank all the Scotch they had on the train and bought several quarts on my way to the hotel. This was on Sunday. I got tight that night, stayed sober Monday until after the dinner and then proceeded to get tight again. I drank all I dared in the bar, and then went to my room to finish the job. Tuesday I started in the morning. . . . I did not want to disgrace myself, so I then checked out. I bought some more liquor on the way to the depot. I had to wait some time for the train. I remember nothing from then on until I woke up at a friend's house, in a town near home.

He awakened at the home of one of his nurses, whom he had telephoned from the railroad station in Akron. The Smith children remember that the sobering-up process took three days. As it happened, Dr. Bob had an operation scheduled for that third day. Bill loaded the doctor up with the classic folk remedy of the time for hangovers—sauerkraut and tomato juice for vitamins and Karo corn syrup for energy. He gave Bob a few beers to steady his nerves and taper him off. On the way to City Hospital the morning of the operation, June 10, 1935, Dr. Bob still had the shakes. Bill gave him another bottle of beer. Alcoholics Anonymous dates its beginning from that day, the day of Bob Smith's last drink.

Both men were eager to "fix" more drunks, as they put it in those days. Eddie R., who lived down the block from the Smiths, was recommended by the Smiths' minister. Young Bob described him as an alcoholic who was also "a borderline mental case and a depressive." During the summer of 1935, Eddie attempted suicide and pursued Anne Smith with a butcher knife from her own kitchen. His "cure" never held. But, Young Bob said, "My father and Bill were determined to make a convert out of somebody."

"They've always got a batch of alcoholics down at City Hospital," Dr. Bob said to Bill. He called the admissions nurse and told her that he had met a man from New York who had found a new cure for alcoholism. "Is that so, doctor?" was her response. "You don't mean to tell me you've tried it on yourself?"

He sheepishly admitted that he had. The nurse relented and informed Dr. Bob that she had a patient, a lawyer, who had been in the hospital six times in the preceding four months. He went out of his mind when drunk, had assaulted two nurses, and was now tied to his hospital bed. Dr. Bob told the man's wife, who, like Mrs. Seiberling, was named Henrietta, that if she had fifty dollars to put her husband in a private room, he would treat him without cost. To get around the rules that channeled drunks into charity wards, the patient had been admitted as suffering from a type of virus.

For almost a week, Dr. Bob and Bill Wilson visited the man daily in his hospital room. Henrietta had told her husband that his treatment, by a staff doctor and a friend who had been drunks, would not cost a cent. He was disbelieving, but he liked hearing them tell their stories about what it had been like to be a drunk. He liked telling his own story, Henrietta recalled. "He was there about five days before they could make him say that he couldn't control his drinking and had to leave it up to God. . . . They *made* him get down on his knees at the side of the bed . . . and pray and say he would turn his life over to God."

Bill Wilson and Dr. Bob had finally saved a third alcoholic. He was Bill D., known in A.A. as "the man on the bed" because he had gained sobriety in a hospital. Three drunks had begun an association, a society that would attract only one hundred members over the next four years. It would not even have a name until 1939.

# 3

▾

# THE EARLY
# CHRISTIANS

"We were groping in the dark."
—Dr. Bob Smith

In the beginning, the tiny band of A.A. pioneers was simply stumbling ahead, day after perilous day, into a way of life without drinking. They had only each other and the precepts of the Oxford Group to guide them. "We were groping in the dark," Dr. Bob said. "I, a physician, knew nothing about [alcoholism] to speak of. There wasn't anything worth reading in any of the textbooks. Usually the information consisted of some queer treatment for the

D.T.'s, if the patient had gone that far. If he hadn't, you prescribed a few bromides and gave the fellow a good lecture."

A.A.'s founding members were ignorant of the past. They had no idea that in this country the concept of alcoholism as a disease went back to the dawn of the American Republic. The United States had been born wet, and by the end of the eighteenth century its citizens were tippling and guzzling and ushering in the era of the heaviest alcohol consumption in American history. At that time it was considered safer than water. Then along came Dr. Benjamin Rush, a signer of the Declaration of Independence, a Philadelphian who was the most respected physician of his time. Rush was the first American to call chronic drunkenness a distinct, progressive disease. His powerful tract *An Inquiry into the Effects of Ardent Spirits on the Human Mind and Body,* published in 1784, identified alcohol as addictive and claimed that once an "appetite" or "craving" for it became fixed, the victim lost all control over his drinking. His argument that drunkenness was the fault of the drinker only in the early stages of the disease, before alcohol took total command, was a radical departure from previous thinking. It became a classic in temperance literature.

Bill Wilson and Dr. Bob knew nothing of Dr. Rush. They had only a dim notion of the temperance movements that had swept the nation in the nineteenth and early twentieth centuries. They had never heard of the Washingtonians, the nineteenth-century group that A.A. came most to resemble, which swelled from 6 drunks meeting in Baltimore in 1840 to 150,000 before the end of the decade. It then shriveled away, opposed by the clergy and by the non-Washingtonian dry movements. The Washingtonians, alone among the temperance groups of that time, did not involve themselves with organized religion, politics or social reform. Their purpose was remarkably single-minded, just like A.A.—sobered-up alcoholics saving other alcoholics who still drank, while teaching them to avoid the temptations that led them to drink in the first place. Abraham Lincoln said of the Washingtonians in 1842: "Those whom they desire to convince and persuade are their old friends and companions. They know they are not demons, nor even the worst of men."

Bill and Dr. Bob were aware only that the temperance crusaders had reached their pinnacle with the passage of national Prohibition, which ended in failure. The law was in force from early 1920 through 1933, years when both men had plunged downward into a quagmire of mindless, helpless bingeing. Then Bill had arrived in Akron in 1935, fired up with Dr. William Duncan Silkworth's "new" theory that alcoholism was neither a moral defect nor a lapse in willpower, but a legitimate illness composed of a mysterious physical "allergy" and a mental and emotional compulsion to drink. The two founders of A.A., slowly and painfully, had further discovered that it took the experience and determination of one alcoholic to help another. They also had the support and the ideas of the Oxford Group. Its importance in shaping A.A. concepts cannot be overstated.

In the mid-1930's, it was the Oxford meetings that gave the little group of alcoholics in Akron and then New York, a philosophical home and a spiritual focus. The core of the Oxford program, adapted by A.A., included unconditional surrender of the human will to the will of God; taking a personal moral inventory; confessing ("sharing") before other members; making amends to people whom a member had harmed, and working with others who needed help, willingly and without thought of financial reward.

The Oxford Group, initially known as the First Century Christian Fellowship and in its final years as Moral Re-Armament, or MRA, was founded by Frank N. D. Buchman. An ordained Lutheran minister from Allentown, Pennsylvania, he was a persistent man, an evangelist, a spiritual showman who called himself a "soul surgeon." He had a high, loud voice, a beak of a nose poking out from a round, plump face and thinnish hair. He believed that God had made him ugly for a purpose. He never married. After being swept away by a Salvation Army sermon in England in 1908, he was inspired to write letters of apology to all he felt he had wronged. Buchman got such relief and joy from the writing that he began to tell others of his transformation. He went forth to save. He tried out his central idea of a return to the simplicity, intimacy and fervor of the earliest Christians as a secretary of the Young Men's Christian Association at Pennsylvania State College, and from then on ranged the world as a missionary. In China in 1918, he brought his persuasive personality to bear on the Reverend Samuel Shoemaker, an Episcopal minister who had been sent there to start a branch of the YMCA. Shoemaker was to become the most powerful leader of the Oxford Group in New York, the rector of the Calvary Church and Mission on lower Park Avenue and an early mentor of Bill Wilson.

Buchman dated the foundation and name of the Oxford Group from 1921, when he met with undergraduates at Christ Church, a college of Oxford University. His tenets were "absolute honesty, absolute purity, absolute unselfishness and absolute love." Those who accepted the "four absolutes" were invited to change their lives by confessing past sins at "house parties," usually held in people's homes or fashionable hotels. They heard others testify to divine guidance in matters both important and trivial. They admitted to jealousy, laziness, dishonesty, willfulness, excessive drinking or smoking. They participated in Quaker-like "quiet times" for thought and prayer. "Listen to God as you would to a radio-phone," Buchman said. "When man listens, God speaks."

House parties in the twenties and early thirties were usually small, informal but guided meetings that greatly resembled the spiritual retreats of today. There was no hymn-singing or rhythmic hand-clapping, none of the dramatic, noisy salvation scenes one would find at a typical revival meeting. Oxford Groupers were not expected to leave their own churches. The movement was non-denominational and embraced no specific theology. It sought only to help people practice a truly Christian moral life, a better life attained in stages. In thirties' slang, adherents spoke of "getting square with God." They were ardent missionaries, but their technique was low-key. When recruiting, they assigned one person to speak of his lapses and his new life to another, not to talk religion or make the prospect feel guilty. They continued their small meetings, but by the mid-1930's some of the house parties grew to fill ballrooms and stadiums on both sides of the Atlantic. Fifteen thousand people attended one such gathering in 1936 in Birmingham, England. That same year, Bill Wilson and Lois were among 5,000 Oxford Group members and potential members who went to the group's First American National Assembly in Stockbridge, Massachusetts.

Popular books swelled the ranks. Among the most influential were Harold Begbie's *Life-Changers (More Twice-Born Men)*, and *For Sinners Only* by Arthur James Russell, a London newspaper editor. Russell's book, which appeared in 1932, described his journey as a prodigal into the Oxford Group and his discovery of its precept that each person's conscience should be his preacher. Three books published during the thirties were devoted entirely to the lives of alcoholics who found sobriety through the Oxford Group: *The Big Bender, I Was a Pagan* and *Life Began Yesterday*. Many found inspiration in Buchman's catchphrases and slogans, which came to him as naturally as to an advertising copywriter and were passed from lip to ear in Oxford circles. They included A Spiritual Radiophone in Every Home.

The small cluster of drunks struggling to get sober within Akron's Oxford Group in the summer of 1935 also turned to the Bible for solace. The reading that they regarded as essential included the Sermon on the Mount, the thirteenth chapter of Corinthians I ("Charity suffereth long, and is kind; charity envieth not; charity vaunteth not itself, is not puffed up . . .") and the Book of James, with its emphasis on mercy, tolerance, the doing of good works, the confession of faults to one another and the healing properties of prayer. A favorite of Bill and Dr. Bob was *The Varieties of Religious Experience: A Study in Human Nature*, by William James, the great American psychologist and philosopher. Bill's old school buddy, Ebby, an Oxford member, had brought him a copy during Bill's final drying out in Towns Hospital in December 1934. He studied *Varieties* for months, was completely gripped by it, and urged everyone in sight to read it and learn from it. *The Varieties of Religious Experience* is the only outside source given credit in Wilson's most seminal, lasting volume, *Alcoholics Anonymous*—the Big Book.

James's dense, difficult yet exciting work, based on an historic series of lectures at Edinburgh University in 1901 and 1902, remains probably the most celebrated of all books on the psychology of the religious impulse. The philosopher's view of God was not Christian. He was not interested in religious institutions. "I have no living sense of commerce with a God," he said, but he added, "I envy those who have." He believed in believing, and in man's personal experience of some power higher than himself. "Call this, if you like, my mystical *germ*," James said. "It is a very common germ. It creates the rank and file of believers. As it withstands in my case, so it will withstand in most cases, all purely atheistic criticism."

From *Varieties* Bill extracted three other ideas that became central to A.A. thought in working with alcoholics. First, change came when a person reached a state of total desperation and collapse. Second was an admission of defeat. Third was an appeal to a higher power, or at least a cry for help to another human being. This might or might not be a religious experience; it could be a lightning flash of exaltation and a lifting of a burden, as in Bill's case at Towns Hospital, or a gradual transformation into a state of peace and comfort with oneself, as happened with Dr. Bob (and most members of A.A.).

Beginning in 1935, Dr. Bob quickly became an extraordinarily effective worker with active alcoholics. He was tough. He was inflexible. He told his prospects: "Do you want to surrender to God? Take it or leave it." Soon, carloads of drunks were coming to Akron from as far away as Cleveland to meet in his house. Recently, Young Bob tried to explain why his father had been so successful at "fixing" drunks: "Remember that he was a doctor and also a very highly educated man. Nobody was going to snow him by trying to shoot over his head intellectually. He also was precise and concise in his thinking and talking. He knew that a drunk coming out of an alcoholic haze would be absolutely overwhelmed by anything but a straightforward program that anyone could understand. It wasn't aimed at college grads—he kept it simple so that anyone was capable of grasping it." The doctor was authoritative, and he was impressive.

John R., who took his last drink on March 1, 1939, told what it was like to see Dr. Bob materialize at his bedside in Akron's City Hospital:

Doc was a big guy, with arms like a gorilla—he looked like he could use them like a gorilla, too. When Doc talked, he talked with the voice of authority. You could bark back and he barked louder. He'd been almost four years sober by the time he saw me. I couldn't figure how a guy could be sober that long. He was sincere. He told me what a damned fool I'd been all those years—he told me about his drinking, and how he'd sneak bottles into the house in his socks. He gave me paraldehyde. It smelled ungodly; it smelled worse than creosote. It knocked me out for forty-eight hours.

(Paraldehyde, a sedative drug, is a liquid with a revolting odor and taste, acrid and overpowering, which physicians treating alcoholics used for many years before the barbiturate era.)

Under Dr. Bob's guidance, the men he sobered up and introduced to the Oxford Group asked themselves about any new alcoholic prospect: Does he want to stop badly enough? Is he mentally sound, aside from his alcoholism? If he was still married, with wife and children living at home, and if he did not have money problems, he was considered probably not desperate enough to be helped.

The young were not welcome then. The feeling was they had not suffered enough, had not lived enough years and lost enough to have "hit bottom." Women alcoholics were not welcome either. Dr. Bob and many early members held to the Victorian idea that "nice" women weren't drunks. But nonalcoholic wives were brought into the picture from the beginning, and usually attended meetings. Typically, when word began to spread that Dr. Bob and his friends were having amazing success with drunks, a wife would telephone and be interviewed by a sobered-up Oxford Group member about her husband's problems. In those days, members also went out and hustled for drunks, in missions for homeless men and in charity hospital wards. The pioneers did not sit back and wait for a cry for help. Hospitalization was considered to be a must. Bob would circumvent hospital rules against putting alcoholics in private rooms by concocting another diagnosis and smuggling them in so that he could work on likely prospects without distractions.

The doctor and his recovering alcoholic friends would pay frequent visits to the bedside. They told their drinking stories. Patients would reply, as one of them reported, "That's me. That's me. I drink like that." Usually the sick man would spend five or six days in the hospital being detoxified (medically withdrawn from alcohol). In the final days his visitors would ask the prospect to give over his life "to the care and direction of the Creator." Then the man would get down on his knees. When he "surrendered to God," he was considered a member. Those who did not "make their surrender" in the hospital did it soon afterward at an Oxford Group meeting, usually in the home of T. Henry and Clarace Williams.

The Williamses were an Akron couple—generous and "a bit churchy," Dorothy Seiberling said—who opened their house every Wednesday night to the Oxford Group and its growing band of alcoholics. Young Bob, in frequent attendance, described the scene:

> They'd take the guy upstairs and bore in on him. The Catholics in the group didn't like that kind of open confession. Then after a while the new member, looking shaken, would come down to the living room where the wives and us kids were waiting. We'd all sit around on chairs and the members would share and we'd all pray. It was kind of like an old-fashioned revival meeting. They didn't let a newcomer lead a meeting until he'd been sober a year.

Within days of their surrender, in obedience to Oxford Group precepts, the neophytes were asked to "take inventory" of themselves, admit their character defects and make amends to those they had hurt while drinking. They spent a lot of time between meetings at the Ardmore Avenue house of Bob and Anne Smith—in fact, the place was bursting with visitors. Young Bob and Sue remembered how it was, and this is a composite of their memories:

> The coffeepot was on day and night. Eight O'Clock Coffee cost twenty-nine cents for three pounds then, and Mother used

up about six pounds a week for her visitors. In the mornings there was "quiet time" for a little group in the living room. They read from the Bible and just sat there, thinking their own thoughts and getting a silent guidance for the day. Mother always sat in a dark corner by the fireplace, which had fake gas logs in it; her eyes were weak and glare hurt them. Everybody was welcome. Everybody was painfully broke.

Dorothy S., the wife of an early member, said, "In those early days most of us didn't have telephones. We were handed a little address book. We were told, 'All our homes are open to you. Drop in at any time.' "

Another wife recalled the hospitality and the pot-luck meals at the Ardmore Avenue house: "The people at the table might have eleven kinds of potato salad, because we were all too poor to buy wieners. Everyone brought food. I wonder if A.A.'s today appreciate how pitifully poor most of us were in those early, struggling days." It was a banner Sunday when the Smiths could offer corned-beef hash.

Bill Wilson lived with the Smiths for the entire summer of 1935, sitting and talking and smoking cigarettes in the kitchen with Dr. Bob until two or three o'clock every morning. Young Bob often sat with them, fascinated, as they picked each other's brains and tried to formulate an orderly program they could present to the next "man on the bed" in the hospital. Fortunately the doctor never scheduled his operations until 11 A.M.

"I thought Bill would never come home from Akron," his wife, Lois, said. "I nagged and nagged him to return."

Finally she took a week's vacation from her job at Loeser's department store in Brooklyn and went west to meet the Smiths. "My mother straightened her out," Sue Smith said. "Lois seemed so resentful at first, but then she seemed relieved at how happy everyone was." Young Bob said, "It was not a somber, serious time. My father and Bill were so excited about their program, and when the drunks began to come into our house they were even more excited. It was definitely not a sad time. It was a joyous, exciting time. I guess what made it happy was that finally, they were free."

On August 26, 1935, Bill returned home to Brooklyn. He had never been so content. In Dr. Bob he had found a friend and brother for life. He was enthusiastic about the work with other alcoholics in Akron. He had come back to the warmth of an Oxford Group welcome in New York. But he did not know that Lois was stifling a growing resentment—a common feeling among the spouses of alcoholics who have stopped drinking. One Sunday, Bill casually said to his wife, "We'll have to hurry, or we'll be late for the Oxford Group meeting."

Lois exploded. "Damn your old meetings!" she shouted.

That fall in 1935, the Wilsons followed the example of the Smiths by making their Clinton Street home—the gift of Lois's father, who had moved out after marrying for a second time—a halfway house for drunks. "When I think back on those days, I wonder WHAT we lived on," Lois said. Her diary included notations such as, "Ebby pid me two dollars for his board. . . . George H., sent by Dr. Silkworth, came to live with us." So did Bill C., a lawyer, who stayed for quite a while.

The long-suffering Lois was losing her temper more frequently. She was resentful that Bill hadn't gotten sober for her sake; resentful that her husband didn't have time for her anymore. "The house was full of drunks; you were always out working on somebody and bringing somebody home," she told Bill years later.

She loved the house. She had been raised there, the oldest of six children. Built in 1848, it was typical of the stately brick row houses that still line the quiet, leafy streets of Brooklyn Heights. It was four stories tall, with steep steps leading up to the front door on the parlor floor. Marble Victorian fireplaces and high, carved ceilings gave it an elegant air. Into this setting came Bill's sloppy, alcoholic friends, demanding more pancakes for breakfast, stashing empty whiskey bottles in the kitchen, where Lois, seething, found them. "We were seldom alone together now," she said. By the fall of 1935, other alcoholics, from New York and New Jersey, were joining the Wilson freeloaders for Tuesday night meetings at the Clinton Street house.

Getting his lodgers to stop drinking proved more than Bill could manage. No matter what he said or did, they kept getting drunk. One of them, Bill C. the lawyer, sold Lois' and Bill's best clothes to buy liquor, then committed suicide.

Slowly, Bill had come to believe that alcoholics needed to work with their own kind, that staying sober while achieving balance and peace in one's life was the only goal that counted. He was growing dissatisfied with the publicity that prominent Oxford Group adherents were getting in the nation's press; he thought such exposure would only puff up an alcoholic's ego and cause him to get drunk again. He did not like the Oxford members' stress on the "four absolutes." He thought that the word "absolute" implied a perfection, impossible to achieve, that was already frightening alcoholics just struggling to remain sober. He resented the constant checking-up on each Oxford member by others in the group to make sure that all were following the prescribed path. Are you 'maximum'?" they would ask each other. He did not like the increasing size of their get-togethers or their growing snobbishness. Power, prestige and money impressed Frank Buchman; he was constantly seeking big-name members for his movement who would testify to its attractions. People were invited to join what was becoming an ever-larger but socially and professionally more exclusive club. Some began calling the Oxford Group an "upper-class Salvation Army."

By contrast, the alcoholics being saved in New York, Akron and elsewhere within the Oxford Group were drunks being dredged up from the bottom of their drinking lives, regardless of how high they had risen previously in their vocations.

Bill never wrote of the bombshell Buchman dropped shortly before the New York alcoholics pulled away. It shook the Oxford Group profoundly and triggered an international controversy that ultimately forced it to hide under another name. The bombshell was an article in the *New York World-Telegram* of August 26, 1936. The reporter, William A. H. Birnie, quoted Buchman as saying: "I thank heaven for a man like Adolf Hitler, who built a front-line of defense against the anti-Christ of Communism. . . . My barber in London told me Hitler saved all Europe from Communism. That's how he felt. Of course, I don't condone everything the Nazis do. . . . I suppose Hitler sees Karl Marx in every Jew. . . . But think what it would mean to the world if Hitler surrendered to the control of God. Or Mussolini, or any dictator. Through such a man God could control a nation overnight and solve any last, bewildering problem." The Oxford ranks Buchman led were decimated despite widespread pacifist sentiments in the United States. In 1939, as the free world went to war against Nazi Germany, the Oxford Group became the Moral Re-Armament movement.

In 1936 and 1937, Bill Wilson, increasingly obsessed about saving alcoholics, did only a few free-lance stock market investigations. They represented his last serious effort to reestablish himself on Wall Street. But soon he received his first offer of a steady job in another field. The offer came from Charles Towns, owner of the hospital where Bill had finally gotten sober and where he was now finding some of his most promising prospects among other hospitalized drunks. Towns asked him to open an office there as a paid lay alcoholism therapist. Bill was ecstatic, then amazed to discover that the alcoholics living in the Wilson household and other members of the Oxford Group who were trying to recover disapproved. Why should he get paid, they asked him, when the rest of them, who were involved in the same sort of labors, would not be? Full of regret, Bill declined Charles Towns' offer. Any real money that came to him from then on until the end of his life was earned within Alcoholics Anonymous, mostly from royalties of the textbooks he wrote for A.A.

In 1937, another opportunity set Bill afire once more with dreams of success. This time they were ignited by John D. Rockefeller, Jr., a teetotaler and earlier, a famous champion of Prohibition. Through Bill's brother-in-law, Dr. Leonard Strong, he was introduced to Willard Richardson of the Rockefeller Foundation. Although Bill had had only scattered luck with those he had tried to sober up personally, it did not seem to discourage this irrepressible dreamer. He began to have visions of hiring men to act as paid missionaries to carry the alcoholics' message, of establishing chains of special hospitals to treat alcoholics, of literature about the slowly growing clusters of recovered drunks, their methods and goals. In December 1937, Richardson and a few other Rockefeller advisers met with Bill, Dr. Bob and some of their recovered alcoholics. Each alcoholic in the room told his own story. The groups' methods of reaching others were described. Scott declared, "Why, this is first-century Christianity!" Later, after Bill proposed paid missionaries and a hospital chain for alcoholics, Scott asked, "But won't money spoil this thing?"

In February 1938, Frank Amos, an Ohio native whose family owned a newspaper there, went to Akron to investigate Dr. Bob's reported successes in saving alcoholics. He presented a glowing report to Rockefeller, urging that he give $50,000 to the movement. Rockefeller was much more cautious. He agreed that both Dr. Bob and Bill needed some personal financial help to free them for such work, and consented to place $5,000 for that purpose in the treasury of Riverside Church. Much of it went to pay off the mortgage on the Smith house in Akron.

Bill, Dr. Strong and the New York alcoholics had further meetings with Rockefeller's friends Richardson, Amos and A. LeRoy Chipman, who offered their own services to the groups of alcoholics led by Bill and Dr. Bob. On August 11, 1938, with the help of John Wood, a young lawyer, they established a tax-exempt, charitable entity called the Alcoholic Foundation. The foundation had little money, but it gave the movement a legally formed, New York-based center.

Bill Wilson's dreams of paid missionaries and special hospitals for alcoholics had fizzled. The idea for a textbook to guide the membership, however, began to be seriously discussed in New York and Akron in 1937 and 1938. The members needed such a book for four very practical reasons: It could set forth a clear statement of the recovery program and prevent distortion of the methods used to help alcoholics; it could be mailed or carried to among sympathetic nonalcoholics; and it could make money. What few suspected was that the title finally chosen for the book—*Alcoholics Anonymous*—would also give a name at last to a little bunch of sobered-up drunks.

Bill began work on the book in the spring of 1938 in the office of the Honor Dealers, in Newark, New Jersey, the last of all his brief, failed business ventures outside A.A. His partner was Hank P., an oil-company executive who had lost his job because of drinking and wound up in Towns Hospital. There Bill, out on one of his missions to save drunks in the fall of 1935, had found Hank and gotten him sober—Bill's first success. Hank and his wife, Kathleen, traveled from New Jersey every Tuesday to the meetings at the Wilson house and had become close friends. Hank and Bill, through Honor Dealers, sought to organize gasoline-station owners in northern New Jersey into a cooperative buying group and, from the profits, help more alcoholics. An energetic, impatient redhead, Hank loved and hated with equal gusto and was brimming over with ideas. He ran the business as Bill became increasingly involved with his manuscript, dictating rough drafts each day to Ruth Hock, the Honor Dealers' nonalcoholic secretary, for typing.

Bill wrote all of the opening eleven chapters. They included his own personal story, as well as "There Is a Solution," "More About Alcoholism," "We Agnostics," "Working with Others" and the crucial fifth chapter, "How It Works," which contained the Twelve Steps to recovery. According to Lois, Bill wrote the first draft of the steps in one night in bed. She often told of how Bill would never stand up if he could sit down, and lying down was even better.

The first draft of the Twelve Steps was very close to its final version in the Big Book, which read:

1. We admitted that we were powerless over alcohol—that our lives had become unmanageable.
2. Came to believe that a Power greater than ourselves could restore us to sanity.

3. Made a decision to turn our will and our lives over to the care and direction of God *as we understood Him.*
4. Made a searching and fearless moral inventory of ourselves.
5. Admitted to God, to ourselves, and to another human being the exact nature of our wrongs.
6. Were entirely ready to have God remove all these defects of character.
7. Humbly asked Him to remove our shortcomings.
8. Made a list of all persons we had harmed, and became willing to make amends to them all.
9. Made direct amends to such people wherever possible, except when to do so would injure them or others.
10. Continued to take personal inventory and when we were wrong promptly admitted it.
11. Sought through prayer and meditation to improve our conscious contact with God *as we understood Him,* praying only for knowledge of His will for us and the power to carry that out.
12. Having had a spiritual awakening as the result of these steps, we tried to carry this message to alcoholics, and to practice these principles in all our affairs.

Like every other part of the book, the Twelve Steps were copied and passed around to the New York and Ohio groups. Every sentence was heatedly discussed. Some thought there was "too much God" in the steps and the early chapters, and that they would offend atheists and agnostics. Bill's first draft mentioned getting down on one's knees to pray, a usual practice even among the Oxford members who were not Catholic or Episcopalian. The reference to kneeling was cut from one step. The phrase, in italics, *"as we understood Him"* was added after the word *God* in two other steps.

Bill would not let even Lois, who was dying to do so, write the chapter titled "To Wives." After all, she was the wife who had endured Bill's drunken years and the houseful of alcoholics he was trying to wrestle into sobriety. "I have never known why he didn't want me to write about the wives, and it hurt me at first," she said.

The "Personal Stories" part of the book contained twenty-eight accounts from the alcoholics in Akron and New York. Dr. Silkworth contributed "The Doctor's Opinion" at the beginning of the book. His letter of endorsement said in part:

> In late 1934 I attended a patient who, though he had been a competent business man of good earning capacity, was an alcoholic of a type I had come to regard as hopeless. In the course of his . . . treatment he acquired certain ideas concerning a possible means of recovery. As part of his rehabilitation he commenced to present his conceptions to other alcoholics, impressing upon them that they must do likewise with still others. This has become the basis of a rapidly growing fellowship of these men and their families. This man and over one hundrend others appear to have recovered. I personally know scores of cases who were of the type with whom other methods had failed completely. These facts appear to be of extreme medical importance; because of the extraordinary possibilities of rapid growth inherent in this group they may mark a new epoch in the annals of alcoholism. These men may well have a remedy for thousands of such situations.

The original foreword, written by Bill, began with this confident yet modest statement:

> We, of Alcoholics Anonymous, are more than one hundred men and women who have recovered from a seemingly hopeless state of mind and body. To show other alcoholics *precisely how we have recovered* is the main purpose of this book. . . . We think this account of our experiences will help everyone to better understand the alcoholic. Many do not comprehend that the alcoholic is a very sick person. . . . We are sure that our way of living has its advantages for all.
>
> It is important that we remain anonymous because we are too few at present to handle the overwhelming number of appeals

which may result from this publication. Being mostly business or professional folk, we could not well carry on our occupations in such an event. We would like it understood that our alcoholic work is an avocation.

When writing or speaking publicly about alcoholism, we urge each of our Fellowship to omit his personal name, designating himself instead as "a member of Alcoholics Anonymous."

The original foreword continued:

We are not an organization in the conventional sense of the word. There are no fees or dues whatsoever. The only requirement for membership is an honest desire to stop drinking. We are not allied with any particular faith, sect or denomination, nor do we oppose anyone. We simply wish to be helpful to those who are afflicted.

With minor changes, that statement of purpose would be repeated aloud as a preamble to thousands of A.A. meetings every day in the years to come.

The title of the book, like much else within its pages, was decided only after strenuous discussion and polling of the groups. By mid-1938, Bill was using *Alcoholics Anonymous* as a working title for both the book and the "fellowship," as it continued to be called by many members even after the enormous influx of women.

Among the dozens of other titles the members suggested were *Dry Frontiers* and *The Empty Glass*. "At one time," said Lois, "Bill was tempted to call the book 'The Wilson Movement,' using his last name and to sign it as author. This natural but egotistical impulse was soon overcome by more mature reasoning."

The choice finally narrowed to *Alcoholics Anonymous* dreamed up by a member who had worked for *The New Yorker* magazine.

Henrietta D. of Akron, wife of Bill D., A.A. No. 3, told one and all that when she first heard the title, it was "the awfullest name I ever heard."

The style of the opening chapters of *Alcoholics Anonymous* consists of simple declarative sentences. There is some outdated slang (one of Bill's favorites was "ten-strike," from bowling, to describe an instantly successful idea) and a boosterist tone of on-ward and upward with George Follansbee Babbitt. The plain and straightforwardly told "Personal Stories" can at times also seem a bit old-fashioned. Yet for half a century the book has had some-thing fundamental to say to alcoholics wanting to get well. It is the one book in A.A. that everybody reads.

The first copies of *Alcoholics Anonymous* rolled off the Corn-wall Press in Cornwall, New York, in April 1939. The plant's owner, Edward Blackwell, suggested an initial printing of 5,000 copies, rather than the unrealistically high figure that Wilson and Hank P. envisaged.

They decided on a list price of $3.50—rather high for 1939 and only $1.15 less than it costs today. (Today, non-A.A. purchasers of the Big Book, which now has a plainer, navy-blue cover, pay $4.65. A.A. members buy it for even less: $4.10 a copy.) The first edition was so bulky that it quickly became known as the Big Book.

The initial reaction of the medical profession was one of con-tempt. A review in the *Journal of the American Medical Associ-ation* for October 14, 1939, called *Alcoholics Anonymous* "a curious combination of organizing propaganda and religious exhorta-tion. . . . The one valid thing in the book is the recognition of the seriousness of addiction to alcohol. Other than this, the book has no scientific merit or interest." Earlier, *The New York Times* had been more charitable. In June 1939, a Sunday *Times* reviewer wrote, "Lest this title should arouse the risibles [sic] in any reader, let me state that the general thesis of *Alcoholics Anonymous* is more soundly based psychologically than any other treatment of the subject I have ever come upon." But Harry Emerson Fosdick of New York's Riverside Church, in a review that appeared in religious publications, threw his enormous national prestige behind the book. Calling it single and remarkable, he urged it on everyone in any way involved with alcohol abuse.

Despite Fosdick's recommendation, nearly all the initial 5,000 copies of *Alcoholics Anonymous* remained in Edward Blackwell's warehouse. Nobody was buying. Bill Wilson and Hank P. ap-proached all the national magazines for coverage, without a nibble.

Finally, Morgan R. of New York, formerly a successful advertising man, said he would get on the air with his friend Gabriel Heatter. Heatter had an enormously popular radio program called *We the People*. He specialized in human-interest interviews, often heart-rending, which he commented upon in fatherly, unctuous tones. Heatter agreed to interview Morgan for three minutes on *We the People* on April 25, 1939. The alcoholics were thrilled. As the hour of the 9 P.M. broadcast drew near, the entire membership of about one hundred men, one woman, and their families, in New York and Ohio, gathered around their radios.

Heatter began: "The man beside me now has had one of the most gripping and dramatic experiences I've ever heard. I'm not going to tell you his name. And when you hear what he has to say, I think you'll understand why. But . . . the Listener's Committee of *We the People* decided to grant him time because they feel if one person is helped by hearing his story, then *We the People* will have done a real service."

Morgan R. began: "Six months ago, I got out of an insane asylum. I'd been sent there because I was drinking myself to death. But the doctors said they could do nothing for me." Four years earlier, he said, he had been earning $20,000 a year. He had a wife, a "swell girl," and a young son. He worked hard and drank to relax like his colleagues. "Only they knew when to stop. I didn't. And pretty soon I drank myself out of my job. I promised my wife I'd straighten out. But I couldn't. Finally she took the baby and left me."

Morgan told how he had wound up on the streets panhandling for liquor. "Every time I sobered up, I swore not to touch another drop. But if I went a few hours without a drink, I'd begin to cry like a baby and tremble all over."

Shortly after he left the asylum, Morgan said, he met Tom, a friend who took him to another friend's home. "A bunch of men were sitting around, smoking cigars, telling jokes, having a great time. But I noticed they weren't drinking," he added. "When Tom told me they'd all been in the same boat as I was, I couldn't believe him."

Tom pointed out a doctor who had drunk himself out of his practice, who now was the head of a big hospital, a grocery clerk, the vice president of a corporation. Morgan continued, "They got together five years ago. Called themselves Alcoholics Anonymous. And they'd worked out a method of recovery. One of their most important secrets was helping the other fellow. . . . Gradually, those men helped me back to life. I stopped drinking. Found courage to face life once again. Today, I've got a job, and I'm going to climb back to success."

Morgan then made his pitch for the Big Book: "Recently, we wrote a book called *Alcoholics Anonymous*. It tells precisely how we all came back from a living death. Working on that book made me realize how other people had suffered—how they'd gone through the same thing I did. That's why I wanted to come on this program. I wanted to tell people who are going through that torment—if they sincerely want to, they can come back. Take their place in society once again!" [Applause. Music up and out.]

Bill Wilson and his friends speculated how they would handle the flood of inquiries. At a cost of $500, they had typed and mailed out 20,000 cards to notify people in the medical profession about the broadcast. They waited three days, to give enough time for the cards to pile up in the Alcoholic Foundation's post-office box. Then they took empty suitcases down to the post office to carry home all the replies.

"When they unlocked the box," said Lois, "they couldn't believe their eyes—only twelve cards. Five hundred bucks had gone down the drain."

It was a terrible spring. The day after Heatter's broadcast, on April 26, 1939, Bill and Lois were forced to leave 182 Clinton Street, her family's home for fifty years; the bank holding the mortgage had finally sold the house, for which the Wilsons had been paying a minuscule rent since Lois's father's death in 1936. For the next two years, they would have no permanent home of their own. They lived like vagabonds, first with one A.A. family, then with another.

There were some bright spots. *Liberty* magazine, one of the most popular periodicals of the time, published an approving article titled "Alcoholics and God" in September 1939. The next month, the *Cleveland Plain Dealer,* a strong Midwest daily, published a seven-part series on A.A. backed up with supportive editorials. Recruits began coming in, but it was a trickle compared to Bill's hopes. It was not until two years later that A.A. got the breakthrough it had been waiting for—a cover article in the *Saturday Evening Post,* the weekly magazine that more than three million Americans read and believed in. Jack Alexander's piece was intelligent, riveting, understandable. The most famous single article in A.A. history, published March 1, 1941, it was thought to be the main reason the membership quadrupled that year, from 2,000 to 8,000.

In 1939 and 1940, however, Bill Wilson had suffered two grievous rejections: one from inside A.A., the other from outside. In the end, both events sharpened his ideas about the way A.A. should go. He decided late in 1939 that the A.A. headquarters and the Big Book publishing operation should be moved from the Honor Dealers office in New Jersey to the Alcoholic Foundation in Manhattan. Hank P. wrote Bill a memo. Affectionate and wry in tone, it asked questions that have echoed down the years in A.A., questions about the separation of a money-making business and work for the love of it; about individualism and the cult of personality that was already beginning to gather around Bill Wilson and Dr. Bob; and about the way it was for those early Christians and might never be again. Hank asked:

"Did Jesus Christ have an office? . . . Would money that would be spent on an office be better spent for traveling expenses for people spreading the good news? Will there be a Grand Poohbah of A.A.?"

Bill's response was courteous but reserved. He was troubled about Hank. His hot-tempered, impulsive friend had started drinking again. He was fighting with his wife. He wanted a divorce. He wanted to marry Ruth Hock, the Honor Dealers' secretary. The rupture between the two men proved irrevocable.

The other blow came from John D. Rockefeller, Jr. Early in

1940, Rockefeller announced that he would like to give a dinner at the exclusive Union Club on Park Avenue in New York for members and friends of A.A. as well as some important people unfamiliar with its work. Bill called the seventy-five men who accepted "a veritable constellation of New York's prominent and wealthy. Anybody," he said, "could see that their total financial worth might easily be a billion dollars."

Dr. Foster Kennedy, head of the clinical division of Cornell University Medical College, spoke. Dr. Kennedy had already written to the *Journal of the American Medical Association* to protest its blistering review of A.A.'s Big Book, saying, "I believe medical men of good will should aid these decent people rather than loftily condemn them for not being scientific."

The listeners included the bluebloods Godfrey L. Cabot and Gordon Auchincloss, the dime-store tycoon Samuel H. Kress and Thomas J. Watson, the founder of International Business Machines. Nelson Rockefeller, then thirty-one, represented his father, who had suddenly taken ill. As the evening wore on, Bill's hopes soared:

Breathlessly we waited for the climax—the matter of money. Nelson Rockefeller obliged us. . . . "Gentlemen, you can all see that this is a work of goodwill. Its power lies in the fact that one member carries the good message to the next, without any thought of financial reward. Therefore, it is our belief that Alcoholics Anonymous should be self-supporting so far as money is concerned. It needs only our goodwill." Whereupon the guests clapped lustily, and the whole billion dollars' worth of them walked out the door.

It is a marvelous story as Bill told it, many hundreds of times, to delighted A.A.'s chuckling about how they escaped the corruption of evil lucre. It has come down as a key scene in A.A.'s oral history. But that is not quite what happened. The minutes of the after-dinner remarks in 1940 show that Nelson Rockefeller did not speak at all. The chairman was Albert Scott, president of Lockwood Greene Engineers and a trustee of the Alcoholic Foundation and of Riverside Church. At the end, one of the guests asked, "Mr. Chairman, before we adjourn will you tell us what you think we can do to help the movement along?" Scott replied:

Well, I confess a little embarrassment at this question. I just consulted with Mr. Nelson Rockefeller on the subject you have just mentioned and he decided he would not say anything on that subject in Mr. Rockefeller's [John D. junior's] absence. . . . Mr. Rockefeller has said he will be very glad to send a copy of this book with his compliments to anyone who would like to see it.

The evening ended with those words. The two accounts, Bill Wilson's and the transcribed minutes, illustrate perfectly Bill's life-long penchant for embroidering the facts while accurately summarizing the gist of an event. The outcome of that extraordinary dinner did dash, once again and for the last time, his dreams of important outside money for A.A.

In 1940, the New York members, weary of wandering from home to home for their gatherings, finally found their first meeting center—in a former stable on West Twenty-fourth Street. The Twenty-fourth Street Clubhouse, its $100-a-month rent guaranteed by two employed members, had a long, tunnellike corridor leading from the front that A.A.'s dubbed "the last mile." At its end was one large room paneled in knotty pine with a fireplace and kitchen. Upstairs were cramped quarters where Lois and Bill lived from November 1940, until they found the first and only home of their own in 1941.

Lois described the Wilsons' tiny digs at the clubhouse: "We painted the walls and curtained two orange crates to use as dressers. From an old friend we bought a bed without a footboard, so Bill could hang his feet out. We had to crawl over the bed to reach our clothes, which hung on hooks on the wall. About ten feet square, the room had a window; but for air it was easier to open the door to the fire escape."

An old member described the atmosphere: "People came from everywhere, driving in from Connecticut or Westchester or just drifting in from the streets of Manhattan. If you came early you sat on chairs in the sitting room or on the stairs to the second floor. There was a picture of Bill above the fireplace with what looked like a halo around his head. We used to kid Bill about it. There were no young people. There were many more men than women, and all of them had been low-bottom drunks. I wasn't made to feel odd because I was a woman."

"In a sense they were all members of an exclusive club," said another A.A., "and only they understood what dues they had had to pay to get there."

On a sleeting night in 1940, a crippled Jesuit priest from St. Louis named Edward Dowling hobbled into the Twenty-fourth Street Clubhouse. Bill, the first to admit he was a hypochondriac, was in bed upstairs with one of his many "imaginary ulcer attacks," as he called them, and he was feeling very depressed. Father Dowling, editor of a Roman Catholic publication called *The Queen's Work*, had read the Big Book and wanted to know more about Alcoholics Anonymous and its program for recovery. The stranger radiated sympathy. Gradually Bill began to unburden himself of the thoughts and guilts he had been able to confess to no one else. Father Dowling, a nonalcoholic, became Bill Wilson's spiritual adviser and one of his staunchest supporters in an intimate friendship that endured until the priest's death twenty years later.

In the spring of 1941, the Wilsons finally found Stepping Stones. The house—an inviting, cozy, Dutch Colonial structure of dark brown shingles with gables sunk into a steep gambrel roof—was set in a hilly, wooded area of Bedford Hills in Westchester County, about an hour's ride north of New York City. The ground floor consisted of a huge living room with a cavernous stone fireplace and French doors that faced east onto a screened veranda. Off this were three small bedrooms and a kitchen. The master bedroom and a long, broad gallery lined with books, photographs and memorabilia were upstairs. Its owner was a woman whose husband had died an active alcoholic and whose best friend had been saved by an A.A. group in New Jersey. She offered the house to the Wilsons for $6,500, no money down, with mortgage payments of $40 a month.

On April 11, 1941, Bill and Lois spent the first night in twenty-three years of marriage in a home that was truly their own. At first they called it "Bill-Lo's Break." Because of the constant climbing up and down the steep slope between the house and garage they finally called it Stepping Stones—with its echoes, of course, of the Twelve Steps. At last they would have a private place to themselves—they thought. Soon, however, A.A. members found their way to Bedford Hills: It was open house every weekend for about thirty or forty of them. There were usually house guests as well, and during the 1940's, Bill brought Helen Evans, his half sister by his father's second wife, to Stepping Stones to live.

Bill, a monomaniac who loved to sit or lie down and think, write and read, while Lois did all the physical work, including shoveling snow off the long driveway at Stepping Stones—finally built a place where he could be alone. It was a little concrete-block studio up a hill on the grounds. He called it "Wit's End." He also began spending several nights a week at the Bedford Hotel in Manhattan. When Bill was preoccupied, little that was going on around him penetrated his consciousness.

His half sister Helen remembered that when she and Lois would get him to the table for lunch at Stepping Stones, "He'd just sit there, and you could see his mind was going around. And he'd pick up a fork to eat the soup with."

In the mid-1940's Bill's depressions were deepening. He was seldom free of black and despairing moods. He was seeing psychiatrists regularly: first Dr. Harry Tiebout, an enthusiastic supporter of A.A.'s recovery program; then Dr. Frances Weekes. For a year, he took Roman Catholic instruction from Monsignor Fulton J. Sheen, a charismatic and influential New York priest, renowned for bringing the famous into the Catholic fold, whose zeal seemed to pour out of his burning, hypnotic eyes. But Bill never was converted and never was comfortable within organized religion, despite his lifelong efforts to gain the friendship and use the power of individual clergymen.

He and Lois spent months on the road every year during the 1940's, crisscrossing the United States to visit and inspire the groups that were popping up in every region. By 1944 there were 10,000 members in 360 groups. *The Grapevine*, A.A.'s monthly magazine, was started and became one of Bill's most important means of communicating his thoughts to readers. A.A. headquarters moved uptown from Vesey street in New York's financial district to Lexington Avenue near Grand Central Terminal. Nell Wing, a giggly, tender-hearted chatterbox who was Bill's nonalcoholic secretary for many years and A.A.'s first archivist, remembered those carefree days in the Lexington Avenue office:

It was March 3, 1947. I was just out of the Coast Guard and in New York to get a temporary job. A woman at the employment agency whispered to me, "How'd you like to work at Alcoholics Anonymous?" I went over to the A.A. office, and there wasn't even a name on the door, just a number. There were thirteen people including Bill jammmed into three teensy little rooms. It was chaos. I remember people horsing around between answering the phones, and somebody named Mary Lou was wearing a paper bag over over her head. I was hired as a typist for thirty-two dollars a week, and I stayed for thirty-six years.

Lelia M., the heiress to one of America's publishing fortunes and one of the first female members of A.A., was equally close to Bill. In 1943, after her psychiatrist forced her to go to A.A., the doctor gave her the Big Book. Lelia had read it, she said, "with a glass in my hand." She hated it. Reluctantly, "squirming for a drink," she went to the Vesey Street headquarters. "Bill had a kind of asymmetrical good looks, sleepy eyes and a lantern jaw," she said. "He often talked a lot, but in a measured way. When he was listening, he held his mouth open a little as if he had had a slight stroke. Anything but. He was witty and alert and terrific and tall. He was infinitely tolerant."

Lelia said to him: "Your book is all about God, and I don't believe in God."

He said gently, "Do you think you are one of us?" She immediately nodded her head. "I hadn't belonged anywhere for a long time," said this aristocratic, cultivated woman years later. "I was an outcast, drinking in bars."

Bill told her: "We have a physical allergy and a psychological compulsion. We can't tolerate it, but we're compelled to drink. You can't help this. You're not bad, you're sick." Relief flooded through her, a feeling of sudden freedom—an emotion experienced by many thousands of alcoholics who have finally faced their most intractable problem.

Lelia's sponsor—the A.A. word for mentor and closest friend —became Marty Mann, an energetic doer and mesmerizing speaker who had joined A.A. in 1939. At her death in 1980, she held the record for continuous sobriety of any woman in A.A. She was the founder and prime mover of the National Committee for Education on Alcoholism and its successor, the National Council on Alcoholism. She repeatedly toured the lecture circuit with her message that the alcoholic was a sick person, and that alcoholism was an illness, a public health problem and a public responsibility. In doing so, she also repeatedly broke her anonymity, initially with Bill Wilson's encouragement and later to his dismay; yet their friendship never wavered. Marty was convinced that educating the public, and laying her life, her full name and expertise on the line, were more important than staying anonymous. She had enriched her knowledge in 1943 at the newly founded Yale School of Alcohol Studies, the nation's first such educational program, and became convinced that it was her calling to change public attitudes toward the disease and its victims.

The concept of anonymity was strongly rooted in A.A. from its fledgling days. So were the ideas of shunning money, property, public controversy and politics; the singleness of purpose; the independence of local groups, and a headquarters where the staff would serve and represent those far-flung groups but not govern them. None of this, however, had been written down. The need for clear guidelines had been discussed at headquarters since 1943; by then, Bill had absorbed a good deal in his visits to groups across the country and through their letters and questions, which he was mainly responsible for answering. Bill then put together the Twelve Traditions, which with the Twelve Steps form the fundamental underpinnings of the philosophy of Alcoholics Anonymous. They were never called "laws," "rules," or "by-laws." "Suggestions" seemed a little weak. "Traditions" they became.

Bill spent years pushing the Twelve Traditions, campaigning around the country. Sometimes the groups did not like his steamroller tactics and his constant harping upon his new set of principles. The Twelve Steps were a program to help heal individuals; the Twelve Traditions set forth a guide to group behavior, and the early, highly individualistic members balked at that. At last, however, they were approved by A.A.'s first international convention in July 1950. By the year's end, Dr. Bob—the only other person besides Bill entitled and expected to speak for the membership—was dead of cancer. He died November 16, and was buried in Akron's Mount Peace Cemetery beside Anne, who had died the year before.

Bill was now the single individual left at the head of A.A. He was fifty-five years old. He would live for twenty more years, would write three more books, the most important and popular one explaining in detail the Twelve Steps and Twelve Traditions. Before him was the 1951 Lasker Group Award given to A.A.; a Yale doctorate of laws offered in 1954 and declined with tremendous regret by Bill, who could not break the Traditions he himself had written; and a proposed cover article on him in *Time* magazine, which he also refused. His Big Book had become the central textbook to guide the movement, his most important and enduring legacy. It was the foundation stone of A.A.'s growing publishing empire and has always been a critical indicator of the numbers of people passing through A.A., since it has been for sale almost entirely within A.A. groups or through A.A. headquarters, rarely in outside bookstores.

The Big Book is one of the greatest publishing successes of all time; by 1985, the year of A.A.'s fiftieth anniversary, five million copies had been sold. Royalties from Wilson's books would ultimately give him and Lois a comfortable income—from $30,000 to $40,000 annually by the late 1960's, and, by the time of his death in 1971, almost $56,000 a year. Beginning in the 1970's, it made Lois rich. In 1986, she received $912,500 from sales of the

Big Book and three other A.A. books her husband had written. Her share had been determined by an agreement made in 1963 between Wilson and A.A. World Services, the publisher: 13.5 percent of the books' retail price for Lois and 1.5 percent for Helen W., Bill's last and most enduring mistress. (Helen W. survived Bill by only a few years, dying in the 1970's.) Lois could not have given her fortune to A.A. even if she had wished to. According to one of the Twelve Traditions her own husband wrote, A.A. must decline all outside contributions. Even Lois was an "outsider": The widow of the co-founder could not leave Stepping Stones to A.A. Finally Lois channeled some of her money into the Stepping Stones Foundation for alcoholism research.

In the last twenty years of Bill's life, he shocked A.A. trustees and old-timers not only by taking lovers but with his experiments with LSD, his crusades for niacin to solve mental problems and the spiritualist seances he organized at Stepping Stones. He could not step down, could not let go of A.A.'s tiller. Dennis Manders, the nonalcoholic comptroller of A.A.'s finances for thirty-five years beginning in 1950, said Bill spent "the last fifteen years [of his life] stepping down." He could remain anonymous at no group meeting, being healed quietly like all the others. They begged him to speak everywhere; he was mobbed at A.A. conventions. Barry L. saw the lines form at one convention so that people could touch him and shake hands; a woman came up to him in tears to say, "You saved my family." "I saw pain on his face," Barry recalled. "He had to be kind. He felt so guilty about his womanizing, and yet he was treated like a saint."

Dr. John Norris, the A.A. trustee, said: "I was amazed, given such adoration, that Bill could retain any shred of humanity and humility. People got a thrill out of touching his coat. It was pretty heady stuff." Finally, a weekly group meeting was organized at A.A. headquarters in New York so that Bill could be one among equals. "Anyplace else, the strength of group support was not available to Bill," Dr. Norris said. He would sit for hours in his office, feet up, the door open, and buttonhole anybody who came along. He might keep them there an hour or two, just chatting. A heavy, sloppy smoker all his life, he developed emphysema in the 1960's. It killed him. He gave his last speech to the International A.A. Convention in Miami in 1970, lifted to the platform in a wheelchair, gasping for breath and sucking oxygen from the tank that was always with him. He died on January 24, 1971, and was buried in his birthplace, East Dorset, Vermont. Neither his headstone nor Dr. Bob's bears any mention of A.A. In his final years and after his death, Bill Wilson became a cult figure within the movement, a role he both dreaded and secretly desired. He had become what Hank P. had feared. He had become the Grand Poohbah of Alcoholics Anonymous.

In 1964, Arthur Krock, the grand old conservative columnist of *The New York Times,* wrote the following about President John Fitzgerald Kennedy shortly after his assassination; it could apply as well to Bill Wilson: "The truth explains what the gathering myth obscures—that [he] was endearingly and admirably human."

# 4

## A.A. TODAY

"A.A. is the only place you can go during the cocktail hour where everybody in the room is getting better instead of worse."
—*A newcomer to A.A.*

"You've got to understand that all these people would be dead if it weren't for each other."
—*Wife of a senior A.A. member*

Only Bill Wilson could have imagined the following scenes, because only Bill among the old-timers in A.A. had such grandiose, impractical dreams. Fifty summers after two men sat in Dr. Bob's kitchen on Ardmore Avenue in Akron, chain-smoking and wrestling alone with their problem, fifty years to the day of Dr. Bob's last drink, thousands of recovered drunks filled the cavernous, echoing twilight of the Cathedral of St. John the Divine in New

York, the largest Gothic cathedral in the world. It was June 10, 1985. The service—or rather gigantic meeting to celebrate A.A.'s first half century—brought as many people to the church on that hot, sunny afternoon as all those who belonged to Alcoholics Anonymous by 1941, six years after its founding.

The gathering was only one of the many local celebrations throughout the nation. A month later, in July 1985, A.A.'s again demonstrated their strength, and their exhilaration in recovery, when 44,000 of them, from fifty-four countries, converged on Montreal for A.A.'s Golden Anniversary International Convention. For hundreds of miles in every direction the highways were long, linear parties of sober alcoholic drivers waving and calling to one another as soon as they recognized an A.A. slogan on each others' cars. IF YOU'RE A FRIEND OF BILL'S, HONK! was a favorite bumper-sticker greeting, and almost every roadside stand was the scene for a reunion of strangers. Upon arrival, they swamped the city and filled the hotels and inns as far as two hours away.

*The New York Times* correspondent, who had come reluctantly to the assignment from the Canadian capital of Ottawa, was astonished. "Far from being a self-righteous assembly of sullen ex-drunkards," he wrote, "the convention, the largest Montreal has been host for, was a chatty, joyful occasion, barely hinting at the individual tragedies that drove 44,000 people together." The reporter, who had covered stories on three continents and had seen many extraordinary sights, was flabbergasted not just at the numbers and the cheerfulness but at the diversity of the convening alcoholics. They showed up in sports shirts and polyester slacks, in designer blouses with tasteful jewelry, in T-shirts and shorts and running shoes, and in tattoos, skull earrings and denim jackets astride big, black motorcycles. There were A.A.'s from Iowa and Florida and Oregon, from Italy, Zimbabwe and Sri Lanka. About a fifth of them were less than thirty years old. Between a third and half were women.

There were meetings in Montreal about the special concerns of gays, blacks, doctors, newcomers, night workers, airline employees, lawyers, prison personnel, women, young people, merchant seamen, the clergy. General meetings, each an hour long, began at midnight July 4 and ran without stopping, night and day, until 8 A.M. on July 7. They were packed. The topics ranged from prayer to pain, from anxieties about money to why the A.A. member never "graduates."

Thousands of wives and children of alcoholics also came to Montreal. Many of them attended the separate Al-Anon International Convention for families of alcoholics. A senior member of A.A. recalled how his wife was asked by friends if she didn't find A.A. conventions depressing. She answered that they filled her with joy. "You've got to understand," she said, "that all these people would be dead if it weren't for each other." That is what gives A.A. meetings their special intensity, their drama and their laughter. All of the members, the world over, have been afraid in the same foxhole. All have come through a test of fire. They try to follow the exhortation of one old speaker at the Montreal convention, Barry L., a flamboyant figure clinking with jewelry who joined A.A. in the mid-1940's. He told them: "The next drunk who comes in the door deserves the same love that you and I got."

A.A. today has almost two million members in 63,000 groups in 114 countries around the world, and its numbers are now doubling every ten years. About half of all A.A.'s are in the United States. Many additional millions have passed through the movement and been made whole by its program, but A.A. headquarters counts only those who currently attend meetings regularly. There are clues to A.A.'s presence everywhere for those who know: the sign on a jeep's hood in a Mexican town that says the "Grupo Bill Wilson" will meet that night; A.A.'s "Serenity Prayer" framed in South African living rooms or embroidered on a pillow in a chic Madison Avenue shop; a West Virginia bumper sticker advising ONE DAY AT A TIME.

The essence of A.A. can only be guessed at in the big, showy gatherings such as those at St. John the Divine and in Montreal. It is in the intimacy of neighborhood meetings that the truth, the flavor and an inkling of the reasons for A.A.'s success can be grasped. Members may meet in groups as small as two or three, or as large as 200, but the usual meeting is somewhere between a dozen and forty people. They meet in Pago-Pago, American Samoa, every Wednesday night, in McMurdo Sound, Antarctica, on Saturdays during the polar summer, and in Lilongwe, Malawi, on Mondays and Thursdays. They find each other just to sit and chat between meetings in a doughnut and coffee shop on the main street of Peterborough, New Hampshire, a town of only 10,000 that has four A.A. groups. One of them is called "Our Town" in honor of Thornton Wilder, who took Peterborough as the model for his nostalgic play about American small-town life. The belfry of a Catholic church near Covent Garden in London and a bank's boardroom in Marin County, California, are reserved for A.A. meetings once each week. Some meet on ships at sea or in port. To these exotic settings must be added the thousands of prosaic basements and halls in churches, community centers and hospitals where most A.A.'s struggle through their return to a life of quality. No handicap impedes them; there are dozens of groups for the deaf in the United States and Canada, whose meetings are held in silence while the members' flashing hands tell their stories. Some can find meetings just by going out their front door. In New York City alone—the most active single spot on earth—alcoholics can choose from among 1,800 meetings held by 725 groups every single week of the year.

The substance of A.A.—its core literature, its program of recovery and its ways of looking at life—has changed very little over the years. Its Twelve Steps and Twelve Traditions exist today as Bill Wilson articulated them more than forty years ago. What has changed is the nature and size of the membership, and the way the public feels about Alcoholics Anonymous.

In the early years, A.A. members were almost exclusively male, white, middle-class, middle-aged and of Western European extraction. They were men who had fallen very far. They were often skid row types, the kind stigmatized as "hopeless" alcoholics. Groups seldom had contact with others any distance away. Then, in 1944, A.A.'s *Grapevine* magazine was founded. It became Bill Wilson's test kitchen for ideas and a monthly forum for all the members, their "meeting in print" and their means of learning about what was going on elsewhere.

Outside A.A. in the 1940's, there was also a series of breakthroughs. These slowly helped to transform A.A. from the butt of public disbelief and even ridicule to an accepted, and then admired, organization—one that attracted an ever more diverse membership, finally mirroring the whole of America, the regions within it, even the neighborhoods of its cities. The first important breakthrough in the outside world came with Jack Alexander's cover article on A.A. in the *Saturday Evening Post* in 1941. It doubled the membership within months. Two years later the School of Alcohol Studies was established at Yale, conferring a new respectability on the subject of alcoholism. Then Marty Mann, one of the most celebrated and loved women in A.A.'s history, founded the forerunner to the National Council on Alcoholism and stumped the country to tell the public that alcoholism was not a disgrace but a disease and a public health responsibility. Handsome, eloquent, convincing, she made friends and converts wherever she went and encouraged many other women to join A.A.

In 1951, the American Public Health Association gave A.A. the Lasker Award, one of the most prestigious in medicine. The citation was unusually prescient for the time. It read in part:

> Alcoholics Anonymous works upon the novel principle that a recovered alcoholic can reach and treat a fellow sufferer as no one else can. In so doing, the recovered alcoholic maintains his own sobriety; the man he treats soon becomes a physician to the next new applicant, thus creating an ever expanding chain reaction of liberation, with patients welded together by bonds of common suffering, common understanding, and stimulating action in a great cause.
>
> This is not a reform movement, nor is it operated by professionals who are concerned with the problem. It is financed by voluntary contributions of its members, all of whom remain anonymous. . . . It enjoys the good will and often the warm endorsement of many medical and scientific groups—no mean achievement in itself for any organization run entirely by laymen.

Historians may one day point to Alcoholics Anonymous as a society which did far more than achieve a considerable measure of success with alcoholism and its stigma; they may recognize Alcoholics Anonymous to have been a great venture in social pioneering which forged a new instrument of social action; a new therapy based on the kinship of common suffering; one having a vast potential for the myriad other ills of mankind.

In 1954, Lillian Roth, the actress and nightclub singer, became the first of a long line of show business stars to confess her alcoholism and her salvation through A.A. Her book, *I'll Cry Tomorrow*, was a sensation. The following year, Susan Hayward's screen performance as Roth brought her an Academy Award nomination.

In 1956, the trustees and the House of Delegates of the American Medical Association declared that alcoholism was a disease. The nation's doctors thus validated a central concept of A.A., further swelling the ranks of its membership.

In 1958, the country's new but vast audience of television watchers got its first inside view of how A.A. worked. *Days of Wine and Roses*, written by J. P. Miller for *Playhouse 90* and starring Cliff Robertson and Piper Laurie, was a shattering film about an attractive young couple's descent into alcoholism and the husband's redemption through Alcoholics Anonymous. Not since Billy Wilder and Charles Brackett made Charles R. Jackson's novel *Lost Weekend* into a movie in 1945 had there been such a merciless portrayal of alcoholic suffering and degradation. *Lost Weekend* had won four Oscars, including one for its star, Ray Milland. The television play *Days of Wine and Roses* was also a critical and public triumph. Five years later, Jack Lemmon and Lee Remick starred in the movie version. A.A. collaborated on both, a first for the organization.

For a long time, Alcoholics Anonymous was believed to be a purely North American phenomenon. It was thought that its themes of self-help, volunteerism, idealism, the Protestant work ethic, optimism and pragmatism would not transfer to more relaxed cultures. Roberto M., born in Ecuador, now the genial coordinator for Hispanic groups at A.A. headquarters, voiced the early point of view among his Latin American friends: "A.A. is okay for gringos, but not for us. In Latin America, everybody drinks. If a man doesn't drink, he's not a macho. We need to drink to live, to do business." To Vicente's surprise, A.A. began to boom in Mexico. Latin, Catholic, revolutionary, its roots in ancient civilizations, Mexico now has 250,000 A.A.'s, a membership second only to that of the United States. Vicente was hard put to explain the phenomenon, except to say that Bill Wilson's precepts and the spiritual message of A.A. seem to work almost everywhere. The growth of Alcohólicos Anónimos in Latin America is reflected in Guatemala, which has 30,000 members, more than Great Britain, where A.A. was started long before. Brazil has 77,000 A.A.'s, more than Canada, the first country after the United States to form A.A. groups.

Until recently, Alcoholics Anonymous had been unable to gain a toehold in the Soviet Union and its satellite nations of Eastern Europe. A.A. had been regarded there as possibly threatening, because of its precepts of anonymity and confidentiality, its religious overtones and the fact that it works outside any government control. Then, under Mikhail S. Gorbachev's policy of *glasnost*, or openness, the Soviet government responded to an invitation from J. W. Canty, co-founder of a fledgling exchange program to combat alcohol abuse. In July 1987 the Soviet Union sent to the United States four doctors specializing in addiction. The delegation visited A.A. meetings in New York, the Summer School of Alcohol Studies at Rutgers University in New Jersey and the Rehabilitation Unit of the Smithers Alcoholism Center in Manhattan. The doctors, whose tour lasted three weeks, said they were deeply impressed by the A.A. meetings. When they returned to the Soviet Union, they took back with them quantities of A.A. pamphlets that A.A. had had translated into Russian for them. In August, a Russian joined an impromptu A.A. meeting somewhere in Moscow held by three visiting Americans. The Russian said afterward that he doubted that A.A. would catch on in the Soviet Union. He told the Americans that if A.A. was not officially sanctioned there, no one would dare to join, but that if it *was* officially sanctioned, alcoholics would still be afraid to join, fearful that the meetings would be monitored and their drinking problems would be used against them.

The only Eastern European satellite to embrace A.A. so far has been Poland, which sprang out of nowhere in A.A.'s membership records in the early 1980's and counts seventy groups today. The Polish government has finally recognized what it calls the "psychotherapeutic" value of A.A., and Polish delegates were an eloquent voice in the 1985 Montreal convention.

Despite the growing popularity of A.A. abroad, even in cultures that would seem to have nothing in common with America, the fact remains that it has flourished most exuberantly in the United States, its home ground. Its founders were American. The nearest thing to a world headquarters that A.A. has is located in Manhattan. A.A.'s precepts, borrowed from all manner of philosophies and religions, were synthesized there by the Vermont-born, adopted-New Yorker Bill Wilson.

In the last decade or so, legions of American stars, particularly in films, the theater and television, have gone public in spectacular fashion. Almost all said their hope was to help other alcoholics to recovery by their own example.

Dennis Wholey, the host of a late-night television show, wrote a book called *The Courage to Change* (the title came from a line in a prayer A.A. uses, called the Serenity Prayer), which collected the testimonies of such famous recovered alcoholics as television comedian Sid Caesar and actor Jason Robards.

Yet the great mass of the membership is composed of more or less ordinary people between the extremes. The great drama of their lives has not been played out in squalid flophouses or behind the footlights. These drunkards have suffered, forever alone, in bars or their own bedrooms or the living rooms of friends who have become increasingly estranged by their behavior. Their redemption, too, has been worked out in obscurity. To fill in the picture of this anonymous membership and how it is changing, A.A. headquarters has conducted a comprehensive survey in the

United States and Canada every three years since 1968. Out of the welter of statistics, three important trends have emerged.

One is that A.A. is no longer a male preserve. The number of women has risen slowly but steadily in the last two decades, and now forms one third of the total North American membership and about half of all members in big cities. The second trend, much more abrupt and dramatic, is that A.A. is no longer just a middle-aged society. Young people have poured in immense numbers into A.A. in the last ten years. Just as dramatic, and much more controversial within the ranks, is that most of the young newcomers are addicted to other drugs as well as to alcohol.

It is common now to hear a young speaker in A.A. say, "My name is Joe, and I'm a drug addict and an alcoholic." This angers some A.A. members, particularly the old-timers. One with twenty years of sobriety said, "This fellowship was formed to help suffering alcoholics, and alcoholics only. That's why it has been so successful—we don't monkey around with other problems. I don't feel that the problems of alkies and addicts are interchangeable."

In a few communities A.A. members have formed "Over Thirty" groups. The message is clear if unspoken: No druggies wanted. John T. Schwarzlose, who runs the Betty Ford Center for substance abusers in Rancho Mirage, California, is infuriated by this development. "A.A. is the epitome of tolerance, flexibility and inclusiveness," he said, "but some of the drug addicts who have been in here have told me about being turned away from A.A. meetings in the Midwest and South when they said they were just addicted to drugs. Now I tell all the addicts to say they are both alcoholics and drug abusers." In the big cities and at A.A. headquarters, the attitudes toward those who are labeled "dually addicted" to drugs and alcohol are much more relaxed and welcoming.

About 60 percent of all newcomers—some still drinking at first, most not—who go to meetings for up to a year remain in A.A. Usually, they stay sober for good. That means, of course, that 40 percent are lost to A.A. after trying out its program. These statistics refute the widely held notion of outsiders that Alcoholics Anonymous is successful with everyone.

The average member attends four meetings a week. After about five years of regular attendance, some A.A.'s go to fewer and fewer meetings. They may stop altogether. This happens because veterans may feel that they have "got the program" and are living their lives comfortably and happily without alcohol. However, some speakers at meetings are full of cautionary tales about how he or she drifted away from A.A. meetings and drank again, sometimes disastrously and for periods of months or years, before returning to the fold.

A.A. surveys do not inquire whether members go to church or temple or if they believe in God. There are no questions about ethnic or racial origins, sexual preferences or whether alcoholism runs in the family. But one fact stands out for anyone attending meetings consistently over a period of years and listening to the "how-I-got-drunk-and-how-I-got-sober" stories. Often, speakers begin with: "My name is Mary, and I am an alcoholic . . . and my father [or my mother] was an alcoholic." It becomes obvious after a while that the children of alcoholics become alcoholics themselves in very high numbers. A genetic predisposition for alcoholism is reflected strikingly both in current research into the disease and within the A.A. membership.

Those long familiar with A.A. meetings also notice that there seem to be disproportionately high numbers of Irish Americans, bred in a culture that looks benignly on its men drinking to drunkenness and doing much of their after-hours socializing in bars. "Alcoholism goes with certain cultures, such as the Celtic or the Scandinavian, that approve of drinking, or at least are ambivalent about it," said Dr. LeClair Bissell, the founding director of Smithers Alcoholism Treatment and Training Center in Manhattan. "There is the heredity part of the disease of alcoholism. There are also settings in which drinking is feasible or encouraged. In some environments or religions, people don't drink on principle. These abstinent cultures in the United States include Baptists, some other southern Protestant sects, and Mormons."

For a long time, there was the belief that Jews did not become alcoholics. It followed, therefore, that they did not need to join

A.A. "Jews have historically used wine sparingly, mostly for religious purposes," said Renah Rabinowitz, a former director of the JACS (Jewish Alcoholics, Chemically Dependent Persons and Significant Others) Foundation. " *'Schikker iz a goy'* [a drunkard is a Gentile] comforted us. It's no longer true—Jews are being assimilated into the American mainstream culture, and they are becoming alcoholics too." The work of JACS is helping to dispel the myth. Jews are present in large numbers at A.A. meetings in such cities as New York, where more than a million people—15 percent of the population—are Jewish. It is still true, however, that while many Protestant and Catholic churches rent rooms to A.A. groups, few synagogues do. Of the 1,800 meetings held every week in New York City, only 24 take place in synagogues or Jewish community centers. For years, only one temple in New York, the historic Central Synagogue in midtown Manhattan, rented out meeting space to Alcoholics Anonymous.

Sheldon B., an alcoholism counselor in New York, told how a few years ago he approached his rabbi with the idea of opening their temple to meetings of an A.A. group. He thought that Jews might be more comfortable about accepting help in a synagogue setting rather than in a church. The rabbi informed him that there was no need: "There are no Jewish alcoholics." When Sheldon B. said, "But I am an alcoholic," the rabbi thought for a moment. Then he said: "Are you sure you know who your real father was?"

Hispanics are flooding into A.A., both in the United States and in Latin America. But few Orientals are seen. Alcoholism has not surfaced as a significant problem in America's Oriental communities, swelled in recent years by refugees from Southeast Asia. As in the traditional Jewish culture, excessive drinking among Orientals is abhorred. In addition, the Oriental "flushing reaction" to alcohol is considered uncomfortable and embarrassing as well as a built-in stopping block to drunkenness; perhaps two thirds to three quarters of Orientals experience uncomfortable feelings of heat and nausea after drinking only a small amount.

Blacks are seriously under-represented in A.A. The black population of the United States is twenty-nine million, 12 percent of the whole. In addition, alcoholism has been documented as a serious problem in poor black communities, particularly in America's inner cities. There are black A.A. groups and mixed groups in northern cities such as Cleveland, Denver, Philadelphia, New York and Chicago, yet the total of blacks in A.A. comes nowhere near reflecting their total in the nation. "Slavery didn't get the black man down," said Paul D., a black doctor from Texas. "Racism didn't get the black man down. But alcoholism is getting the black man down. We have a total epidemic of alcoholism and drug abuse. We have hundreds of A.A. meetings in my city and only one of the groups is black. There are one hundred and forty black doctors where I live, and I'm the only black doctor to go to A.A."

Carl W., a teacher in Pennsylvania, said: "There is a great stigma in being black and being drunk, even recovered. I haven't seen one black alcoholic come out of the closet nationally. There is a stigma. There is a penalty. I am a teacher. I made the mistake of telling my principal that I had a problem. I checked myself into a treatment center. She used a hatchet on me." Carl's voice became thick with tension as he added, "I see bumper stickers that say 'It's Okay Not to Drink.' Maybe we should have one that says 'It's Okay to Be Black and Not Drink.' It's okay for white folks to have a nervous breakdown and go to treatment centers. They're welcomed back. If black folks have a breakdown or go to a treatment center for alcoholism, they think you're malingering."

At the 1985 Montreal convention, Wade L., a muscular, dignified black man from New York, said, "I do not see minorities in the hierarchy of A.A., nor did I see them on the dais the night that all us A.A.'s gathered in the stadium. Nor did I see blacks in as many numbers as there should have been in the seats. I think we should stop pretending that there is not a racial issue at this convention. Not every gay, not every woman, not every Jew, not every black lives just in New York. These alcoholics need entrance into our great fellowship all over the country."

Ray B., a Wisconsin social worker, said: "The black community is afraid that if blacks admit their alcoholism, it will reinforce the white stereotype that they are shiftless, no good and unemployable.

The black community likes to think that oppression causes their alcoholism. Many gays and other oppressed minorities use the same argument. 'Who wouldn't drink?' they say. 'Our lives are so goddamned awful. Society hates us. We can't get a break. Oblivion is the only way out of our pain.' "

Homosexuals also addressed this issue at the Montreal convention in a standing-room-only meeting that drew 1,000 A.A.'s. The topic was "Gays in A.A.—Are We Really Different?" The first gay speaker was black. He said, "When I first went to meetings I was foaming at the mouth like a dog. I was saying 'motherfucker' on purpose. Some people don't like that shit. [Laughter.] In twenty-three years of uninterrupted sobriety I have been criticized and ostracized and humiliated—but I didn't drink on it." Growing up in Alabama, he said, "I was taught to hate myself. I was a nigger sissy. In A.A. I learned that the *only* requirement for joining was a desire to stop drinking. I learned that God loves us all. My business in A.A. is to stay sober and help you if you want it."

The second speaker was Jewish. He grew up in a small town in Florida. "All through college, the army, medical school, I was closeted," he said. "I was drinking and drugging to fill up that big empty hole inside of me. No amount of sex could fill up that hole inside of me. The one thing I hope I never get enough of is this program. For the very first time in my life, I do not feel isolated and different."

The third speaker, from Ontario, said with a sheepish grin "I'm sorry not to be black, or a Jew—but I *did* drink, and I had an R.C. upbringing. [Laughter]." When he learned of the topic on which he was to talk, "Are Gays in A.A. Really Different?" he said, "I couldn't get a handle on it. I was dying, and this program gave me hope. I no longer felt that difference. I was getting acceptance. I was getting love that went to the depth of the fellowship." Then in 1974, he started a gay group in Ontario with six meetings a week. "The central office of A.A. didn't understand special interest groups," he said. He spoke of "macho" attitudes there, and the disapproving question, "You wouldn't be an interior decorator, would you?" He said, "I wondered if the day would come when the divisions would not seem so deep. Now I see that gay people are up front in this convention."

Other gays speaking spontaneously from the floor said their own attitudes were, "If you want to drink, fine—but don't blame it on being gay." Or, "You're an alcoholic—and being gay isn't going to change it." A man from California's Central Valley said, "I was the only gay in my group. They used to tell jokes about queers in meetings." Then, he said, a lesbian friend who was in another A.A. group told him, "Some people are sicker than others. You can confront them, or you can stay silent. But whatever way you choose, it's not worth drinking over."

A.A. has been described as an ill-defined, loosely formed sub-culture of alcoholics who are no longer drinking. When you try to stretch the definition much beyond that, you get into trouble. There are many things that outsiders believe A.A. to be that it is not. To begin with, it is not a temperance organization.

A.A. does not want to save the world from gin. Nobody invites you to join A.A. You are a member if you say you are, or if you walk into an A.A. meeting with the thought that you have a drinking problem and you want to stop.

Members do not aggressively recruit newcomers. They wait until they detect a reaching out for help from the active alcoholic, his or her family or close friends. The reason for this is that experienced persons in A.A. believe it is hopeless to drag another into sobriety if the alcoholic is determined not to be helped or refuses to believe he or she is ill. (Even so, the courts in some states are using A.A. as a drunk tank, sending thousands of offenders such as drunk drivers to A.A. meetings instead of to jail. This has created problems for A.A., swamping meetings in states such as Maryland with hordes of resentful newcomers. By tradition, only those with a *desire* to stop drinking are welcome. Nonetheless, the A.A. program sometimes catches on with unwilling alcoholics whom the courts have forced to attend meetings.)

A.A. is not a religious cult. It is not an evangelical movement. Some members are religious, and some are agnostics or atheists.

Many members choose to believe that their "higher power" is their A.A. group.

On the whole, members are flexible, tolerant of eccentrics, suspicious of "rules" and "musts." Those who have become comfortable in their sobriety often serve liquor in their homes to friends who are not alcoholic and are not upset when others drink moderately around them. Their attitude seems to be, "I wish I could drink as you do, but I can't."

A.A. has no ties with political parties, foundations, charities or causes; does not sponsor research into alcoholism; does not follow up or try to control its members.

Unlike most tax-exempt organizations, A.A. does no fundraising. It does not accept money from outsiders. There is even a limit on what a member can give. Each group is self-supporting, passing a little basket at every meeting to help pay for coffee, snacks, literature and renting space. Those present often give a dollar. Some are not able to give anything, or may drop a coin into the basket. No living member may give more than $1,000 to A.A. in any year. (This has crept upward from the $100 annual limit set in 1950, which was one tenth of 1 percent of A.A.'s budget of $100,000 that year. A.A. now runs an $11.5 million operation, which means that at the percentage originally fixed, A.A. could accept about $11,500 annually from a member. "Every so often, raising the ceiling on gifts comes up at the yearly A.A. conference," says Dennis Manders, a round-faced, kindly accountant and a nonalcoholic who, as A.A.'s comptroller, ran its finances for thirty-five years. "The delegates practically scream the idea down."

No member may bequeath more than $1,000 to A.A. No property may be given to A.A., which has never owned real estate. The fear of corruption by wealth, property, power and politics as expressed in the Twelve Traditions is as strongly rooted in A.A. practices today as it was more than a generation ago.

In the early years, Bill Wilson dreamed of A.A.-run chains of hospitals and treatment centers for alcoholics. He, his band of pioneers and their increasingly influential nonalcoholic friends sought money from the rich and took contributions from outside. By 1950 those ideas and methods had vanished as the Traditions Bill zealously promoted in the 1940's, hoping to keep A.A. "pure," gained acceptance within the membership.

Manders described the mind-set about money as "the corporate poverty philosophy." It suffuses the words and actions of those who do the business of A.A. They feel that money, power and property would divert the organization from what Bill called "its primary spiritual aim" of helping the still-suffering alcoholic without thought of financial reward. According to Manders:

> The whole bottom line of this corporate poverty philosophy is not to show a profit. We say, "Hey, we're not in business to make money." Through the years we've turned down hundreds of thousands of dollars in gifts, and it's made plenty of people angry. The lawyers of one Texas millionaire threatened to sue A.A. when we said we couldn't take his money, no matter how grateful the guy was.
>
> The reason we discourage gifts and bequests is that we don't ever want some person dropping a million bucks in the A.A. hopper and saying, "Now, *I'm* going to call the tune."

Some of A.A.'s money is contributed by groups in the United States and Canada to New York headquarters (which doesn't like to call itself a headquarters at all and so is known as the General Service Office). "Nobody *runs* A.A." is the refrain at GSO. "We provide services to the membership." Yet almost half of the groups in North America contribute nothing at all to their headquarters for these services. They feel that carrying the expenses of their groups through voluntary, pass-the-hat contributions is enough. Many members don't know that such a thing as a General Service Office exists. This kind of autonomy and decentralization is typical of Alcoholics Anonymous.

Less than a third of the 114 foreign countries with A.A. members have a national headquarters; those that do exist are almost completely independent of the New York office. This may be one of the most important reasons for A.A.'s success abroad: a laissez-faire attitude that allows different cultures to pursue their own roads to recovery, using the Twelve Steps and the Twelve Traditions as guideposts.

It is publishing that makes A.A.'s services possible. A.A. headquarters in New York is sitting atop a multimillion-dollar publishing empire that is growing bigger every year—and is the cause of some trepidation among those who have taken what amounts to a vow of poverty.

The publishing operation now brings in $8.8 million annually. This is 76 percent of A.A.'s yearly corporate income. It has carried the corporation since 1939, when the just-written Big Book was the only thing A.A. had to sell.

Almost from the beginning, A.A. decided to be its own publisher, putting out all its own books and pamphlets and its own magazine, the *A.A. Grapevine*. Each year the publishing empire distributes seven million copies of more than forty pamphlets and almost a million and a half copies of six books and two booklets. The literature not written by Wilson has been written by anonymous members. New works are rigorously discussed and edited in manuscript through committees at headquarters, and then approved or rejected by North American delegates meeting at the yearly A.A. conference. If rejected, a new work goes back to headquarters for more editing. The process takes years, involving the resolution of many conflicting opinions before printing is ordered. No book or pamphlet is considered unless it is felt that the subject a work covers—such as young people or drugs other than alcohol—has become one of compelling interest to a significant number of A.A.'s members.

Who runs A.A. today? It is close to the truth to say that A.A. consists of a million Indians and no chiefs. Or that it is organized anarchy. Or that it is less an organization than an organism that keeps splitting, amoeba-like, into ever more and more groups. If a member doesn't like the way things are run in his group, he can start another one with people he finds more compatible. This gave rise to an A.A. saying, "All you need to start a new group is two drunks, a coffeepot and some resentment."

There *is* a structure in Alcoholics Anonymous, and Bill Wilson designed it. However, like the philosophy of corporate poverty, it sets any conventional notion of how to run a business on its head.

*The A.A. Service Manual*, used as a text by staff members at New York headquarters, lays out the structure of A.A. in a most significant illustration. A chart on page twenty shows "A.A. Groups" at the *top* of the pyramid—the 36,000 groups in the United States and Canada. Symbolically, the Board of Trustees, which is made up of fourteen A.A. members and seven nonalcoholics, is at the *bottom*. Also at the bottom is A.A. World Services, the nonprofit corporation that manages the General Service Office, publishes all its literature and serves groups in foreign countries that do not have national headquarters of their own. The inverted pyramid, in which power is seated in the mass of members, not in the trustees or the managers of A.A.'s business, would drive any ordinary executive to ulcers. But that is the A.A. way.

The manner in which A.A. directs its collective affairs and sets policy can be seen most clearly—or in all its democratic confusion—at its yearly General Service Conference. This meeting, which is intended to be the voice and collective conscience and the closest approximation to a governing body of A.A., takes place for six crowded days in April at a New York hotel. It is closed both to the public and to other members. About 135 people attend, including ninety-one delegates elected at regional assemblies in the United States and Canada who may serve for only two years. There are also the trustees of the General Service board, the directors of the two A.A. corporations (A.A. World Services and the *A.A. Grapevine*), and members of the headquarters staff who run the day-to-day business.

Through a series of reports from interlocking trustee and conference committees—divided into subjects of concern such as literature, treatment centers, prisons, finance, public information, and cooperation with professionals—the assembled delegates vote on "advisory action." The movement from year to year can be glacial; seemingly minuscule decisions such as whether to publish the Big Book in a paperback edition have been put off year after year by delegates unable to achieve the required "substantial unanimity"—an idea embedded in Bill Wilson's booklet *Twelve Concepts for World Service*.

Whatever policies are decided at the April conference are carried out the rest of the year by the staff at the General Service Office. "Act for us, but don't boss us," said Bill Wilson. And just in case there is danger of somebody becoming overly fond of a job, establishing a little fiefdom, or being overeager to perpetuate his or her point of view, nearly all jobs are rotated. This principle is followed at almost every level, including the 63,000 groups worldwide. (One exception is the general manager, who is the chief executive officer at headquarters.) Officers in groups, such as the chairman and treasurer, usually step down after six months or at most a year. Most of the paid members who hold top positions at the New York headquarters must switch jobs every two years in a kind of musical chairs. They are called staffers or coordinators. They are never called top officials or spokesmen, because they are equal in rank and because, since Bill Wilson's death, no one person is supposed to speak for A.A. Each of the ten staffers has one area of responsibility: literature, the annual conference, overseas groups, the professional community, "loners" and seagoing members, public information, prisons, rehabilitation centers, the headquarters staff and Spanish services. The last is the newest post, created in 1984, and the man who occupies it does not rotate. He is a consultant on any committee providing services to A.A.'s ever-expanding Hispanic population.

Twenty-one trustees, who meet four times a year, are not paid. The seven nonalcoholic trustees are usually expert in some profession such as medicine, finance or social work. They may serve for up to nine years. Fourteen alcoholic trustees, drawn from the membership's own much larger pool of prospects, may serve for only four years.

Joan K. Jackson, a nonalcoholic trustee and a sociologist with decades of work among alcoholics behind her when she joined the board, considered the nonalcoholic trustees uniquely valuable for several reasons: "We are the front men of A.A. We can use our full names in public. We can accept the awards A.A. keeps getting all the time. We are not perceived by outsiders as having any vested interest. Privately within A.A., our greatest function is as gadflies and questioners—there are many things we don't understand that A.A.'s take as a given. For instance, I wouldn't get all the nuances of a fantastic concept like anonymity."

There has been criticism that A.A. headquarters are overly sensitive to pressure from the most rigid and narrow-minded members, particularly old-timers, who regard the Big Book and other authorized A.A. literature almost as Holy Writ. "If anything is going to destroy A.A.," said Dr. John Norris, for years an A.A. trustee, "it will be what I call the 'Tradition lawyers.' They find it easier to live with black and white than they do with gray. These 'bleeding deacons'—these Fundamentalists—are afraid of and fight any change."

Writing in *The Nation* in 1964, Jerome Ellison charged that A.A.'s top councils had lost touch with the ever more diverse rank and file. The same year, Arthur H. Cain, a New York psychologist, in a book and articles for various magazines, called A.A. a "cult" that enslaved its members to self-righteous sobriety. Bill Wilson's reaction was typical of the man's tolerance. The co-founder, trying to calm the fuss at headquarters, said, "In all the years this is the first thoroughgoing criticism A.A. has ever had. So the practice of absorbing stuff like that in good humor should be of value."

The day-to-day business of Alcoholics Anonymous has been carried on since 1970 in a solid brick building at 468 Park Avenue South in midtown Manhattan. Until 1980, when it was refurbished and expanded, the headquarters were dingy, noisy and overcrowded. "People were sitting on top of one another," one of the veterans said. "When visitors came, their reaction usually was, 'What a dump!' " Now the premises, occupying several floors, are plain, light and cheerful, with beige walls and plenty of windows.

About twenty of the 110 salaried employees at the General Service Office are recovered alcoholics in A.A. They hold all the top jobs, except those involving money. Bill Wilson and the early A.A.'s were afraid that if anybody in a managerial position fell off the wagon, that would be bad enough, but if he were handling finances as well, the results could be disastrous. The philosophy has endured. So has the concept that clerical and menial work can be done by anybody, but only members have a true grasp of strictly A.A. matters. "In this office A.A.'s occupy all the key positions and nonalcoholics occupy all the menial positions or those in office management," said Clyde P., a senior adviser. "I guess what we're doing is illegal, because it's a kind of discrimination. A.A.'s do no typing, filing, wrapping packages, taking dictation, adding up columns of figures, operating data processors or cleaning the latrines."

Until very recently, the staff of nonalcoholics in the financial office were even physically separated from the alcoholics carrying out policy and answering members' mail in an adjoining but connecting building at headquarters. "It was almost like saying 'Render unto Caesar the things that are Caesar's and render unto God the things that are God's,' " said one staffer.

The ten staffers—including former teachers, editors, a scientist, a sea captain, a nurse and a public relations man—and the general manager of the General Service Office sit in small individual offices, usually with their doors open, in an L-shaped row on the eighth floor. The atmosphere at headquarters, as at meetings, is informal and friendly. People drift into each others' cubicles without notice to seek information and exchange ideas. Every Friday morning those who wish to gather at the A.A. meeting held by GSO staffers in the conference room on the fifth floor.

The coordinator on prisons answers about ninety letters a week from inmates, wardens and guards. Some of the letters from prisoners are heartbreaking, truly cries from the belly of the beast. There are 45,000 A.A. members in prisons today; almost all of them joined or formed groups after going behind bars. A headquarters staffer gives information about how to start a group in prison; once the group gets rolling, it is turned over to A.A. members. About 1,000 A.A. members "outside" around the country have become "sponsors" to prisoners—a relationship similar to a big brother or big sister. They write regularly to inmates, visit them when possible and are waiting for them at the prison gates the day of their release to bring them to their first meetings as free men and women. One of the difficulties in reaching prisoners is that much A.A. literature is above their heads: the average reading level of those in America's prisons is below the seventh grade and many are almost illiterate. "This assignment is to carry the A.A. message to those at the very bottom, locked up and with little hope," the prisons coordinator says.

The staffer assigned to "loners"—people too sick or isolated to be able to attend meetings—and "internationalists"—seagoing members—edits a newsletter that in effect is the biggest single special meeting anywhere in Alcoholics Anonymous. Twenty-five hundred members subscribe to the *Loners-Internationalists Meeting,* a bimonthly newsletter in which people thousands of miles apart exchange their most private thoughts, fears, joys, birthday dates, notices of deaths, addresses and expressions of affection with each other by mail.

The A.A. archives and the *Grapevine* occupy most of the fifth floor. The *Grapevine* remains one of the world's most popular publications in the alcoholism field, with a circulation of 123,000. Regular features of the early issues were a "guest piece" by a nonalcoholic friend of A.A., a "Time on Your Hands" column to give useful hobby suggestions to help fill the new free time that sobriety brings and, during World War II, one complete page headed "Mail Call for A.A.'s in the Armed Forces." The first issue of the *Grapevine*'s present digest-size format was published in 1948.

Along with the news of A.A.'s growth were articles on subjects that still preoccupy the membership. For instance, pieces in 1945 covered "the sleeping pill menace," and Bill Wilson was writing about "Those Goof Balls." One member wrote in to urge that special groups be formed for "older members"—those with more than three months' sobriety. The Preamble that is read at the beginning of all meetings to remind members and inform newcomers what A.A. is and is not first appeared in the *Grapevine* in 1947.

Nonalcoholic friends of A.A. have contributed over the years. They ranged from Sister Ignatia, Dr. Bob's chief nurse in the alcoholic ward of St. Thomas Hospital in Akron, where he served in the last decade of his life, to Aldous Huxley, Reinhold Niebuhr and Dr. Karl Menninger.

The *Grapevine* has reflected both the changes in the membership and professional views in the field of alcoholism. Its "About Alcoholism" section, or "gray pages," carry information on what is current in treatment and research. Often these items are contrary to A.A. philosophy, and a disclaimer on the first page of the section states that they are there purely for information and do not imply endorsement or approval by A.A. "We are criticized occasionally for including this section, but every time we ask our readers, they vote overwhelmingly to keep it," a *Grapevine* editor said.

This is a glimpse of Alcoholics Anonymous as it is today. To understand the secret of how it works and why it has been so successful with hundreds of thousands of people who were afflicted with what was once considered a hopeless condition or a heinous moral lapse, one must look within the A.A. meetings themselves.

# 5

## HOW A.A. WORKS

"Don't drink, a day at a time. Go to meetings."
—*Every A.A. old-timer to*
*every A.A. newcomer*

It is not quite that simple, but almost. In fact, what goes on at an A.A. meeting seems so simple at first that some people are baffled. "Is that all there is?" they may ask themselves. Well, no, but a newcomer is in no shape to absorb anything complicated.

All meetings are alike, and every one, like a fingerprint, is different. Alcoholics may enter the room as strangers, but if they sit there an hour to ninety minutes—meetings rarely last longer than that—they will probably not leave it feeling completely foreign. This may not happen at once. For a while they may not hear anything helpful because alcoholics who are still drinking, or who have just put the cork in the bottle but done nothing more, are listening only to themselves and that insistent little voice within them. It is their friend, the bottle talking—their only friend.

People new to A.A. are angry. They are frightened. They are ashamed to be there. And they are ill.

A doctor many years in A.A. said, "When we first come into A.A., we are all brain-damaged." Another recovered physician said, "After years of drinking, we alcoholics become cognitively impaired. In plain language, we can't think straight. The root of 'intoxicate' is the Latin word *toxicum*—'poison.' We have systematically poisoned ourselves, damaging the central nervous system."

Sometimes alcoholics who know nothing about medicine can say more dramatically than any doctor what compulsive drinking has done to them. "I was committing chronic suicide," said a woman speaking to other A.A.'s in the basement of an Episcopal church in an East Coast city. "I was putting a liquid bullet into my brain every night."

Anyone who wants to stop drinking can become a member of Alcoholics Anonymous. That is all there is to it. Nobody puts the arm on people to join, or asks why they have come, or signs their names to a piece of paper, or makes them speak or take a pledge of abstinence. People simply go to a meeting. They sit there. They listen. They sit in the back if they want to, although they may not hear very well what is being said up front if the meeting is big. They are there for a reason. The reason is *not* why they drank.

"To ask why is the wrong question," members sometimes say. The question is not why or how or when or how much a person drinks, but rather how it distorts any important part of that person's life—marriage, children, work, friendships. Listen to what veteran A.A.'s, speaking in actual meetings around the country, have suggested to beginners:

Martin said, "My feeling is that you have to ask yourself, 'How does drinking mess up my life?' If drinking screws up your life and you do things that you wouldn't do if you weren't drinking, then you have a problem. And if you have a problem, this program can help you if you work at it."

Ellen said, "If we could do it alone, we wouldn't be in these rooms."

Steve said, "If you come into these rooms you belong here. Well, maybe one person in a million doesn't belong here. But if you think you're that person, you really *do* belong here."

For a time, psychiatrists, though a respected source of help, were the butt of jokes at meetings. The reason was that many alcoholics who had gone through psychotherapy felt their doctors had been interested only in *why* they drank. Ken's comment at one meeting was typical: "My shrink told me, 'Your drinking is only a symptom of your underlying problems.' Five years later I had solved the problems and I was still drinking like a fish." The A.A.'s listening to Ken dissolved in laughter. But nowadays, more and more therapists appear convinced that no important problems can be truly confronted until alcoholic patients stop anesthetizing themselves with liquor and clear the fog from their brains. A doctor who is a recovered alcoholic said, "Alcoholism is the primary thing that has to be fixed. If it isn't, *nothing* will work. We're endlessly interested in why, but it's not the first order of business. What you find out fast in A.A. is that you're all through drinking. As well as drugging. If you accept that—that you *must* do that—it is totally different from why you drank, or the hope that you will miraculously get better. There are no long-term chemical answers to life."

One straightforward reason people have always drunk alcohol— both alcoholics who eventually cannot stop and social drinkers who can—is given by physicians who specialize in the treatment of alcoholics. People drink, say the experts, because they like the effect of alcohol. It can make them euphoric, ease their pain, and allow them to forget whatever it is that may be bothering them. The thing that distinguishes alcoholics, they say, is that alcoholics keep on drinking long after the payoff of ease and comfort they get by taking a drink or two has vanished. Ultimately, they drink to get drunk. Only major adjustments of outlook can save them from this pattern.

This is what Alcoholics Anonymous believes its program of recovery supplies. It does not work for everyone, but then, nothing does. Over the years, the best estimate experts have been able to settle on is that more than half the people who give A.A. a real chance—going to meetings regularly for three to twelve months, sitting up front, listening closely, speaking up occasionally, perhaps filling the coffee urn, cleaning the ashtrays or folding the chairs afterward—will recover. And they will want to stay in A.A.

Like the movies, meetings begin on time. People are allowed to wander in late or leave before it's over, but they might miss a crucial scene. Even a sentence uttered by one member may suddenly reach out and comfort another, like the time Katherine said gently to a woman full of remorse and self-loathing: "Forgive yourself." Or when Annie, reporting to her group on an "absolutely shitty day" at work and at home, finished by saying, "The only perfect thing I did today was, I didn't take a drink."

Lots of people in A.A. have taken strength from the often-expressed thought that "There is nothing so bad that can happen to me that a drink won't make worse." In one of those comments that can strike home with their truth, Melanie said: "I was not present for most of my life." A man named Bobby responded, "I am finally participating in my own life." In one meeting, Frank, the leader for the evening, told a furious, shaky eighteen-year-old, sober the same number of days: "You will get the program by osmosis, whether you like it or not. You will get hope here."

The lack of rules and rituals can be a surprise. So is the absence of confrontation, finger-pointing, shouting, blame-laying, angry debate and chronic whining. A.A. is one of the most successful examples in history of a self-help, behavior-changing movement. It is group therapy, it is very dramatic at times (and often very funny), but it is not psychodrama and there is no central target. There are, however, powerful and unspoken codes of behavior in meetings. Nobody tells a beginner what those codes are; they are revealed solely through the example of other, more experienced members. Saying "you must" or "you should" is taboo. "This what I did" is the preferred way to give advice.

Recovered alcoholics in A.A., unlike all too many ex-smokers, are not given to preaching, bullying, moralizing, lecturing, knuckle-rapping or making somebody else feel wrong, stupid or threatening to the moralizer's lungs and liver. For example, one autumn Sunday in Chicago, Susan, a dark young woman sitting in the front row at a meeting, poured out her anger at not being able to drink. When she had finished, in tears, an elderly man seated near her said, "My name is Greg, I'm an alcoholic, I've been in this program a long time, and I don't think anger is a proper thing for a beginner to talk about." His comment was greeted by a thick, stunned silence. After a moment, a middle-aged woman in the back row spoke up. She said gently and with a smile, "My name is Adele, I am an alcoholic, and I think anything that bothers any of us is an acceptable thing to talk about at a meeting. I get angry a lot, and when I do, I pick up the phone and call a friend in A.A." There was an audible sigh of relief throughout the room. When the meeting ended, Adele and half a dozen others went up to Susan, hugged her and asked her out to a nearby coffee shop for what members call "the meeting after the meeting." Greg stood alone.

That Chicago meeting is but one instance of the tolerance most members exhibit toward each other. A.A.'s know alcoholism is a life-and-death affair. They know from experience that it ruins not just their health but everything in their lives that matters. Anger and frustration are common reactions as they enter a new world without alcohol. In the end, they learn to be flexible, both in the A.A. environment and in an outside world where drinking is the norm.

This has been true since A.A.'s earliest years. In the Big Book, Wilson emphasized: "We are careful never to show intolerance or hatred of drinking as an institution. Experience shows that such an attitude is not helpful to anyone. Every new alcoholic looks for this spirit among us and is immensely relieved when he finds we are not witch-burners."

Those new to A.A. gatherings will hear a good deal of laughter there—a kind of foxhole hilarity. They will find listening of rare intensity. It is a courteous, profound silence of a quality found in Quaker meetings. A.A.'s will listen to a speaker's shocking story—and in some sections of the country, notably New York, to his foul language—in respectful silence. Anybody may speak up about anything from the floor, but he or she is not encouraged to go on too long; the feeling is that there are others who are hurting, too, or who want to communicate some joy, or a present sorrow. If that evening's leader of the meeting is skillful, he or she will find a way to thank the person speaking too long from the floor and then quickly recognize another upraised hand. At a typical closed meeting (for alcoholics only), the speaker and those wanting to say something from the floor remain seated while talking. In a round-robin meeting, where people seated around a table talk in turn, the reluctant person need only say "I pass." The point is not to put anybody on the spot and not to make anybody uncomfortable.

Here, constructed from notes and recollections of hundreds of meetings over the years, are quotations from members. They have been wrapped into an account of what might be considered a typical meeting:

The place is a church basement with an attached kitchen, anywhere in the United States. Tacked on the walls are children's bright posters. A green plastic rocking horse stands in one corner along with a tumble of blocks and a pile of tattered little books: evidence of the day-care center that occupies the space during the daytime. The time is twenty minutes to eight on a spring evening. Several men and women straggle in: volunteers from the "Serenity Group," which meets every Thursday.

They will create an A.A. environment in moments. Two people begin making an urn of coffee; then they lay out the bags of cookies they have brought with them on plates. Other volunteers take folding chairs stacked along the walls and set them up facing a Formica-topped table where the Serenity Group's current chairwoman and the evening's speaker will sit. The coffee urn is placed on a table near the door with piles of paper napkins and plastic cups. Next to it is a table for A.A. literature ordered from headquarters: pamphlets as well as several copies of the Big Book and *Twelve Steps and Twelve Traditions,* a slimmer volume containing essays by Bill Wilson explaining the precepts of the program. The volunteers hang little placards on the walls. They say ONE DAY AT

A TIME, KEEP IT SIMPLE, I AM RESPONSIBLE. One volunteer confides to another, "You know, when I was new I thought these slogans were corny and downright dumb. 'Nothing can be that simple,' I thought. Now I think they're little nuggets of wisdom." He places the biggest sign of all, headed THE TWELVE STEPS, on an easel up front near the speaker's table. The steps—A.A.'s program for recovery—mention alcohol only once, in the first step. God is alluded to rather often.

Shortly before the meeting begins, more people wander through the door in twos and threes, head for the coffee and cookies, and stand in clusters laughing, chatting and often embracing. Those who come in alone sometimes look bewildered, shamefaced or frightened. They sit at the back. They are new. The more friendly veterans go over to them and greet them: "Hi, I'm Vincent. Can I get you some coffee?" Finally all settle into their seats. Diane, the Serenity Group's current chairwoman, a slender, intense woman in her twenties, dressed in jeans and a neat Shetland sweater, looks at her watch; it is exactly eight o'clock. She raps for order and says, "Hello, everybody, and welcome to the regular Thursday night meeting of the Serenity Group. My name is Diane and I am an alcoholic." She reads the A.A. Preamble from a card.

Diane cranes out over the crowd of thirty attentive people and says, "Is anybody celebrating a birthday this week?" One young man with a black pirate's mustache shoots up his hand. He smiles sheepishly and says, "My name is Len, and I'm an alcoholic, and I'm two years in A.A. next Monday." Everyone claps; the man next to Len puts an arm over his shoulders and says, "Way to go!"

"Is there anybody here with less than ninety days in the program?" Diane asks. Another hand goes up. The man is cadaverous, flushed, shaking and serious. "My name is George," he mutters. "Nineteen days today." Everybody bursts into applause and turns toward him, smiling. The newer a person is, the more enthusiastic the clapping, because all members know that the first days and weeks without a drink are the hardest.

"Is anybody at this meeting for the first time?" asks Diane. "Anybody from out of town?"

A woman in a turquoise pantsuit raises her hand and says, "My

name is Anna, and I'm an alcoholic from Wichita Falls, Texas."
More smiles, applause. "Hi, Anna!" people chorus.

Diane says, "Anna, we're glad to have you here," and turns to
the speaker seated at the head table, a rangy man in his thirties
with sparkling blue eyes and a shock of unruly blond hair. "Our
speaker for this evening is Tommy," Diane says. "He's an old
friend who's helped me a lot. I'm proud to have you, Tommy."
The audience gives him a big hand. Tommy leans over the table
to tell his story. He will speak for twenty or thirty minutes and
without notes; this lends a freshness and spontaneity to the accounts of many members, who may surprise even themselves when
an experience they hadn't thought of for months or years pops
into their minds. Arrangements for speakers are casual, as is everything in A.A. The group's program chairman simply asks acquaintances or friends if they are free to speak on a certain date.
If the speaker does not show, someone is picked at random from
the floor, usually moments before the meeting begins.

Tommy leads off with the sentence with which all A.A.'s introduce themselves at a meeting: "My name is Tommy, and I'm an
alcoholic." And then he says, "And let me tell you, it's been a
bitch." He grins wickedly, and people laugh, settle back and relax.
Tommy tells about the good years, the fun he had drinking and
drugging on the rock music circuit with his high-living pals. As he
goes on, his story darkens. "For eleven years, I wanted drugs and
booze to take me somewhere," he says, "but I never got there."
At the end, he sat alone all day long in one room of his house,
with blacked-out windows and wall-to-wall mirrors. "And there
were thousands and thousands and thousands of me reflected back
from those mirrors, guzzling and snorting. I had a telephone number that nobody had because I didn't want anybody to know I
was home." One day five years ago, he went out to a bar. "A guy
asked me as we were standing there, 'What's your name, man?' I
thought and thought and I couldn't remember," Tommy says. "I
couldn't remember the name I was born with." That day he picked
up a phone book and called Alcoholics Anonymous.

Tommy glances at the clock on the wall. It is twenty-five minutes after eight, time to end his story. "There are days when I just don't want to do this anymore," he says. "Days when I don't want to go to another fucking meeting. And then I think about that room with the mirrors. I can't tell you how to fix your life. I *can* tell you how to stay sober. I've been here for five years. I should be okay by now. Sometimes I'm not okay. But it's better than it was—a lot better. I owe you people plenty. Thank you." Loud applause.

The ninety-minute-long meeting has another hour to go. The secretary of the Serenity Group stands up and says, "We'll take a coffee break after we pass the baskets. There are no dues or fees, but we do have expenses, for rent and coffee and the snacks." Baskets are passed hand to hand along the rows. One dollar is the most anybody puts in. Some throw in a coin or two, but nobody notices; it is assumed that those who can't afford to contribute now will do so later. A.A. is free to anybody who wants it and needs it. For five or ten minutes, people stretch, surround the coffee urn for another cup, gab with each other, and wander back to their chairs. Then the floor is open to discussion. Unless it is a meeting in which the speaker sets a topic—"self-pity," for example, or "gratitude"—anybody can talk on any subject that is close to his or her heart that day. Many do just that anyhow, ignoring the suggested topic. People talk about their fears, their jobs, their mothers-in-law, their lovers, about something wonderful or awful that just happened to them. The revelations can be as intimate as those told to a clergyman or a doctor, and the trust that they will be kept confidential is as absolute. The difference is that at the meetings there is no authority figure listening. In A.A., everybody is equal. Everybody has the same cunning, baffling, powerful disease; there is no rank higher than membership, and nobody has sway over anybody else. A.A.'s talk frequently about how they fought off or succumbed to a temptation to drink. This is called a "slip" in A.A.; it is viewed seriously, but the slipper is forgiven in advance.

Tommy, back in his seat after the coffee break to lead the meeting, decides that he will chose the topic "temptation." "For the beginners here, why don't we talk for a while about how to avoid taking that first drink?" he suggests. Hands pop up all over the room. Tommy points to one.

"Try HALT," says the woman he has indicated. "It stands for Hungry, Angry, Lonely, Tired. If you feel any one of those things, it will trigger the urge for a drink. Grab a candy bar, ice cream, a sweet soda. Nobody wants a Scotch after that."

"Try telephone therapy," says another woman. "Ask us for our numbers after the meeting. We'll be glad to give them to you. If you feel a compulsion to drink, call us at any time. We'll just keep talking until the urge passes. And it always does, believe me."

More hands wave to catch Tommy's eye. A man says, "Avoid people, places and things that remind you of drinking. Get busy, or you're in danger. Go to a meeting, call an A.A. friend, take a brisk walk. Don't go anywhere you used to go. If you were a bar drinker and you see a bar, steer yourself around the block."

Suggestions are coming fast from the hand-wavers. "Postpone the drink. Say to yourself, 'I won't take a drink *now*.'" "Stick with the winners—the people you see around here who are obviously getting better and are serious about their recovery. Emotionally needy neurotics can drag a beginner down. Pay attention to *your* recovery, not theirs." "Find a sponsor—an A.A. member with a year or more of sobriety, if you can—who looks like she's enjoying life without drinking." (Veteran A.A.'s suggest the sponsor should be a member of the same sex, because romantic or sexual entanglements seem to complicate the life of a recovering alcoholic and threaten sobriety. The lucky newcomer's sponsor will be a best friend, mentor, confidant and guide in A.A.)

An old-timer with a face like a split rock finishes off the topic of how to avoid a slip. "Even if you do slip," he says, "there's nobody here who will punish you. The drink is punishment enough."

Tommy opens the floor to a general discussion. "Anybody hurting today?" he asks. "Anybody need to get something off their chest?"

A forlorn teenager in a sweat suit raises her hand and says, "I'm Denise, sober thirty-eight days." Then she blurts out, "I miss the craziness. I miss my friends. I miss me!" She sinks her head in her hands.

The man next to her lifts his own hand. "I'm Don, and I'm an alcoholic. I used to say to myself, 'How could you go through everything you went through all those years and still miss it?' Well, I did miss it. Honestly it gets better, a day at a time, as you go along."

Another man says with a laugh, "Just remember—don't drink if your *ass* falls off!"

A snowy-haired priest in black suit and clerical collar smiles sympathetically and speaks up. His tone is self-mocking. "I used to think," he says, " 'what are my sufferings compared to what Our Lord went through?' But then it occurred to me—except for the last three days, he had a pretty good time!" He brings down the house; the forlorn teenager's mouth falls open, and then she giggles.

Tommy looks at the clock. It is nine-thirty. "Thank you all. It's been a great meeting, and it's time to close," he says. "Would all those who care to, join me in the Serenity Prayer?" Thirty people rise and clasp the hands of those on their left and right. They say aloud:

> God grant me the serenity
> To accept the things I cannot change;
> Courage to change the things I can;
> And wisdom to know the difference.

Everyone squeezes the hands he or she is holding and says, "Keep coming back. It works!" Friends gather in knots, suggest going off to the nearest coffee shop, sweep up a few beginners with them and drift away. A few always stay behind to stack the chairs back against the walls, empty the ashtrays and wash up the coffee urn and the serving platters. The meeting is at an end.

Everyone—beginners and old-timers alike—is told, over and over, "Don't pick up the first drink." "Don't drink, a day at a time." "Go to meetings." Those three instructions are the nearest things to commands anyone will ever find in A.A. They seem absurdly simple. But in them lies one of the greatest reasons for A.A.'s success: rather than confronting newcomers with the grim and unthinkable prospect of a lifetime of abstinence, A.A. reduces the problem to manageable size. Members are asked only to stay away from the first drink, for today only. Yesterday is a closed chapter; tomorrow's events are yet to be written. No temperance or prohibition movement ever thought of *that* before; "the pledge" was always taken for life.

The beginner is taught by example and anecdote how to avoid a drink for twenty-four hours only—or for an hour, if the thought of even one day without drinking is intolerable. If a person slips and drinks again, he or she can silently make the twenty-four-hour promise once again. Members learn how to protect themselves from that first drink, and thus the next, and the next. They try to live in the now. "Anybody can go one day without drinking," newcomers are told. "Yesterday is a closed chapter. You can't know what will happen tomorrow. Live today, today." Once that kind of thinking is established, A.A.'s find that they can apply the "live-in-just-these-twenty-four-hours" exhortation to many other seemingly intractable problems.

The power of experience and example that members demonstrate in and out of meetings cannot be overestimated. An active alcoholic, even though reluctant to listen to someone in Alcoholics Anonymous, knows that the A.A. member has been in the same dark place where the drunk still lives. The new person also quickly learns that he or she will not be judged and is not unique. For some, this is an astonishing discovery.

In *The A.A. Experience: A Close-up View for Professionals*, by Milton A. Maxwell, a sociologist who served A.A. as a nonalcoholic trustee, alcoholics both new to A.A. and sober for some time described what they were like and how they felt at their first meeting:

Woman, forty-two, sober six months in A.A.: "I went to my first meeting considerable [sic] laced with wine because I was terrified. I didn't know what I was going to find. I don't remember who the speakers were or what they said. Having believed that there was no chance that I could ever stop drinking—and convinced that I was going to die and there was nothing I could do about it—I left the meeting with a feeling of hope. I also felt that these were people who cared, which was a kind of new feeling for me, because I never felt like anybody really cared."

Woman, forty, sober six years: "I was still upset, nervous and sick when I attended my first meeting—a large meeting with quite a few women there. I was overwhelmed. All I can remember was not the speaker but the people. I looked at the women. One I figured was a social worker, and the others must be the wives or relatives of the alcoholics. I thought I was the only woman drunk there, and it was absolutely unbelievable when these women came over to me and told me they were alcoholics. It was really like a ton of bricks off my head, knowing that there were other women who drank and got drunk—mothers like I was. That's really all I remember except that I saw love and something there that I wanted."

Man, newly sober: "The first wonderful thing in A.A. that was opened to me was that there were millions like me and that it wasn't something to be ashamed of, because there was something that could be done about it."

Man, thirty-five, sober two years: "At my first meeting I was amazed to hear all these people talking about fears and problems that I had had and had never talked to anybody about. It gave me a feeling of being very comfortable. I felt that I had arrived at a place where I was very much at home and that these people knew what they were talking about. They had come through the mill that I had."

Woman, thirty-two, sober four years: "At my first meeting, my hands were shaking like a leaf. I had reached the point where I was afraid of crowds, and I almost panicked when I walked into this room. But the people looked happy and friendly. Then a woman asked me if I wanted a cup of coffee. I panicked because

I knew I couldn't hold the cup without spilling it. She put her hand on my arm, and she looked in my eyes and said, 'I'll hold it for you.' When I looked in her eyes, I knew she understood."

Members suggest that newcomers just sit still and listen for a while. They also ask beginners to "identify, don't compare." This means that the listener is asked to look for what is similar, not what is different, in a speaker's drinking story and the listener's own. Often, alcoholics new to A.A. and wanting out desperately try to find satisfaction in those contrasts. Here is a typical example from the Maxwell survey:

Man, forty-seven, eight years sober: "My first meeting was a discussion meeting. I heard people talking about denting fenders on their automobiles, getting divorces, and beating their children, and I thought 'My God, I've never done these things.' But the thing that stuck in my mind more than anything else was someone's mentioning the blackout. I asked, 'What do you mean?' They said this is a period of time which you can't remember. I said, 'My God, I have been having them for years.' I had gotten into a lot of trouble through the years. I would make promises to people and never keep them—and they would say, 'Don't you remember you said this?' and I'd have to say that I can't remember. I guess I identified more with the blackout than anything else."

Almost always, it is wrenchingly hard for new members to admit aloud that they are alcoholics. But once they see that there is no shame, no blame, but hope, the statement, "My name is [first name], and I am an alcoholic," becomes a proud affirmation of membership in A.A. The shame gradually vanishes with constant repetition. What the statement says is: We share a common disease, we accept that we cannot control it, we will arrest it this day with the help of a power greater than each one of us. It also reminds members that each recovered alcoholic is only one drink away from a drunk.

In addition to the closed meeting, there are open meetings, where friends and families are welcome. In open meetings the custom is to have three speakers and a leader who works in some of his or her story between speakers, or as a prelude. Some members do not go to open meetings because there is rarely discussion from the floor and because they feel that the real no-holds-barred drama and humor of Alcoholics Anonymous can be better savored in closed meetings. The open meetings do serve a purpose, however, for the wavering prospect: They usually give a newcomer three speakers who tell their story in depth rather than one speaker followed by a scatter-shot discussion from the floor. These accounts from the Maxwell survey help explain further:

Man, forty-one, sober five years, describing his first meeting, which was open: "The first speaker was a robust, typical heavy drinker, a type of drinker I could not identify with at all. As a matter of fact, after listening to him I didn't think I was in the right place. However, the second speaker was a woman who had a drinking problem very similar to mine. She also came from a family of nondrinkers and drank very little while in college. But her drinking got under way and progressed during her twenties. So I was able to identify with her very quickly—which got me very interested in A.A. and kept me coming back to hear some more about this."

Woman, fifty-two, sober four months, who initially went to a closed meeting: "My first meeting was in a home, mostly men and only four women. I was afraid I couldn't relate to the men because their experiences would not at all be like mine. But I couldn't relate to the women either. The language I heard was frightening, and I really thought that maybe I had made a mistake, like I wasn't going to fit in there. The next day I called the minister-counselor I knew, and he put me in touch with a woman he thought I could relate to. That was good. She is still my sponsor, [best friend and mentor in A.A.], and she's great. At the time, she introduced me to other groups where I felt more at home. But since then, I have gone back to the original group, and I like it."

Many newcomers "shop around" until they find one or more groups that suit their temperament and background and in which they feel both stimulated and comforted. The group they come to most is called their home group. Other members are so fascinated by the unending diversity of groups, particularly in big cities, that they keep on table-hopping from meeting to meeting to sample the enormous smorgasbord. It is harder to form close friendships that way, however, and a home-group affiliation is considered a useful anchor for any member. One woman artist who table-hopped for years, "falling in and out of A.A.," she said, finally got serious and found a group of about thirty people she loves. She attends their meetings several times a week at seven-thirty in the morning before going to her studio, and rarely goes to other groups. She explained why: "I have gotten absolutely hooked on them. It's like a soap opera—I have to keep coming back again and again to see how it all comes out."

In the subculture that is A.A., most of the world's yardsticks for success do not count. Members usually do not ask others about their age, occupation or profession, where they work or where they went to school. The clothes a person wears, the way he handles language, the size of his bank account, the honors he may have won are not important in A.A. Additionally, there is a kind of "keeping down with the Joneses" attitude. The language is plain and everyday. There is a wariness of intellectualizing, of using big words and psychiatric jargon. In one Manhattan group that draws a large number of creative or would-be creative people, the members were talking endlessly one evening about their writing blocks, their wounded egos, their psychological problems. A lot of heavy-duty words were being flung around. Near the end of the meeting, a big, tough veteran named Joe spoke up from the sidelines. "My name is Joe and I'm an alkie," he said. "I've been listening to yez talk all night, and ya know what I t'ink? I t'ink yer all fulla bullshit." Almost everyone laughed.

The members dress simply. In the cities, very casual clothes such as jeans and sweatshirts are totally acceptable. It looks odd to see someone dressed to the nines at an A.A. meeting. One deviant from the norm is a group that reflects the ritzy, WASPish tone of the Church of the Heavenly Rest, a stately, cathedral-like Episcopal church on Manhattan's upper Fifth Avenue. The group that meets there weekly is known mockingly in some New York A.A. circles as the Church of the Overly Dressed.

Self-esteem is encouraged, but vanity about what a person does or has achieved in the outside world is not. A physician in the "Caduceus" group of doctors in A.A. described how each self-inflated newcomer gradually changed: "All the new doctors who come into Caduceus seem to be under tremendous compulsion to recite their curriculum vitae: their medical schools, their hospital affiliation. They try to make it clear to everyone else that they have great medical knowledge. They make references to some medical issue. In some way, without anybody saying anything, this kind of behavior gradually tapers off. The newcomers begin to realize that instead of 'I am what I do,' the group's silent message is, 'You are how sober you are today—and the rest of it doesn't matter.' "

Members at a meeting will listen courteously to any speaker, including those engaged in self-puffery or vaunting. After a few moments, however, the glazed eyes, the slight restlessness, will indicate to all but the most self-absorbed that it might be wise to shut up or take another tack. Nobody wants to bore an audience. On the other hand, there are many ways in which a group rewards members who are struggling to maintain their sobriety and become better people. They are urged to tell their troubles and ask for help at any time of day or night that they feel the need. They are protected by anonymity and forgiven for relapsing. Nobody pushes reluctant members to tell their story in a meeting or even to utter a word unless and until they feel ready. A.A.'s say, "Just bring the body to a meeting and the mind will follow." That means a newcomer will ultimately understand what is going on and wish to contribute. Another A.A. saying is, "Act your way into good thinking. You don't think your way into good actions in this program."

In due course most members feel they want to speak up, helping themselves and others. "A.A. is not a hiding place," said one. "It's a place for action, for getting well." The habit of masking one's deepest self, of lying about everything and to everyone in order to continue the habit, is deeply ingrained in drunks. Therefore the value of talking honestly to others who will understand is a crucial strength of Alcoholics Anonymous. Retelling a personal story while discovering new truths about oneself continues to lighten the burden of years of guilt and denial.

A priest long in A.A. warned, however, that this kind of catharsis cannot be compared with Roman Catholic confession. "It's not a structured thing," he said, "where the big sins and the little sins are identified and you confess to those defined sins and there is a specific amend or punishment for each of them such as doing X number of Hail Marys and Stations of the Cross and then you go out the church door absolved until your next confession." When an alcoholic said to an A.A. priest after speaking at the meeting they had both attended, "Father, I feel so good about making my confession," he replied, "Vomiting all over your hostess at dinner is not a sin."

Damian McElrath, a dauntingly bright former Franciscan priest who heads residential services at the Hazelden Rehabilitation Center near Center City, Minnesota, said:

> The essence of A.A. is conversation, dialogue, one alcoholic talking with another in a meeting or over a cup of coffee elsewhere. The problem with the active alcoholic is that his life is a monologue—he connects with his addicted self, and that is all. Ninety percent of the recovery process is through peers talking with one another. The beginning of all wisdom is self-knowledge. In A.A., you connect first with yourself. Then with another human being. Then with your Higher Power. You can't say, "I love God and hate my brother."

Although few alcoholics are considered hopeless, there are some who will never make it in A.A. Dr. Anne Geller, who directs the Smithers treatment center in Manhattan, defined them:

"People who are psychopathically isolated and closed off even when not drinking will not do well in A.A.," she said. "People who persist in seeing themselves as unique and different from everybody else will not do well. People who repeat behavior that is maladaptive, who are not able to hear what the A.A. community is telling them in words or by example will have difficulty in A.A. Those who are angry or paranoid won't be happy there. You have to have some degree of empathy. You have to be able to see the universality of your own experience. If you can't see yourself in others, you're in trouble."

Dr. Geller has observed and treated thousands of alcoholics since she came to Smithers in 1977. Born in England, educated at Oxford, she is a neurologist with psychiatric training. She has a sharp, intelligent face and twinkling eyes that disappear into slits when she laughs, which is often. Her manner is thoughtful, and she is a careful and sympathetic listener. She is a feminist who has participated in many consciousness-raising groups, and she has examined what is similar and what is different between those groups and A.A. "They are alike," she said,

in that they both clearly provide a place where a stigmatized person can go and be accepted and talk openly about the stigmatized condition. There is a narcissistic injury involved here —a wound to one's conception of self. The alcoholic has it, the woman who grew up learning to demean herself has it. What A.A. provides is a way of repairing the wound that is unique among self-help groups, which often disintegrate into coffee klatches. What gives A.A. its clinical edge is: You are accepted for who you are, not what you do; the group reinforces you in many, many ways simply for remaining sober; and finally, you are in a position to help others. That last edge to me is critical and is the source of the tremendous strength of A.A. Any neophyte can progress through the program of recovery to become a respected elder. It gets away from the set roles of "treator" and "treatee." Lots of self-help groups don't have that component.

Many alcoholics have sought help elsewhere before they first walk through the door of an A.A. meeting. But those helpers almost invariably have been "superior" people—doctors, bosses, members of the clergy, representatives of the law, counselors of all kinds, spouses who don't drink or who drink moderately. It is quite wonderful for the newcomer to find himself in a place where everyone has once sunk as low as he has—indeed, often lower. After a short time, it can be very comforting to hear people tell what stinkers they were before a roomful of sympathetic listeners.

The help works both ways. Bill Wilson wrote in the Big Book: "Practical experience shows that nothing will so much insure immunity from drinking as intensive work with other alcoholics. It works when other activities fail. This is our *twelfth suggestion*: Carry this message to other alcoholics! You can help when no one else can. You can secure their confidence when others fail. Remember they are very ill."

"Life will take on new meaning. To watch people recover, to see them help others, to watch loneliness vanish, to see a fellowship grow up about you, to have a host of friends—this is an experience you must not miss. We know you will not want to miss it. Frequent contact with newcomers and with each other is the bright spot of our lives."

Wilson often said and wrote that there was nothing original in A.A.'s principles, that the Twelve Steps were a synthesis of ideas drawn from religion, medicine and experience. Nonetheless, the idea that one drunk could help another, the only qualification being that the first one was sober, was considered laughable only a few years ago. This and other A.A. ideas have been successfully imitated by groups such as Al-Anon and Alateen for the families of alcoholics, Narcotics Anonymous, Gamblers Anonymous and Overeaters Anonymous.

In 1939, only four years after the founding of A.A., Wilson was already explaining in the Big Book why A.A. was succeeding with seemingly impossible drunks:

That the man who is making the approach has had the same difficulty, that he obviously knows what he is talking about, that his whole deportment shouts at the new prospect that he is a man with a real answer, that he has no attitude of holier than thou, nothing whatever except the sincere desire to be helpful; that there are no fees to pay, no axes to grind, no people to please, no lectures to be endured—these are the conditions we have found most effective.

The Twelfth Step of Alcoholics Anonymous reads: "Having had a spiritual awakening as the result of [the previous] steps we tried to carry this message to alcoholics, and to practice these principles in all our affairs."

"Twelve-Stepping," or "doing a Twelfth-Step call," is simply A.A. jargon for visiting an alcoholic who has asked for help. Members are asked not to do this alone, if possible, or to pay such a visit to an active alcoholic who is a member of the opposite sex. Experience has shown that two people of the same gender can be effective. More than two can be intimidating. And approaching an active alcoholic alone can be frightening. It is useless to try to talk to someone who is drunk; nothing will penetrate. The "morning after" is a good time, as many drunks can be more receptive when depressed, jittery, remorseful or just hung over. A.A.'s usually visit a prospect without any monitors such as a family member. (Treatment centers and other alcoholism agencies, however, are increasingly using a technique called intervention, whereby loved ones confront the alcoholic. The intervention method, developed in the 1970's by Vernon Johnson, founder of the Johnson Institute in Minneapolis, was used successfully in 1978 on Betty Ford, the former First Lady.)

More than half a century ago, Wilson described in the Big Book how to pay a Twelfth-Step visit, and his suggestions seem as valid today as ever. It was addressed to men, because there was only a sprinkling of women alcoholics among the A.A. pioneers. Wilson wrote:

At first engage [the subject] in general conversation. After a while, turn the talk to some phase of drinking. Tell him enough about your drinking habits, symptoms, and experiences to encourage him to speak of himself. If he wishes to talk, let him do so. You will thus get a better idea of how you ought to proceed. If he is not communicative, give him a sketch of your drinking career up to the time you quit. But say nothing, for the moment, of how that was accomplished. If he is in a serious mood dwell on the troubles liquor has caused you, being careful not to moralize or lecture. If his mood is light, tell him humorous stories of your escapades. Get him to tell some of his.

When he sees you know all about the drinking game, commence to describe yourself as an alcoholic. Tell him how baffled you were, how you finally learned that you were sick. Give him an account of the struggles you made to stop. Show him the mental twist which leads to the first drink of a spree. . . . If he is alcoholic, he will understand you at once. He will match your mental inconsistencies with some of his own.

If you are satisfied that he is a real alcoholic, begin to dwell on the hopeless feature of the malady. Show him, from your own experience, how the queer mental condition surrounding that first drink prevents normal functioning of the will power. Don't at this stage, refer to this book, unless he has seen it and wishes to discuss it. And be careful not to brand him as an alcoholic. Let him draw his own conclusion. If he sticks to the idea that he can still control his drinking, tell him that possibly he can—if he is not too alcoholic. But insist that if he is severely afflicted, there may be little chance he can recover by himself.

Continue to speak of alcoholism as a sickness, a fatal malady. Talk about the conditions of body and mind which accompany it. Keep his attention focused mainly on your personal experience. Explain that many are doomed who never realize their predicament. Doctors are rightly loath to tell alcoholic patients the whole story unless it will serve some good purpose. But you may talk to him about the hopelessness of alcoholism, because you offer a solution.

A.A. members paying a Twelfth-Step call still follow Wilson's suggestion not to put pressure on prospects, make them feel under any obligation, or insist that there be future visits if the alcoholic is unwilling. Wilson wrote:

> If your talk has been sane, quiet and full of human understanding, you have perhaps made a friend. Maybe you have disturbed him about the question of alcoholism. This is all to the good. The more hopeless he feels, the better. He will be more likely to follow your suggestions. . . . do not wear out your welcome. Give him a chance to think it over. . . . If he has trouble later, he is likely to say you rushed him. . . . Never talk down to an alcoholic from any moral or spiritual hilltop, simply lay out the kit of spiritual tools for his inspection. Show him how they worked with you. Offer him friendship and fellowship. Tell him that if he wants to get well you will do anything to help.

This is not to imply that A.A. members memorize or rigidly follow what Wilson had to say. Much more often their only example is a more experienced member with whom they make a Twelfth-Step call. As with reportorial interviewing or a doctor's bedside manner, a member learns by listening and by doing. Some people, by instinct and temperament, are good at it. Others never get the hang of it.

A.A. members will come quickly and without question to the aid of problem drinkers who ask for help. There are many reasons, some perhaps not immediately understandable to outsiders. One is that it's fun to play God. Another is that the sheer shock and dramatic intensity of working with active drunks helps A.A.'s to avoid the overconfidence that could trigger their own return to drinking. Twelve-Stepping is also the only practical way that all members can pay back their debt to the persons who helped *them* get sober. This debt of gratitude is enormous. Another important satisfaction is that the purely altruistic act of helping other human beings with no thought of reward is deeply fulfilling. Mahatma Gandhi said that every human action acquires a meaning when it is performed as a service. Most A.A. members have also experienced the joy of seeing drunks who were considered "hopeless" change and grow and get well within Alcoholics Anonymous. "Alcoholism is not contagious," goes an A.A. saying, "but recovery is."

Another A.A. pamphlet about beginners points out, "Newcomers are rarely helped by ponderous sermonizing about the Twelve Steps, or by complicated interpretations. The Steps speak plainly for themselves, and all newcomers are, of course, free to interpret and use them as they individually choose." Members refer to the Twelve Steps as not a set of "musts" or rules but a kind of road map to an enjoyable sober life. Boiled down to six instantly understandable principles, the A.A. program might read:

1. We admit we are licked and cannot get well on our own.
2. We get honest with ourselves.
3. We talk it out with somebody else.
4. We try to make amends to people we have harmed.
5. We pray to whatever greater Power we think there is, even as an experiment, or think of our A.A. group as our "Higher Power."
6. We try to give of ourselves for our own sake and without stint to other alcoholics, with no thought of reward.

Often, even for longtime members, the steps can be hard to grasp. At a recent meeting in New York, a young woman was agonizing about incorporating the steps in her turbulent life. She was having particular difficulty with the first three: "We admitted that we were powerless over alcohol—that our lives had become unmanageable"; "Came to believe that a Power greater than ourselves could restore us to sanity"; and "Made a decision to turn our will and our lives over to God as we understood Him." After she had maundered on for several minutes, a veteran spoke up. "The first three steps," the old-timer said, "are: I can't. He can. Let Him."

It is a common fear among newcomers that to be sober is to be bored—and boring. A young man new to A.A. told of saying to a nonalcoholic friend, "What a bore I'll be, now that I'm in A.A." The friend replied, "What do you think you were when you repeated yourself twenty times a night?" One member calls this fear the "I'll-never-laugh-again syndrome." "How can I ever enjoy a party again?" many beginners ask. The answer is that recovered alcoholics *do* have fun at parties, in much the same way that children get dizzy with sheer high spirits at a lively gathering without touching a drop of alcohol. "When the adults are having a great time at a party," said a father of two, "the children get drunk."

"It's true that A.A. will ruin your drinking," a wise former sot said at a meeting. "You can't pretend anymore that it was any good at the end or that it'll ever be good again." A woman continued his thought: "On the other hand," she said, "after smothered years and smothered emotions, you get into A.A., and *life* occurs to you—good, bad, anything—but it occurs." People are also afraid that their sex life will suffer in sobriety, when they can no longer drink away their inhibitions. This, too, passes. One member responds to this common question in an A.A.-produced film by saying that he was not there for his lovemaking before. "Sex is a better experience when you're there," he said, "and you know who you're with."

Some beginners, newly free from alcohol, often go through what members call a pink-cloud experience. It may be merely a chemical change—sudden sobriety after years of heavy drinking—but the world can look absolutely marvelous. Gripped by gratitude and zeal, they often feel they have found the one Perfect Answer, the Magic Formula, the Instant Fix. Older members see this state of exaltation as a possible danger sign, because it could lead to overconfidence and a slip. A.A. is not an Instant Answer. It is a process, a long-term and at times very difficult and frustrating process. Nobody learns Russian in a day. "This program is a delicate little gift, given to you one day at a time," one member advised a group of beginners. "You learn to go through life without chemicals."

Outsiders often want to know how many meetings members are supposed to attend in a given period. In recent years, A.A. has suggested that "ninety meetings in ninety days" will give any newcomer a flying start. For the rest, the answer is as many meetings as a member may want or need. After a while—a period determined by each individual—some may feel one or two meetings a week will be satisfactory.

People ask whether members have to attend meetings for the rest of their lives. One common answer is, "No, not necessarily, but most of us want to and some of us need to." Meetings can bring comfort and relief, a welcome pause in life, an emotional refreshment and stimulus that others may find by going to church or temple, or through psychotherapy, running or any other kind of therapeutic activity. Life in A.A., however, is more than attending meetings. It is more than being grateful survivors in the same lifeboat, although that is part of it. "A.A.," said a pioneer named Sam, "gives me the ability to live comfortably, peacefully, joyously with myself."

Dr. Joseph A. Pursch, former director of alcoholism rehabilitation at the Navy Regional Medical Center in Long Beach, California, where Betty Ford began her treatment, was bold enough to give a timetable for recovery. "Recovery means switching from pills and booze to people and feelings," he declared. "It's a process that takes from two to three years. After successful treatment, and especially if he works the Twelve Steps of Alcoholics Anonymous, the recovering alcoholic no longer uses alcohol or other mood-altering drugs, becomes honest with himself (which reduces psychological stress) and changes his life-style (work, eating, exercise, hobbies, et cetera), which also reduces living stress. In that sense, recovery forces the alcoholic to become a more ethical and healthy human being than he would have been had he not had alcoholism. That's what I mean by [getting] 'weller than well.' "

For a few, A.A. can become a substitute addiction. One meets people in the program who have moved their whole lives into it; whose spouses and friends are part of it; whose activities are focused on meetings, dances, Bill Wilson memorial dinners, coffee shop hangouts, regional get-togethers. "It is heresy [to these people] to say you don't go to meetings anymore," said a member with more than thirty years of sobriety in A.A. "They are full of horror stories about how us oldies drifted away from the program and came back with our tails between our legs after we tried to drink socially—and then went down the chute for months or years."

When asked about this, another member responded mildly, "Yes, I'll admit it can be a substitute addiction for some, but I guess it's better than drinking up your salary, beating your wife or neglecting your children."

Perhaps the total-immersion types may not lead lives that are otherwise richly rewarding. Or possibly they are afraid of the outside world, although A.A. teaches them to live fairly gracefully in a society where most people drink. In any event, A.A. at its best returns members to busy, happy, productive lives, both inside and outside the membership.

Marty Mann, founder of the National Council on Alcoholism, wrote in her classic book, *A New Primer on Alcoholism*:

> The alcoholic who seeks help . . . will be shown the A.A. way to sobriety. Further, he will be convinced that he too can learn the way, by seeing about him dozens, or hundreds . . . who have trod that way successfully before him. This is perhaps the first great lesson the newcomer is taught: that it can be done. He sees with his own eyes numbers of people who have done it, and he hears with his own ears stories that he must believe, of past drinking as bad as or worse than his own. . . . Of almost equal importance to the newcomer is the obvious fact that these people are apparently *enjoying* their sobriety.

She knew from her own experience. Marty was the first woman to get permanently sober in Alcoholics Anonymous. She came into it in 1939 at the age of thirty-five, "looking at the world out of the blackest pit of hell," she said. "I was homeless, friendless, incapable and utterly alone." A child of privilege, she was born in 1904 in Chicago, into a rich and socially prominent family that had been in America for over three hundred years. Her father, William Henry Mann, was general manager of Marshall Field and Company, Chicago's greatest department store. She went to the Latin School for Girls, followed by a life of dates and parties and drinking out of her escorts' hip flasks. Prohibition was no problem. "I was fortunate," she said. "I had a father who had laid in a big supply when Prohibition came, so there was plenty of liquor at home."

After three years of being treated for tuberculosis, she went to finishing schools in California and Florida and was polished off with a year at Miss Nixon's School in Florence in 1925-26. She came out a handsome, poised, articulate, straight-backed flapper, with cropped blond hair. She made her debut, became a member of the Junior League and was briefly married. She was proud of the way she held her liquor. "I could drink everybody under the table," she said. "I took everyone else home."

The Wall Street crash of 1929 put an end to her opulent, carefree life, so she took jobs with an interior decorator and a fashion magazine. In 1930, she sailed for London and set up a photography studio with a woman partner. She began to have blackouts. At a party, she fell out of a window and fractured her jaw and hip, bit off both sides of her tongue and spent six months in a hospital. "I came out with a brace and the conviction I was insane," she said. Her friends threw a party to celebrate her homecoming, and she got drunker than she had ever been. For days afterward, she would lurch off to London's Hyde Park with a bottle. She went to a series of psychiatrists; they all recommended she go to a mental institution—"meaning I really was a lunatic and would never come out," Marty said. "Not one word was mentioned about alcoholism."

In 1937, she returned to the United States. She wound up spending fifteen months in a Connecticut sanitarium run by Dr. Harry Tiebout, one of the first psychiatrists to support A.A.'s program publicly. One day in 1939 he gave her a copy of the just-published *Alcoholics Anonymous*. "I rejected it at first because it had God in it," she said. "I threw it on my bed." As she looked around in fury, her eyes focused on the book and one sentence: "We cannot live with anger."

"I cannot tell you how or why, but suddenly I was on my knees," she recalled. "Outside the grass looked greener; everything seemed to sing. I was overwhelmed with a complete, utter sense of belief. For the first time, I felt free."

Frightened, she ran to Dr. Tiebout. "Do you think I'm really crazy?" she asked.

"No," he replied. "You've only found what we've all been looking for."

# 6

▼

# THE GOD PART

"My sponsor told me this was a spiritual program so I tried est and yoga and Zen; I tried Catholicism and incense sticks and meditation. The only place I ever found God was here—in your faces, and the way you talked."

—*Sally B., at an A.A. meeting*

"I came in here to save my ass. And then I found out it was attached to my soul."

—*Lawrence Block*
*"Eight Million Ways to Die"*

Nothing makes a member of Alcoholics Anonymous more uncomfortable than the comment that A.A. is "religious." Members constantly hear nonalcoholics expressing admiration for A.A. They say, "It's a magnificent organization . . ." And then they say, ". . . Only I couldn't take the God part." The public perception that A.A. is composed of a bunch of smooth-talking Christers is even more deeply rooted than the image of members as skid row bums. It is easy to understand why. The two basic texts of Alcoholics Anonymous—its Twelve Steps to recovery and the Big Book, which contains the steps—are studded with references to God. Six of the Twelve Steps mention God directly or by implication. Bill Wilson summons God frequently in his Big Book: "God will determine that . . ." "Your real reliance is always upon Him . . ." "Abandon yourself to God as you understand God . . ." One of the crucial chapters of the Big Book, "How It Works," leads into a discussion of recovery with these words: "Remember that we deal with alcohol—cunning, baffling, powerful! Without help it is too much for us. But there is One who has all power—That One is God. May you find Him now!"

Neither Wilson nor Dr. Bob Smith was a religious person in any conventional sense of the term. In "Bill's Story" in the Big Book, Wilson described how he felt about organized religion until he was almost middle-aged:

With ministers, and the world's religions, I parted [company]. When they talked of a God personal to me, who was love, superhuman strength and direction, I became irritated and my mind snapped shut against such a theory.

To Christ I conceded the certainty of a great man, not too closely followed by those who claimed Him. . . . The wars which had been fought, the burnings and chicanery that religious dispute had facilitated, made me sick. I honestly doubted whether, on balance, the religions of mankind had done any good.

During the final months of his drinking in 1934, his old schoolmate Ebby, who had gotten sober in the Oxford Group, suggested to his resistant friend, *"Why don't you choose your own conception of God?"* Wilson recounted his reaction: "That statement hit me hard," he wrote. "It melted the icy intellectual mountain in whose shadow I had lived and shivered many years. . . . *It was only a matter of being willing to believe in a Power greater than myself. Nothing more was required of me to make my beginning."*

Shortly thereafter, in Towns Hospital in New York in December 1934, after his final disastrous binge, Wilson experienced what he believed to be a religious conversion. He recounted this spectacular experience thousands of times, in person and in print.

But Bill later emphasized, in his writings and teachings, that Alcoholics Anonymous was a *layman's* group. He felt that no one should have to believe in any particular religious faith or dogma; that each member was entitled to a personal interpretation of the words "God as we understand Him," including the concept of the A.A. group as a "Higher Power." Dr. Bob, despite all his reading of the Bible and the spiritual-uplift books of the 1930's, always longed to have a sudden life-changing religious experience like Bill's. "He kept hoping, but it never happened," his son said. "He just got it bit by bit." One day, however, the doctor told Young Bob, "I was sitting in my office at my desk, and I had a feeling of profound peace that was inexpressible."

Bill's own life was filled with religious and spiritual ambiguity and consumed by the search—never again rewarded—for the exalting and transforming ecstasy he had experienced in 1934. Almost to the end, he engaged in serious and prolonged experiments with spiritualism, hallucinatory drugs such as LSD and megavitamin doses of niacin.

A doctor in A.A. who treats both alcoholics and drug addicts has commented that Wilson's surge of religious exaltation in 1934 could have been a toxic, hallucinatory reaction to the sobering-up drugs given him in Towns Hospital. "Or it could have been the kind of ecstatic experience mystics have reported on through history. The cause is ultimately not important," she said. "What's important is what you then do with that experience. People who have temporal lobe seizures are often flooded by emotional exaltation just prior to the seizure. Also, when you talk to cocaine users—especially people doing crack—they report a kind of oceanic rush. What *they* then do is go and get more crack. It's how you *use* the experience that matters. For some people, it leads to an opening up—an awareness of a different sort, often of your own potential. I do think that people in early recovery are in a state of great emotional instability."

(She added, "Unfortunately, one result of reading in A.A. literature about Bill's ecstatic experience is that a few members are waiting for this to happen—for something to descend upon them from heaven. It's like the vaginal orgasm—they're waiting for an experience that never comes.")

It is true that early on, Alcoholics Anonymous was a more conventionally religious society. Among other things, its pioneers prayed together on their knees. By the 1940's, however, a half-dozen years after the founding, this practice was abandoned. The Manhattanites in A.A. in particular were generally not as devout or as traditional as members in smaller communities. They never have been, and they are not today. But then, neither is Manhattan, the most sophisticated borough of the nation's most zestily individualistic and diverse metropolis. (It also has the world's densest concentration of members and meetings.) From the very beginning, and despite the heavy references to the Deity in the key opening chapters of the Big Book, Wilson also appealed to nonbelievers and doubters. In the chapter called "We Agnostics," he wrote, "[This book's] main object is to enable you to find a Power greater than yourself which will solve your problem." He went on:

> It means, of course, that we are going to talk about God. Here difficulty arises with agnostics. Many times we talk to a new man and watch his hope rise as we discuss his alcoholic problems and explain our fellowship. But his face falls when we speak of spiritual matters, especially when we mention God. . . . We know how he feels. We have shared his honest doubt and prejudice. Some of us have been violently anti-religious. . . . Much to our relief, we discovered we did not need to consider another's conception of God. Our own conception, however inadequate, was sufficient to make the approach and effect a contact with Him.

The first printing of the Big Book left the impression with some readers that a kind of cataclysmic spiritual upheaval had to take place before a drunk could throw off the burden of alcohol forever. This discouraged many. So Wilson included an appendix on "Spiritual Experience" two years later, in 1941, which he urged all to read. Part of it says:

> Among our rapidly growing membership of thousands of alcoholics such transformations, although frequent, are by no means the rule. Most of our experiences are what the psychologist William James calls the "educational variety" because they develop slowly over a period of time. Quite often friends of the newcomer are aware of the difference long before he is himself. He finally realizes that he has undergone a profound alteration in his reaction to life; that such a change could hardly have been brought about by himself alone.

The concept of "surrender" and the relinquishing of the egotistical need for control implied in A.A.'s first and subsequent steps comes straight from William James's *The Varieties of Religious Experience.* In his chapter titled "The Religion of Healthy-Mindedness," he wrote:

> [The] way to success, as vouched for by innumerable authentic personal narrations, is . . . by the "surrender" of which I spoke in my second lecture. Passivity, not activity; relaxation, not intentness, should be now the rule. Give up the feeling of responsibility, let go your hold, resign the care of your destiny to higher powers, be genuinely indifferent as to what becomes of it all, and you will find not only that you gain a perfect inward relief, but often also . . . the particular goods you sincerely thought you were renouncing. This is the salvation through self-despair, the dying to be truly born, of Lutheran theology. . . . To get to it, a critical point must usually be passed, a corner turned within one. Something must give way, a native hardness must break down and liquefy; and this event . . . is frequently sudden and automatic, and leaves on the Subject an impression that he has been wrought on by an external power.
>
> Whatever its ultimate significance may prove to be, this is certainly one fundamental form of human experience. Some say that the capacity or incapacity for it is what divides the religious from the merely moralistic character. . . .

A form of regeneration by relaxing, by letting go, psychologically indistinguishable from the Lutheran justification by faith and the Wesleyan acceptance of free grace is within the reach of persons who have no conviction of sin and care nothing for the Lutheran theology. It is but giving your little private convulsive self a rest, and finding that a greater Self is there. The results, slow or sudden, or great or small, of the combined optimism and expectancy, the regenerative phenomena which ensue on the abandonment of effort, remain firm facts of human nature, no matter whether we adopt a theistic, a pantheistic-idealistic, or a medical-materialistic view of their ultimate causal explanation.

It is all very well to read about A.A. and to learn about what inspired its founding members. But it is not the same as living A.A. And one of the realities of being in A.A. today, of seeing it and experiencing it in action, is how accepting its members are of each other's religious or nonreligious points of view. A.A. is an accommodating, flexible and inclusive society. This has struck most newcomers who have given it a serious chance. From its earliest days, this has also struck members of the clergy.

In an interview in 1986, Gordon Grimm, a Lutheran chaplain at the Hazelden rehabilitation center for alcoholics in Minnesota, had this to say about A.A.:

If you know anything about A.A., you cannot evade its spirituality. Spirituality is much more about humanness than about Godliness. It is about getting involved with one another. So much of our religion takes us back up to God when our purpose on this earth is primarily to reach out to others. It is the only way we have to know God. My personal belief is that we have to get involved with each other. It's what's left out of so much organized religion. For me, a lot of organized religion is escapist—"Just me in the prayer closet." In that caring dimension, the church hasn't done as well as I think A.A. has.

Spirituality has to do with a deep contact with other human beings and with the appreciation that we participate in some issues that cannot be rationally explained. For me, spirituality is how I deal with problems, pain, difficulties in my life—I don't have to escape it; there is meaning and purpose in going through rejection and change. Throughout history—all you have to do is read about the religious wars—people have been "doing God's will" by killing somebody else. That's not what spirituality is about. To me, spirituality is the living out—the putting into practice—of our greatest responsibility. That responsibility is to love. At their best, the members of A.A. are trying to live up to that responsibility. They are also living out my definition of grace: being loved when we don't deserve it. I think all of A.A.'s Twelve Steps are spiritual. The first step is as spiritual as the last.

Grimm has been ministering to alcoholics for thirty years. He is a huge man, six feet four inches tall, weighing 250 pounds, with a benign, down-home manner and gentle ways. His father was an alcoholic, an engineer who lost job after job until he wound up on a farm in Iowa. He spent the last seven years of his life sober in A.A. One July morning in 1986 as Grimm gazed out of his office window at the sparkling lake on Hazelden's grassy campus, he recalled a day in 1951 at the Cherokee State Hospital in Iowa. "My drunken father had been brought there," he said. "A doctor told my brother and me, 'Your father has a disease—his disease is alcoholism.' From that moment on, I had no problem with my dad. Finally, there was a reason I could accept for the way he acted." As a theological student, Grimm spent a year's internship at Willmar State Hospital in Minnesota in the late 1950's, where an enlightened director, a physician, separated the inebriates from the insane and began programs of treatment with the cooperation of Alcoholics Anonymous. In 1965, Grimm came to Hazelden, where he has been a pastoral counselor to thousands of alcoholics. He has dealt there daily with nonbelievers who were troubled by the "God part" of A.A.

"I will always remember a man in A.A. named Fred," the minister said.

He was an alcoholism counselor who struggled with the spiritual for thirteen years in sobriety before he could get comfortable with it. Very early in my training, Fred taught me not to push on the religiosity, not to be rigid. He shared his story with me, and pointed out that the only thing he could hold on to for thirteen years was that he didn't have to believe everything. He just hung on to the things that made sense to him. To Fred, A.A. was a process. Most people in A.A. don't have the thunderbolt religious experience that Bill Wilson had. I have counseled many agnostics and atheists, both Christian and Jewish, who were turned off by fire-and-brimstone preachers in childhood. I keep telling them, "A.A. is a daily experience; it will grow; stick with the group; stick with the process. If this comes to you, it will come." It's out of our hands. You can't inject people with spirituality.

*Spiritual* and *spirituality* are words one hears a lot of in A.A. "It's not a religious program, it's a spiritual program" is a sentence A.A.'s utter over and over again to newcomers and nonmembers. Many of them feel the difference without being able to define it. An atheist member of A.A. said, "People use the word *spiritual* in ways that define themselves. I think it means the ability to get outside one's own immediate concerns to perform an altruistic act."

What is it like to be an atheist in A.A.? Sometimes it is uncomfortable. A distinguished professional woman with more than a decade of sobriety, who has participated in A.A. meetings all over the world, described her dilemma. "It's hard to be an atheist in A.A.," she said.

Agnosticism is a more respectable intellectual stance. But to be honest, I really am an atheist. I am as committed an atheist as others are theists. I really do not believe. I realize that not believing is as irrational as believing. However, I am not comfortable when people start talking about meditation or formal religion. Outside of New York particularly, there's that Big Book, "even-the-most-confirmed-atheist-will-change" mentality. It is unspoken, but there. People don't hassle you, but you get the idea that they're thinking, "Don't worry, if you hang around long enough, you'll get it." By "it," they mean you may come in an atheist, using the group as the higher power, but eventually you will succumb.

What I've learned to do is just not to respond. In the beginning I was angry. I felt very attacked, because part of me was my atheism. The only time I haven't felt accepted in A.A.—the complete me—is in that area.

Another woman with a similar background, more than thirty years sober, also said she did not feel approved of in some A.A. groups:

In some places away from the big cities, I am aware of a not-so-subtle pressure to be saved. Despite A.A.'s protestations to the public, a lot of groups are quite religious. In the South, the Bible Belt area, there's a lot of dogma, a lot of liturgy. A.A. headquarters in New York doesn't like to talk about this. But in many small towns, there's no "God-as-we-understand-Him" stuff. It's just plain God. Every speaker that gets up in some Southern meetings has found God. They say if I'm an atheist I can't stay sober. I've been sober in A.A. since 1953.

Arguments against the "religiosity" of A.A. are also heard from people in the program who are still drinking, or feel deeply uneasy in A.A.; they find this the most acceptable reason for dropping out. It is a favorite rationale with intellectuals. One of the most outspoken and persistent critics of this aspect of A.A. in the 1960's was a New York psychologist, Arthur H. Cain. Charging that A.A. was a "dogmatic cult," he wrote in the *Saturday Evening Post* in 1964: "Behind the A.A. fence the original principle that alcoholics must be humble before God has been turned into the dictum that alcoholics are God's chosen people. This theme is preached in meetings and through books and pamphlets." Then he quoted a pamphlet called *Around the Clock with A.A.*, which he said was put out by a group in California.

Twenty years later, in 1984, an A.A. speaker from California used the same text at an A.A. Founders Day luncheon in Akron, Ohio. The Founders Day weekend, always held in June, attracts

thousands of members from all over the nation to the city where
Alcoholics Anonymous was born. This is what was read aloud
that day:

> God in His wisdom selected this group of men and women to
> be the purveyors of goodness. In selecting them ... He went
> not to the proud, the mighty, the famous or the brilliant. He
> went right to the drunkard, the so-called weakling of the world.
> Well might He have said to us: Unto your weak and feeble hands
> I entrust a power beyond estimate. To you has been given that
> which has been denied the most learned of your fellows. Not
> to scientists or statesmen, not to wives and mothers, not even
> to priests or ministers have I given this gift of healing other
> alcoholics which I entrust to you. It must be used with tolerance,
> for I have restricted its application to no race, no creed and no
> denomination. Personal criticism you must expect. A lack of
> appreciation will be common. Ridicule will be your lot; your
> motives will be misjudged, and you must be prepared for ad-
> versity. For what you call adversity is the ladder we must use
> to ascend the rungs toward spiritual perfection. . . .
> You were selected because you were the outcasts of the world.
> And your long experience as drunkards has made or should
> make you more humbly alert to the cries of distress that come
> from the lonely hearts of alcoholics everywhere. And keep ever
> in mind the confession you made on the first day of your profes-
> sion in A.A. Namely that you are powerless, and it was only
> through your willingness to turn your will and your life unto
> My keeping that relief came to you.

As the member from California droned on from the dais, a glazed
look, a varnish of polite ennui, brushed over the faces in the audience. Some shifted slightly in their chairs or picked at tablecloths,
but they listened to the peroration, as A.A. members learn to do,
in courteous silence. When it was over, much relieved, they settled
back to applaud the next speaker, a witty, raffish and extremely
irreverent veteran.

The pious self-congratulation that trickled from the Californian's text cannot be found anywhere in the dozens of A.A. books and pamphlets that are "conference-approved"—that is to say, the "official" A.A. literature, which is rigorously screened and finally voted upon by American and Canadian delegates at the yearly General Service Conference in New York. Conference-approved literature tends to avoid preening except on the most subtle level.

The degree of discomfort that a doubter or nonbeliever in God may experience in A.A. meetings depends greatly on the group. How much members talk about God and religion varies enormously. But, as a Hazelden pamphlet on unofficial "etiquette" for attending A.A. meetings says, "No one makes an effort to keep [a speaker] from referring to God at meetings, and no one makes an effort to force anyone to talk about God when they don't want to. You need not feel any obligation to participate in prayers or spiritual discussions at A.A. or Al-Anon meetings. You are asked merely to allow others to do so if they wish."

Milton Maxwell, a sociologist who was a nonalcoholic trustee of A.A. for many years, said: "To understand A.A. and its language use, it is also necessary to recognize that A.A.'s generally use 'spiritual' in a broad sense. When they speak of 'spiritual growth,' they include growth away from what Freud called the narcissistic self —growth away from self-centeredness." The way members feel about this was simply expressed by a forty-year-old woman, six years in A.A. She told Maxwell, "To me, spirituality is a feeling of acceptance of myself, of loving the other human being, and accepting what goes on in my life. It is the spirit of giving, the spirit of living."

Only two prayers are commonly said aloud at A.A. meetings: the Serenity Prayer, attributed to the American theologian Reinhold Niebuhr and now sometimes called the A.A. Prayer, and the Lord's Prayer. The Serenity Prayer, unlike the Lord's Prayer, is not part of church liturgy. But it has proved comforting, a kind of anchor, for many alcoholics. It also cannot be interpreted as belonging to any particular religion. The same cannot be said of the Lord's Prayer heard so frequently at the end of A.A. meetings. "It is very clearly a Christian God who is being invoked," said one member. "It is not a Jewish God for sure."

Renah Rabinowitz agrees. A short, energetic and merry woman, she is an observant Jew, the wife of a rabbi in New Jersey and a former director of the JACS Foundation. JACS, founded in 1980, is a spearhead of the effort to educate Jews nationwide about the alcoholism that is in their midst. Its headquarters is at the tail end of a brick-walled basement corridor under the Educational Alliance Building on Manhattan's Lower East Side, which became the first home neighborhood for millions of Jewish immigrants fleeing persecution in Europe in the late nineteenth and early twentieth centuries. She commented on why Jews might feel uneasy in A.A.: "Jews do not have the Lord's Prayer in their liturgy. The words 'Thy Kingdom come, Thy will be done' are difficult for a Jew. Christianity sees the Messiah as having come. We are praying that the Messiah *will* come. That is a major, major difference."

She and the JACS Foundation are firmly oriented toward A.A.'s recovery program. "It's not a shanda [Yiddish for "shame"] to have alcoholism and drug abuse in the Jewish community," she said. "What *is* a shanda is to know that it exists and to do nothing about it." This does not mean that the people in JACS are ignoring the obstacles posed by A.A.'s Christian flavor. For one thing, the vast majority of A.A. meetings in the United States are held in the basements and parish houses of Christian churches. "An orthodox Jew is brought up not to enter a house of worship in another religion's building," Rabinowitz explained.

We may admire the outsides of great European cathedrals, but many of us have suffered from being forced to go into a church and kneel. We try to convince Jews that if you're walking into a church basement for an A.A. meeting, you're not walking into a church to pray. On the other hand, the idea in the Twelve Steps of turning yourself over to God is a Christian-based philosophy. The average Jew, myself included, does think of it as a largely Christian idea. In this day and age there are so many Christian fundamentalists and Jews for Jesus that many Jews

are afraid they're going to be sucked into brainwashing in A.A.
And then people say, "You're not only asking us to walk into
their buildings, you're asking us to say their prayers."

Rabbi Carol Glass, director of the American University B'nai
B'rith Hillel Foundation in Washington, D.C., is another Jew involved in the alcoholism field who has become aware of this am-
bivalence. "I have noticed," she said,

a confusion experienced by many in the initial stages of the
recovery process in A.A. Some Jews have expressed fear that
the beliefs and principles of the Twelve Steps are in conflict with
the tenets of Judaism. Some have even confided to me that they
thought it would be necessary to abandon their religion in order
to be a successful member of A.A. or Al-Anon. It's my intention
to assure all recovering Jews, as well as the rabbis that would
offer them counsel, that nothing could be further from the truth.
Indeed, Twelve Step ideology clearly echoes established beliefs
found in mainstream Jewish liturgy and thought. In addition,
this sequential process for altering addictive behavior bears a
striking resemblance to the Jewish step-by-step method for
changing so-called "sinful" behavior.

Rabbi Glass pointed out specific analogies between Maimon-
ides's Laws of Repentance, Rabbenau Yonah of Gerona's *The
Gates of Repentance* and the Twelve Steps of Alcoholics Anonymous.

The last of the Twelve Steps (which can be "taken," that is to
say, studied and when possible acted upon at one's own speed and
in any order that is comfortable after the newcomer takes the first
step) is a very important one. In it alcoholics are urged to help
others who still suffer, and to apply what they have learned in
A.A. to their daily lives. The twelfth step says: "Having had a
spiritual awakening as a result of steps, we tried to carry this
message to alcoholics, and to practice these principles in all our
affairs." But what is a spiritual awakening? Perhaps Bill Wilson
should answer. He wrote in the Big Book:

"If a mere code of morals, or a better philosophy of life were sufficient to overcome alcoholism, many of us would have recovered long ago. But we found that such codes and philosophies did not save us, no matter how much we tried. We could wish to be moral, we could wish to be philosophically comforted, in fact, we could will these things with all our might, but the needed power wasn't there. Our human resources, as marshalled by the will, were not sufficient; they failed utterly.

"Lack of power, that was our dilemma. We had to find a power by which we could live, and it had to be *A Power Greater Than Ourselves.*"

PART

# TWO

# 7

## THE FAMILIES

I didn't cause the alcoholism.
I can't control it.
I can't cure it.
—*The "Three C's" of Al-Anon*

There should be a fourth "C" in Al-Anon's credo: "But I *can* change myself." Those four sentences are the central message of Al-Anon, the biggest and oldest self-help group in the world for families and close friends of alcoholics.

Spun off from Alcoholics Anonymous in 1951, using A.A.'s Twelve-Step program for recovery yet completely independent of A.A., Al-Anon now numbers half a million members. Four fifths of them live in the United States and Canada. Eighty-eight percent are women. One third are children of alcoholics, many of whom went on to marry alcoholics too, despite their childhood vows that "It will never happen to me." And when they come into Al-Anon they are every bit as sick as the alcoholic husbands, wives, lovers, fathers and mothers who have been ruining their lives. Moreover, they have been unconsciously allowing, even aiding the alcoholic in his or her downward plunge.

Al-Anon is not nearly as well known as A.A. Yet the need for it is numerically greater, because the drinking of every one of the eighteen million alcohol abusers in the United States devastates the lives of at least four other people—seventy-two million Americans in all. In a poll taken by Gallup in 1987, almost one out of four Americans sampled—24 percent of the total population of 220 million—said that alcohol abuse had brought trouble to their families. A much smaller percentage of Americans questioned in other recent samplings said abuse of any other drug, from marijuana to cocaine, was a cause of family disruption.

Those tens of millions out there, most of whom are unaware even of the existence of Al-Anon, let alone what it does, are in desperate straits. The name of their illness is obsession.

It is common and understandable for people who love an alcoholic to protest, "Now wait a minute! *He's* the sick one, not me!" Yet they have become as powerless over alcohol as any compulsive drinker, and their lives have become as unmanageable as any drinker's life. Al-Anon members use an image that perfectly captures their obsession, the way they were before they sought help. It is, "The drunk wraps his arms around the bottle. And the family wraps its arms around the drunk."

Those trying to break free in Al-Anon have lived and suffered with the devastation that alcoholism wreaks both on its primary victim, the alcoholic, and on its secondary victims, themselves. In the end, almost everything the family does is a reaction to what the alcoholic does. They become fixated on the drunk, fixated on his disease. They become enablers. A wonderful word, *enabler*. It may not appear in the dictionary, as *enablement* does. But no other word is so apt for the person who loves and unknowingly abets the alcoholic. An enabler pays the alcoholic's overdue bills, cleans up his messes, calls the boss on Monday morning to say he has the flu, hides his liquor, pours it down the sink, assures him he wasn't such a clod the night before when he made a pass at his best friend's wife. An enabler lies for the alcoholic, protects and rescues him. An enabler, without realizing it, makes it possible for the alcoholic to continue drinking. An enabler believes, perhaps, that the power of love ("If you loved me, you wouldn't drink"), or prayer ("God, if only he stops, I'll never again . . .") or threats not carried out ("I'm leaving and taking the children") will bring the alcoholic to his senses.

Al-Anon's co-founder, Lois Wilson, expressed the compulsion for control over her own husband, Bill, very well. "I failed in every attempt to control his drinking," she said. "I wanted to get inside his brain and turn the screws in the right direction." She tried for almost two decades of an increasingly rocky marriage. She couldn't do it. In the end Bill Wilson got sober by himself in 1934, with some outside help.

The mid-thirties were the years of the Great Depression in America. Few people had money then. The alcoholics of that time, desperate men who were being helped by Bill Wilson in New York and Dr. Bob in Akron, had long since drunk their savings away. Many of them had drunk their jobs away as well. So they met in each others' homes. Their nonalcoholic wives came with them.

"In the beginning A.A. was a family affair," Lois Wilson wrote in her autobiography, *Lois Remembers*:

> Mates, parents and children attended the meetings. . . . Many of the wives tried to live by the [A.A.] program themselves and made much progress, but this was in a general way only. There was nothing to help them understand their own reactions nor to realize how similar these were to the feelings of other A.A. wives. There was little sharing of experience. . . . Back in the early days anyone lucky enough to still have a home shared it with those who had lost theirs. Our house was as busy as an

anthill. . . . There was much visiting between groups and traveling back and forth.

Al-Anon was not even a concept then, but the need for it was growing in the hearts of those who had seen the men they loved saved by A.A. Like many wives of alcoholics since, Lois discovered that the end of her husband's drinking was not the end of her problems. He was, among other things, shutting her out, neglecting her for his A.A. buddies. She was suppressing enormous resentments. Bill did not become the long-lost companion she had dreamed of for so many years. A born homebody, she was forced to be away most days at her job in a department store, earning money for Bill and the drunks he was trying to sober up at their house in Brooklyn. "I was jealous of his newfound friends," Lois said. She was running a hostel for rummies, not a tranquil oasis for two.

In Akron, Anne Smith, Dr. Bob's wife, was also receiving streams of visitors at the Smith house. Unlike Lois, however, Anne was at home all the time, mothering everybody while Dr. Bob attended to his patients at the hospital. Archie T., an early A.A. member, recalled:

> I was literally taken off the street and nursed back to life by Annie. . . . When a couple undertakes the sort of job that Annie and Dr. Bob took on when they took me into their home, it is the wife who is going to bear at least a slightly heavier part of the burden. This is particularly true when the recipient of such an extraordinary act of kindness is not only jobless and penniless, but too ill to get out of the house during the day and hunt for work. Such was my case; and so great was Annie's love, so endless her patience with me, that ten months later I left the house a new man.

As the all-male membership grew (A.A. pioneers believed the myth that "nice" women were never drunks), the nonalcoholic wives followed their men to meetings in bigger homes. Then, in Akron, they tagged along to the King School, the first public building anywhere to house an A.A. meeting. The women were the kitchen brigade. As one member put it, "[They were allowed] to wash dishes, make coffee, organize picnics and things like that." Anne Smith, by nature quiet and retiring, always did more. Dan K., an early member, said, "Annie always looked to the newcomers. She'd spot you, and after the meeting she would go to your table and introduce herself. 'I want to welcome you and your lovely wife to Alcoholics Anonymous. We hope you'll keep coming back.' "

Dorothy S. M. said Anne remembered everybody's name, and their children's names.

> It was that terrific personal interest she took. . . . Even when she was almost blind [from cataracts], there at the last, she'd go up to them, and even if she couldn't distinguish who they were, she could tell by their voices, and she would recall every single thing about them. . . . She used to gather clothes for anyone who didn't have anything to wear. I had a summer coat, and I had to wear it as a winter coat. Annie ripped the fur off somebody's old suit, and we sewed that on. Then came summer, and we just ripped off the fur collar and put on a white collar.

Anne Smith died in 1949, a year before her husband's death, and two years before Al-Anon came into being as an organization separate from A.A. Shy as she was, close to home as she stayed, this generous and profoundly spiritual woman left an enduring legacy to the families of alcoholics. She genuinely believed that God was love. She took to heart the biblical message that faith without good works was a dead faith. Although not recognized as a founder of Al-Anon, she was certainly a guiding angel during the years that preceded it, comforting the wives as well as the earliest A.A.'s who were trying to reconstruct their shattered lives without liquor.

All during the 1940's, Bill and Lois, a more adventurous and outgoing couple than the Smiths, barnstormed the country like a pair of campaigners, giving strength and hope to fledgling A.A. groups that seemed to be sprouting up everywhere. At the same time A.A. Family Groups and A.A. Auxiliaries were forming, both names implying close ties with Alcoholics Anonymous. These groups adapted the wording of Bill's Twelve Steps to accommodate their own recoveries. The book carried the message in print to even the most isolated alcoholic while the Wilsons brought it in person. First Bill would talk at meetings and press the flesh. Then Lois would cheer up the wives at luncheons and coffee klatches. But forever beckoning to Lois was Stepping Stones, their house back in Westchester County, New York, the only home of their own the Wilsons would ever know. Lois loved the gardening, the fixing and painting and sewing, the hours alone with her books and music. She wanted to settle down. Once she counted that she had given talks in sixty-two cities and towns between 1939 and 1951.

Bill had other plans for Lois. In 1950, he suggested that she open a service office in New York where the Family Groups could register, get literature and become more unified. It would also be a place where any distracted wife could come for help. "Bill's suggestion did not appeal to me at first, because I was still excited about having a home of our own," Lois said. "But as I began to think about the need, the idea grew more and more appealing."

With the help of Anne B., who was a close friend, the wife of an alcoholic and a Westchester neighbor, Lois sent letters in May 1951 to eighty-seven A.A. Auxiliaries and Family Groups, expressing the resolve to unify them under one organizational umbrella with a name of its own. Forty-eight groups responded. Among the names they suggested were A.A. Helpmates, Triple A.A. and Non A.A. Finally Al-Anon, a contraction from Alcoholics Anonymous, was chosen. Together, Anne B. and Lois wrote *Purposes and Suggestions for Al-Anon Family Groups,* which included a principle altogether new at that time—the focus on oneself, rather than on the alcoholic. Eventually Anne moved away from the New York area and became much less active in the movement. For those early efforts, however, she is considered to be Al-Anon's co-founder. She died in 1984 at the age of eighty-four.

The earliest Al-Anon groups, composed exclusively of families of men sober in A.A., met in each others' homes. Later, they often gathered to discuss their problems and share their joys in small anterooms outside the much larger A.A. meetings. According to Al-Anon's official history, *First Steps,* published in 1986, "All too

frequently A.A. members viewed the development of Al-Anon sus-
piciously, fearing that past alcoholic episodes would be held up
to scrutiny. This suspicion could have some odd results." In the
book, there is a description of what the A.A. paranoia could lead
to: "Lehua W. of Hawaii tells how A.A. stationed a man outside
the Al-Anon meeting to lie on the couch and pretend to sleep, so
that he could listen in on what the wives were talking about." In
the early days in North Bend, Oregon, an Al-Anon group preferred
to take the fire escape to their meeting place rather than the normal
route, which passed through an A.A. meeting room heavy with
hard looks from the recovering alcoholics. "Those looks said, 'You
women are going to roast us,' " one early Al-Anon member remembered.

Mayme S. told how A.A. and Al-Anon finally got a home eco-
nomics room in a North Bend high school that could be divided
in two. "A.A. gave us permission to use the second half of the
room," she said. "In return, we were to make the coffee and furnish
the cake for A.A. In those early days in Al-Anon, we did a lot of
weeping. We sat around and every time we started a meeting, some
of us would just break down, but finally we got it out of ourselves."
Later, the North Bend A.A.'s and Al-Anon members went to a
bigger location. "Again, Al-Anon had a little back room and still
made the coffee, provided the cake and did the cleanup for A.A.
afterwards," Mayme recalled. "We said we weren't going to do
this, but we still did it."

For years, Al-Anon trotted in the footsteps of A.A. like a faithful
little poodle. In 1952, Lois and Anne moved themselves and their
increasingly voluminous correspondence from Stepping Stones into
A.A.'s Twenty-fourth Street Clubhouse, on Manhattan's West Side.
They had their own typewriter, two drawers in a filing cabinet
and a half share in A.A.'s mimeograph machine. They called their
tiny operation the Clearing House. They were desperate for volunteers and money. "[We] were ready to take in anyone who could
count to nine," Dot L. said. Occasionally, members from groups
across the country would slip a dollar or two for the Clearing
House's expenses into the letters they sent. Lois brought in card-

boards from Bill's shirts, back from the laundry, to stiffen packages of pamphlets for new groups. Other volunteers saved wrapping paper and string. The Al-Anon women brought in sandwiches for lunches in the cockroach-infested kitchen and would hold meetings on the spot. The ventilation was terrible in the Clearing House; in the summer they called it Lois's Sweatshop, and in the winter Lois's Refrigerator. Margaret D., an early member, said that when a cry for help came in over the telephone, she would look up the nearest town with an Al-Anon meeting in an atlas and be glad if the meeting was only 400 miles away. Then it was 200; then less than fifty.

In the late 1950's Al-Anon finally broke away to independent headquarters on East Twenty-third Street, expanding quickly to two floors. Myrna H., the current executive director, who went to work at headquarters in 1963, recalled the dumbwaiter: "If you wanted something from the shipping department downstairs, you would ring a bell and then stick your head into the shaft to talk with the shipping supervisor. You had to be careful not to get knocked out when the dumbwaiter zoomed up with the shipment."

The late fifties and early sixties brought a spate of publicity for Al-Anon; there were articles in newspapers, the immensely popular *Saturday Evening Post* magazine, an episode on the Loretta Young television show called "The Understanding Heart." Nobody helped as much as Ann Landers, the zesty, commonsensical advice columnist. Somehow, she pierced the public's unawareness about the plight of those who live with an alcoholic. Lois Wilson called the columns "undoubtedly the most effective publicity we have enjoyed." Landers first wrote about Al-Anon in 1962, and 4,000 letters poured into headquarters "like a shock wave," a staffer said. Later, an Illinois member wrote to her about how Al-Anon had changed her life. She began:

Dear Ann:

It is Sunday afternoon, our 13-year-old boy went to a ball game, the 10- and 12-year-old girls are in the neighbor's pool, and my husband went to his favorite tavern to get drunk. . . . A few years ago I would have been crying my eyes out, or pouring out my anger to a friend on the telephone. But today I am calm, content and very happy with my life. Why? Because I listened to you and joined Al-Anon. Every woman who is married to an alcoholic must at some point decide whether she is going to allow his problems to defeat her or learn how to live with it. . . . Please, Ann, keep telling people about Al-Anon. It's a life-saver . . . in every sense of the word.

—Gage Park member

Landers replied, "Not a week goes by that I don't receive at least three or four letters from readers in praise of Al-Anon." She gave the Al-Anon address for those who wished to write for literature, adding, "You have nothing to lose but the price of a stamp." That one column brought 10,000 letters flooding into Al-Anon. When Landers reprinted it, 11,000 more came into the New York office. "Most of us toted letters home in shopping bags," one volunteer said, "as we all felt the need to provide some answers as soon as possible." In the years since, Landers has been a frequent, ardent champion of Al-Anon, its subgroup for young people, Alateen, and Alcoholics Anonymous.

In 1966, Al-Anon published its own Big Book, *Living with an Alcoholic;* the title was later changed to *Al-Anon Family Groups.* In 1978, a fast-growing Al-Anon established its World Service Office in a stately building at One Park Avenue in Manhattan, only a block from the General Service Office of Alcoholics Anonymous. In 1985 it moved to even bigger quarters across town in New York's bustling garment district. Its sleek modern interior, done up in ladylike tones of mauve and cream with tasteful prints on the walls, is a perfect background for the well-dressed, well-spoken women who run the day-to-day business of Al-Anon.

The growth and change at Al-Anon headquarters clearly reflect the transformation of the membership in recent years. Al-Anon is tired of fading into the wallpaper, tired of fixing the coffee, tired of saying, "Yes, dear." It mirrors women's journey upward in status and their growing sense of their own worth. Half of its members have had some college education, most are employed and more than a quarter are in executive, professional or managerial jobs. It is not for nothing that Al-Anon's first videocassette, produced in 1986, is called *Al-Anon Speaks for Itself*.

"I used to be a doormat for my husband," said Hildegarde V., a handsome, articulate woman who served as editor of *The Forum*, Al-Anon's monthly journal. "But anybody who goes to Al-Anon and learns to think for herself or become her own person is going to be a difficult person to deal with." She left her still-drinking spouse after thirty years of marriage and has since happily rewed. She continues to be very active in Al-Anon. "It helps me cope," she said, "in every aspect of my life."

In recalling what the membership was like in the early 1960's, Myrna H., the executive director, said, "The average member was a housewife. Some had small children, others children in school. By and large they didn't work, or they held part-time jobs. Very few members were divorced. They are definitely younger now, ranging from the twenties on up, with many more professionals. We seem to attract lots of nurses, teachers, social workers—it's that caretaking need that is so typical of people who live with alcoholics." One of her aides said, "You see Al-Anon today, you see young women, young men who say, 'Hey, I can love him or her forever, but I don't have to stay with this alcoholic.' They don't stay. They refuse to be some therapeutic tool to fix somebody else."

Earlier, the emphasis even in Al-Anon's official literature was on how to keep a marriage together. The members for many years were exclusively the wives of men in A.A. "It was a closed society," said Al-Anon's archivist. "Now we have all kinds of relationships—husbands, parents, children, brothers and sisters, 'live-ins' [lovers], employers and employees. The drinker they care about can be sober or not; in A.A. or not. The only requirement for membership is that an important person in your life be an alcoholic."

The choice of meetings is enormous. There are 28,000 Al-Anon groups worldwide, 15,000 of them in the United States alone. As in A.A., they reflect the general populations of countries, regions, even neighborhoods. All of them meet at least once a week. Al-Anon Information Services operate in every major city and offer up-to-date lists of meetings near the caller's home or office.

The veterans who work at Al-Anon's World Service Office say that those who come to a meeting for the first time usually have no idea of what's going to happen. Or they may have several notions. The most common are: It's part of Alcoholics Anonymous. I'm going there to get my alcoholic sober. It's religious.

The reality is different. Al-Anon is not a religious group or a counseling agency. It is not a treatment center, nor is it allied with any organization offering such services. It is not a club to get the alcoholic sober through some kind of magic. "It is a place," said Lydia M., "to get your life and your soul sorted out." Lydia, who handles literature at headquarters, is an irrepressibly bubbly and talkative person, the mother of five, who finally separated from her alcoholic husband of many years. Three of her children went into Alateen, a part of Al-Anon. Two joined Al-Anon in different parts of the country when they were in their twenties. She still goes weekly to her own Al-Anon meeting in a New Jersey exurb.

"When I see a newcomer at an Al-Anon meeting, with that typical look of fear and anxiety, my heart goes out to her," wrote a member in *Al-Anon Faces Alcoholism,* a basic text. "I want to tell her that serenity and peace of mind do not depend on her husband's sobriety. I would like to spare her the years of anguish I lived through before I learned that my serenity depends only on me."

Meetings usually take place in church parish houses, schools or community centers. The people gathered there are of every age, size and condition, seated around a table for intimate discussions or, in bigger meetings, facing a speaker's table. They are mostly women, with only a scattering of men. This is the single, striking difference between the look of an Al-Anon and an A.A. meeting, where the sexes are represented about equally in big cities, with fewer women members in smaller towns. The membership of Al-Anon has stayed unwaveringly at 88 percent female for some years, a disproportion that worries many Al-Anon members. "I've tried and tried to figure it out," said Al-Anon's executive director, Myrna. "I think the reason is that men seem reluctant to discuss their problems in a group largely made up of women." Some of the more uncomfortable males end up in Al-Anon stag meetings, or form a new one themselves.

The meeting begins on time. One person reads aloud the suggested Al-Anon Preamble to the Twelve Steps: "The Al-Anon Family Groups are a fellowship of relatives and friends of alcoholics who share their experience, strength and hope in order to solve their common problems. We believe alcoholism is a family illness and that changed attitudes can aid recovery."

Another person then reads the Al-Anon Welcome, which says in part:

I welcome you to the [name of group] and hope you will find in this fellowship [they are still using the A.A. term "fellowship" in Al-Anon, although it is clearly more like a sisterhood] the help and friendship we have been privileged to enjoy.

We who live, or who have lived, with the problem of alcoholism understand as perhaps few others can. We, too, were lonely and frustrated, but in Al-Anon we discover that no situation is really hopeless, and that it is possible for us to find contentment, and even happiness, whether the alcoholic is still drinking or not.

We urge you to try our program. It has helped many of us find solutions that lead to serenity. So much depends on our own attitudes, and as we learn to place our problem in its true perspective, we find it loses its power to dominate our thoughts and our lives.

The reader then says the program is based on the Twelve Steps (which have been only slightly changed from the A.A. version) and promises anonymity: "Everything that is said here, in the group meeting and member to member, must be held in confidence. Only in this way can we feel free to say what is in our minds and hearts, for this is how we help one another in Al-Anon."

The speaker for the meeting, seated at the head table, begins.

She tells her own story, the story of what it has been like to live with an alcoholic husband, lover, child or anyone important to her. She tells how she is trying to help herself to grow. She talks, usually without notes, with a kind of honesty and straightforwardness that impresses many new to Al-Anon.

In a meeting in Ohio, a young woman named Dora told what she and many newcomers were like on first coming to Al-Anon. "When we come into our first Al-Anon meeting, we are broken," she said. "We are a mental and physical wreck. We in Al-Anon are like people crowding into a doorway, trying to get in out of the rain that is coming down on us in our lives. . . . Al-Anon handed me an umbrella and made me see who I could become. They didn't care if I looked haggard and was frowning. Or if my conversation was filled with anger and frustration. Or that I had tears in my eyes most of the time. They helped me to get in out of the rain. They dried me off with their fellowship; they gave me hope for a new life; they offered healing for my emotional wounds. They promised recovery from the person I was to the person I could become."

Her pain and the arguments, Dora said, began only three months into her marriage: "The guys would call Ray on the phone and ask him to go out with them, and I would say to him, 'Now Ray, listen. Those single days are over—we're a couple now.' But against my arguing, my pleading, and sometimes even my crying, out he'd go." One night, he struck her for the first time.

There were good times, alone and with friends. They happened less and less. The drinking bouts came closer together. "And then I was back at the window at two-thirty in the morning, watching for his car to come down the street. And I would promise myself, 'I will not stop my tirade until I get through to him this time.'" Her verbal abuse, his violent responses, became the norm. "I had a great vocabulary and I was using it extensively," Dora said. "I was out to hurt and hinder his drinking. And then I would wallow in my martyrdom." She began to cover up with outsiders. "Everyone thought of us as the perfect little family," she said. "I made sure of that. My life was made up of lies."

Finally, she stopped going out to meetings of her various clubs, out to dinner with her friends. "I wasn't real anymore," she said. "If I went out, he might sneak out while I was gone and then I wouldn't be there to say, 'Ah, ah, ah, Momma says no.' I couldn't have my friends over to the house because what if he came in after drinking and they'd notice it? I went from a self-sufficient, strong, happy person to a dependent, weak, miserable one. I began to lose me. My whole existence started to revolve around the alcoholism. I became Ray's dictator, and he became my charge."

Three months after Dora joined Al-Anon, a friend, seeing the change in Dora that had taken place already, brought her a poem called "Come the Dawn," by Veronica A. Shoffstall. The poem inspired and comforted Dora, and she read parts of it out at the Ohio meeting:

After a while you learn the subtle difference
Between holding a hand and chaining a soul,
And you begin to accept your defeats
With your head up and your eyes wide open,
With the grace of a woman, not the grief of a child,
So you plant your own garden and decorate your own
    soul instead of waiting
For someone to bring you flowers.
And you learn that you really can endure . . .
That you really are strong,
And you really do have worth.

The next speaker at that same meeting was Paulette, a woman with a mischievous glint in her eye. She told of the kind of woman she had become with her alcoholic husband, hugging her grievances to her as tight as a teddy bear. "Before Al-Anon, I could justify," she said. "I knew there were things about me that weren't so nice, but I could justify them. Therefore I could keep them. One day I said something to my husband when he was busy watching the news on television. I know he likes the news, and he didn't hear me. Finally he pulled himself away and he said, 'What was it you said?' Well, I wasn't going to tell him. And I looked at him and said, 'You're not going to have me to kick around anymore.' And I left the room. And he said, 'Good night, President Nixon.' " [Burst of laughter and clapping.] Paulette, grinning, went on: "I didn't want to laugh. I wanted to stay angry." [Understanding murmur and more laughter.] The next morning, Paulette said, she told her sponsor—her best friend in Al-Anon—what had happened. The sponsor laughed and then said, "Oh, Paulette, how could you be so petty?" Paulette went home that night to tell her husband she had been "a real A-S-S." It was the first time in a long while that she had said, "I'm sorry." He accepted her apology, at once and with love. Another weight had lifted off Paulette.

The speaker, or speakers, in an Al-Anon meeting talk for about twenty minutes. In the time left—meetings last between sixty and ninety minutes—the floor is open to anyone who has something on her mind. Usually she raises her hand and speaks briefly, remaining seated. Everyone listens courteously. Arguments, debate, wrangling between members or long monologues are gently discouraged. Every newcomer soon learns these unspoken rules, set by the example of others.

At a recent meeting in a church basement in Denver, a small, miserable-looking woman was the first to raise her hand. "My name is Harriet," she said. "This is my third meeting. I thought you'd give me pointers on how to get my husband to stop drinking. I don't understand that First Step—the one that says, 'We admitted we were powerless over alcohol, that our lives had become unmanageable.' I hardly drink at all." Her voice broke on the last words. The leader, Nadine, pointed to another raised hand. Jane spoke up from her seat, turning to Harriet. "The First Step means that we are powerless over the person who drinks, how much he drinks and when. We're powerless to make them stop, and we're not responsible for them becoming alcoholics, either, no matter what they say. I don't know how many times my husband has told me, 'If you were better in bed, I wouldn't drink so much.' In here, I learned it wasn't true, what Dennis was saying. It's not true. If someone tells you something enough times, you're going to believe it. In here, I'm also learning that my own recovery does *not* depend on Dennis's recovery." A look of discovery began to dawn on Harriet's intent face.

A woman stuffed into an orange jumpsuit waved a hand and began, "My name is Louise. Before I came into these rooms, I thought, 'I've got to fix everything. I've got to fix everybody.' " Heads nodded. "Then I woke up one morning and I told myself, 'You're going to live this day as if you were living alone.' I used to sit and worry: My husband's out somewhere. What's he doing? Or he's at home. He's watching TV. What's he got on the other side of the sofa? The man at least is watching a TV program. All I'm doing is watching him watch TV. *Who* has the problem?"

Norma was next. "When they asked me here in Al-Anon how I felt, I'd tell them what my husband was doing. It took me a year and a half before I could answer the question of how I was doing. I was living in a funny-house of mirrors. Everything was distorted. I doubted myself. I blamed myself for everything. I began to wonder if I was crazy. Now I know that if only one member of the family gets better, life will improve for the whole family. This will happen whether the alcoholic in my life gets sober or not."

One of three men among the twenty women in the room, tall and rumpled, raised his hand. "My name is Donald. I heard the word *detachment* a lot when I first came in here and wondered what the hell it meant. I love Margo. I'll always love her. I guess detachment means you've got to stop being some kind of prison guard, or nurse. It doesn't mean I love her less, but I've stopped yelling at her, preaching at her. I've stopped pouring her booze down the drain, looking for the bottles she's hidden behind the books. I don't hassle her anymore, particularly when she's drunk —it's the bottle talking, not Margo. She never remembers anyway the next morning what the hell I said the night before. I'm getting on with my life and being as good to her as I can. If I'm lucky, she may go to A.A. one of these days. I'm not holding my breath."

A woman in her early twenties gave a toss of her fine blond hair and blurted out: "I'm Daisy. This is my first meeting. How long do I have to come here before I feel better?" The woman leading the meeting said, "I can't tell you that, Daisy. I only know that my life was unbearable, and it's better now. The process of getting well takes time. I wouldn't go to a shrink for only one session, or to temple just one Saturday. I've been working out at the gym for years. Go to as many meetings as you need to—nobody's going to check up on you. Keep coming back. If this group doesn't work for you, try going to others until you find one or two that make you comfortable. It doesn't cost anything, and all you have to do is listen. I hope you'll make friends here. See me after the meeting, and we can swap telephone numbers."

The leader smiled at Daisy, checked her watch, rose and said, "I'll read the Al-Anon Closing: 'I would like to say that the opinions expressed here were strictly those of the person who gave them,' " she began. " 'Take what you liked and leave the rest. . . . A few special words to those of you who haven't been with us long: Whatever your problems, there are those among us who have had them too. If you try to keep an open mind, you will find help. You will come to realize that there is no situation too difficult to be bettered and no unhappiness too great to be lessened. We aren't perfect. The welcome we give you may not show the warmth we have in our hearts for you. After a while, you'll discover that though you may not like all of us, you'll love us in a very special way—the same way we already love you.' " She then said, "Will all who care to, join me in the Serenity Prayer?" The group arranged itself in a circle, joined hands and chorused:

"God grant me the serenity
"To accept the things I cannot change;
"Courage to change the things I can,
"And wisdom to know the difference."

Little clusters drifted off to a nearby coffee shop. The leader, Nadine, beckoned to Daisy. "If you'd like to have a look, here's some literature on the table," she said. "The pamphlets don't cost anything. And this little book is called *One Day at a Time in Al-Anon.*" Daisy thumbed through the pamphlets, took two, exchanged telephone numbers with Nadine and swept out the door.

Like A.A., Al-Anon runs its own big publishing operation, with books and pamphlets written by and for members. Pamphlets are often given away at meetings; books are on sale there or can be ordered from Al-Anon's World Service Office in New York. Among the ten books for Al-Anons and Alateens are *Al-Anon Family Groups*, which is the equivalent of the Big Book and sets out the history, purpose, reasons for being and personal stories of Al-Anon; *Al-Anon Faces Alcoholism*, in which additional personal stories from those living with an alcoholic are reinforced by powerful opinions from professionals who work with alcoholics and their families; *The Dilemma of an Alcoholic Marriage*, which discusses how alcohol distorts a couple's thinking and actions in every intimate situation, including sex, and what to do about it; and *Alateen—Hope for Children of Alcoholics*, a basic text for teenagers. Most of these cost five dollars or less.

None is as popular and beloved as *One Day at a Time in Al-Anon*, familiarly known as ODAT. ODAT is a book sturdily bound in dark blue, about six inches long and four inches wide—small enough to slip into a pocketbook. There is one page for each day of the year. The page for January 1 reads in part:

> This year is a book of clean blank pages on which I will write a record of my experiences and my growth through the daily use of the Al-Anon idea. I turned to Al-Anon as a last resort because I was living with a problem that was too much for me. I know I can deal with this problem through applying Al-Anon to myself, to my thoughts and actions, every day. If I allow myself to be influenced by what the alcoholic says and does, I will make blots and smears on the pages of my year. This I will try to avoid at all costs.

"Today's Reminder" for January 1, below the opening paragraph, says: "I can live my life only one day at a time. Perhaps my confusion and despair are so great that I will have to take it one hour at a time, or one minute at a time, reminding myself constantly that I have authority over no life but my own."

Each daily reading is focused on a topic: anger, anonymity, blame; forgiveness, freedom, frustration, fear; humor, sarcasm, self-control, self-deception and self-pity; selfishness and selfless-ness. The quotations that follow "Today's Reminder" are from the Bible, Shakespeare, Thomas Merton, Kahlil Gibran, Thomas à Kempis, Epictetus, Lewis Carroll ("The horror of that moment," the King said, "I shall never, never forget." "You will, though," said the Queen, "if you don't make a memorandum of it"), and from anonymous Al-Anon members. Every member has a copy of ODAT, some as worn out with fondling and thumbing as the Skin Horse in the nursery tale. Three million copies of ODAT, at $4.50 each, have been sold since it was first published in 1968. About 350,000 copies were sold in 1987 alone.

Al-Anon publishes more than fifty pamphlets, on subjects rang-ing from *Al-Anon IS for Men, Freedom from Despair* and *Alco-holism, a Merry-Go-Round Named Denial* to *How Can I Help My Children?, To the Mother and Father, A Guide for the Family of the Alcoholic* and *Al-Anon Is for Adult Children of Alcoholics.* Many of these are given away at meetings, and almost all that are for sale cost less than fifty cents. None of the literature is sold in outside bookshops.

One pamphlet, *Alcoholism, the Family Disease,* contains twenty of the questions most commonly asked by those who love an alcoholic, such as "Is there a time when we can talk to our alcoholic about his drinking or any other serious problem?" Al-Anon's an-swer to that one is, "This, in most cases, should be played by ear. Many have found him to be more accessible after a heavy drinking bout." To another question, "Should we coddle our alcoholics?", Al-Anon replies "No. The more attention they get, the less they will do for themselves, and the longer they will go on drinking."

Some answers deal with what to do when the alcoholic gets sober. This may come as a surprise to people unfamiliar with A.A. and Al-Anon. The reason lies in a crucial misunderstanding, a myth believed by almost all those who have ever been close to an alcoholic. It is: If only he/she would stop drinking, everything would be all right.

Wrong.

Sobriety is not the answer or the end. It is only the beginning.

The alcoholic has taken years to get drunk; it will take months and years for him or her to clear cobwebs out of the brain, to get comfortable with the idea and practice of abstinence. Other problems that have been smothered by alcohol also tend to surface within the alcoholic and those who love that person. An alcoholic's family is a neurotic family with neurotic habits of coping with one another. Very few people in such a household can deal sanely and realistically with life's demands all at once. Bill Wilson realized that; his own marriage nearly foundered on his sobriety. A newly sober alcoholic immersed in A.A. meetings to save himself can neglect his wife and children, or be full of rage and self-pity for a while because he cannot drink. There also can be an attitude of self-congratulation. No wonder: Not drinking, a day at a time, is a continuing series of courageous acts.

The discovery that sobriety also brings problems for a while can be symbolized by Lois Wilson's shoe, unquestionably the most famous object in Al-Anon history. The story of how she threw it at her husband shortly after his drinking years ended, shouting, "Damn your old meetings!" has been told over and over. She was envious of Bill's new friends in A.A., she was sick of being shut out, and besides, the man was beginning to do things on his own. She could no longer play her roles as the drunken Bill's mother, nurse and decision-maker.

Lois was beginning to learn what almost every person married to a sober alcoholic has realized since: that a recovering drunk can wrap his arms as tightly around Alcoholics Anonymous as he did the bottle. He must, for a time, because A.A. has become his life preserver and sobriety the most important thing in life. During this recuperation period, the family's love and support—and its members' own efforts to get better for their own sake—are crucial. That is why one half of the membership of Al-Anon is composed of people whose alcoholics are no longer drinking. Many who rush out of Al-Anon as soon as their drunk sees the light have been shocked by the realization that their problems are not over. If the spouse or lover continues to drink, fewer and fewer women—and men—are willing to keep the family together. They leave and seek divorce. Whatever the outcome, the members of Al-Anon are learning to heal and help each other, to work toward getting better a day at a time, to find a life that is focused on themselves and not on the alcoholic.

"They told me about the slogans," said a member named Polly at a meeting in Ohio. "You know, Live and let live. Easy does it. Do this just for today. Keep it simple. I'd never done anything simple—I used to think, if he does this, then I'm going to do that, and maybe if he does that, I'll act this way. I heard the slogans and the Serenity Prayer fifty times, and I thought, 'My God, can't they be a little more creative?' I'd lived yesterday, I'd lived tomorrow, I'd lived next year. But today, today—it was a place to begin. I began to feel in Al-Anon that I wasn't in this alone, that I no longer had to take this heavy burden and carry it around with me."

Polly's feelings of relief, of being just one of many who will strengthen and support her, can be sensed in most Al-Anon meetings and other events for members only. Among the oldest and most cherished, which takes place every December in New York, is the annual Lois W. Luncheon. It is sponsored by the Greater New York Family Intergroups. On December 7, 1986, Lois Wilson, despite her great age, was there. The block-long Tower Suite on the penthouse floor of the Time & Life Building in Manhattan was jammed with women and a sprinkling of men. Watery winter sunlight streamed through the glass walls; other skyscrapers poked up all around. Lois sat on the dais, eating heartily. The speeches began.

A tubby Alateen member stood up. He cited the hundreds of weekly Al-Anon and A.A. meetings in the New York area and wondered why there were only six or seven Alateen groups still thriving there. "Something's wrong," he said, and sat down to a spattering of applause.

Norman came to the microphone. He was gay. He was thrilled to be there. He had been in Al-Anon seven years, and his lover had just died. His remarks combined enthusiasm, hope and a kind of bitchy self-mockery that sent the women into gales of laughter.

The men exchanged sidelong glances. "My lover's drinking got worse and worse," said Norman. "So did his life. I started getting better with the Serenity Prayer. I figure if I haven't gotten life straight, I blame God and turn it over to him." Norman told how, after his lover died, he cleaned out all the closets; he painted one yellow, one lavender, and one bright red. Then he went on to paint the whole apartment silver, blue and orange. His life had become like that apartment, he said—"the rainbow at the end of my storm." Ovation. Lois smiled benignly.

The microphone was brought to Lois, too frail now to stand at the podium. Out came that unexpectedly strong and resonant alto voice. She ended her brief thanks by saying, jauntily and with total confidence, "See you next year!" She was three months short of her ninety-sixth birthday.

Lois had seen it all, fifty-one years of Alcoholics Anonymous and thirty-five years of Al-Anon. Her husband had founded one group and she the other. With this matchless experience, she knew that surprises always lay ahead. For Al-Anon, the surprise of the 1980's has been the rise of the Adult Children of Alcoholics movement. It has whirled up out of nowhere like a Kansas tornado, looming larger all the time.

"It's a phenomenon," said Myrna H., Al-Anon's executive director, "and it's going to get bigger."

There were fourteen Adult Children groups registered with Al-Anon headquarters in 1981, and 1,100 by 1986. As late as 1984, delegates to the annual Al-Anon national conference thought it was a passing fad—nothing to worry about. Now they are changing their minds and struggling to catch up.

The Adult Children of Alcoholics, who call themselves ACAs or ACOAs or COAs, are stampeding into the movement by the thousands all over the country. Some are in Al-Anon, many are not. Men and women are coming in equal numbers. Al-Anon cannot produce literature fast enough for them, so they are creating their own. In 1983, the nonprofit National Association for Children of Alcoholics was founded in South Laguna, California, put together by a team of therapists, teachers, authors and physicians.

Their aim was, they said, "a network of information and caring for the sake of young, adolescent and adult children of alcoholics everywhere." NACOA had drawn almost 7,000 dues-paying members by the end of 1987.

This movement has begun to fill a void. Somehow, despite the success of Alcoholics Anonymous and Al-Anon, where fully half the members are children of alcoholics, and Alateen, with almost all of its 45,000 members also offspring of alcoholics, there are vast numbers of suffering people being overlooked. The U.S. government's National Institute on Alcohol Abuse and Alcoholism estimates that twenty-eight million Americans have at least one alcoholic parent. Six million of them are eighteen or younger and still under parental control. "The wounded are everywhere," said Sharon Wegscheider-Cruse, a guru of the movement.

The children of alcoholics are gobbling up the new books about them: Wegscheider-Cruse's *Another Chance;* Claudia Black's *My Dad Loves Me, My Dad Has a Disease* and *It Will Never Happen to Me;* Charles Deutsch's *Broken Bottles, Broken Dreams;* Herbert Gravitz's *NACOA Handbook for Adult Children of Alcoholics;* and *Children of Alcoholism: A Survivor's Manual* by Judith Seixas and Geraldine Youcha. All these are selling well, but there is still another, Janet Woititz's *Adult Children of Alcoholics,* that has become a true publishing wonder. Since it first came out in 1983, 700,000 copies have been sold.

The four "classic family roles" coined by Wegscheider-Cruse— the Family Hero, the Scapegoat, the Lost Child and the Mascot —are being echoed in other books and in the ACOA meetings, where speakers often begin by saying, for example, "My name is ... and I was the scapegoat of my family." Often, the meeting will open with what has come to be known among adult children of alcoholics as the Laundry List. It defines, in fourteen points, the kinds of characteristics they tend to take on because of the drunks in their families. "We judge ourselves harshly and have low esteem," says one point. "We have become addicted to excitement after years of living in the midst of a traumatic and often dangerous family 'soap opera,' " says another. "We confuse love with pity, and tend to love people whom we can pity and rescue," goes a third. The last point is, "We had to deny our feelings in our traumatic childhood; we thus became estranged from all our feelings, and lost our ability to recognize and express them."

Now, in Adult Children of Alcoholics meetings, members are giving those feelings full vent. They have been raised in families where they learned very early not to trust, not to feel, and above all not to talk about the specter that haunted their households. Full-grown and still frustrated, they are angry, and their anger is making Al-Anon deeply uncomfortable. It does not matter to the ACOAs that the majority of the members of A.A. and Al-Anon are children of alcoholics themselves. The focus in the first society has always been on the drunk, and in the second, mostly on wives. Many children of alcoholics feel their own problems have been ignored or shunted aside in A.A. and Al-Anon. Often, parents recovering in both groups do not want their children to attend even Al-Anon's own offshoot, Alateen; they see Alateen members as "troublemakers" who are "talking about us" and perhaps hatching rebellions against parental authority.

The Adult Children movement is so new that there are few veterans, except for strays from Al-Anon or Alateen, to set an example in meetings. Like the pioneers of Alcoholics Anonymous and Al-Anon before them, the members are groping. Someone unfamiliar with the Adult Children but knowledgeable about A.A. or Al-Anon may be unsettled by the rage. It is directed not just against the drunken father who raised them but also against the nonalcoholic mother—the martyr, the scold, the dominator. In one such ACOA meeting in a Greenwich Village hospital, a thin young man who identified himself as a "sexaholic" with experience in Al-Anon said, "I want nothing more to do with 'positive' groups." His voice rising to a near shout, he went on, "Screw Al-Anon! I want Al-Anon to leave us to our resentments—leave us to our pain!"

Then an obviously distraught woman delivered herself of a heartbreaking story about family incest and violence. Instead of responding to her, or pointing to the next person with a hand up, the meeting's leader said, "I have here a bunch of ACOA souvenirs.

They cost three dollars, if anybody's interested." He began to slide them along the long table around which the members were sitting. Furious at this abrupt commercial interruption, the woman burst into sobs. She slammed her fist on the table and shrieked at the leader, "You are negating my suffering!"

The leader muttered an apology. "I don't think I can continue to run this meeting," he said. "Would somebody else take over?"

Such scenes frighten and upset many Al-Anon old-timers, who have been bombarding their headquarters with questions about the Adult Children. They are used to listening, to courtesy, to tolerance. Some of the more flexible ones with long years in Al-Anon, however, recall their society's own muddled and tearful beginnings. "I think it will change—and I've already seen changes," said Sandra F., who holds the number-two position at the World Service Office. "Part of the insanity that you see in these Adult Children groups is that it's untreated anger, and it's been repressed, and like a pressure cooker it blows. Picture an Al-Anon or an A.A. meeting where eighty percent of the population is newcomers: What are you going to have there?"

Sandra added: "When I went to my first Adult Children group in my hometown in New Jersey," she said, "the atmosphere was crazy. Now, a year later, it's beautiful. They've worked through their anger at their parents, and they're beginning to concentrate on healing themselves."

Patricia O. has been in the thick of the movement since the word go. She is forty-one years old, but with her creamy skin, masses of curly dark hair and luminous brown eyes, she looks like a colleen half that age. She grew up in the second-floor rear of a tenement on New York's West Side, frightened for as long as she could remember. The neighborhood was in flux, a tough and menacing place. Hispanics and blacks were moving in as the Irish immigrants who preceded them fled to still-white districts elsewhere in the city. Highbridge Park across the street was infested with teenage gangs who would stop at nothing; once they slashed another teenager, Michael Farmer, to death there; he was crippled by polio and helpless. Pat knew the boys who murdered him.

Sometimes it seemed even worse to her inside. She described her mother as a "Ukrainian Lucille Ball, delightful and wonderful," a friend to all the neighbors. She was a seamstress, stitching up bird cage covers and dog coats in a tiny sweatshop two doors away. Pat's father was a drunk from a family riddled for generations by alcoholism, a small, muscular Irishman with a defiant tilt to his chin who looked like James Cagney. His wild bingeing lost him one job after another—as a nightclub singer, fireman, steeplejack, salesman—until finally he sat in the house all day, drinking, feeling inadequate, fantasizing that his wife was seeing other men. When the rage would boil up in him at bars, he would take on ten brawlers at a time until he was battered to the floor. If his wife came early to fetch him home, he would turn his fists on her. Bartender after bartender told him to go elsewhere for his booze. He blacked his wife's eyes regularly. When Pat, the oldest of three children, stood in his way, he would pick her up and throw her across the room against a wall, twice hurting her so badly she was hospitalized. "Nobody in my family spoke," Pat said. "We all screamed. We all screamed at each other at the top of our lungs. When the police came, everybody in the building knew my father had threatened to kill my mother again."

Pat took it out on her little sister and brother. "If they asked me to help them with their homework, I would make them bow to me," she said. "I was cruel and demanding." When she was nine years old, she called her father an alcoholic: "I hurled the word at him—alcoholic! I must have learned it from my mother." Her father called her a whore. She would go to the nearest Roman Catholic church to pray, bargaining with God for her mother's safety. Every day she would come home from school to fix lunch for the family. "I felt like I was holding up the family," she said. "We children all felt we had to make the family work."

When Pat was about fifteen, her mother joined Al-Anon, and soon thereafter, in 1962, Pat began going to one of the earliest New York Alateen meetings in the same church building. A man named Joe from Alcoholics Anonymous was the sponsor (mentor) of the group along with his wife, a member of Al-Anon. "It was the most incredible, powerful experience of my life," Pat said. "Joe was the first sober alcoholic I had ever met. I asked him, 'Why did you do the things you did? Didn't you love your children?' Joe told me, 'I loved my kids. I didn't know what I was doing. I was sick.' " Pat's healing began with Joe. "He made me feel better about my dad," she said. She felt herself growing up in Alateen, leading meetings, becoming less afraid. But when she was invited to speak at a New York state convention of Alcoholics Anonymous, the members could not look her in the eye after she had told her story. "They saw in me what they had done to their own children," she said. "They couldn't bear to face me."

When she was eighteen, her parents separated. At twenty, she joined Al-Anon. She began training as a child psychologist and saw family after family shattered by alcoholism. "Nobody I was working with then in the field of mental health was interested in what alcoholism was doing to kids," she said. In 1974, she was asked to run the prevention and education section at the National Council on Alcoholism. "When they offered me the job," she said, "I felt like a piece of shattered glass—all senses alive. I was shivering with joy." She went on to Washington, to serve in the government's National Institute on Alcohol Abuse and Alcoholism. A founding member of the National Association for Children of Alcoholics, she is now a clinical psychologist working with alcoholic families.

"Anger brought me into the alcoholism field," Pat said. "Anger at what had happened to me and my family. Anger at what I saw in other suffering families. Anger that for the longest time, psychiatrists and psychologists were incredibly narrow-minded, thinking that alcoholism wasn't the proper topic for research and treatment."

Now Pat is seeing that same anger multiplied thousands of times in the swelling Adult Children of Alcoholics movement. She believes that if the members do not learn to channel their released emotions into recovery, they will go under:

Non-Al-Anon meetings [Pat said] tend to degenerate into emotional upheavals, ritual purgings. Some are leaderless. It's a bunch of new people, nobody with longevity. They blame, they point fingers, they comment on each other—"My Christmas was worse than your Christmas."

In ACOA it's a we-them situation: "You did this to me, and it's your fault," and the payoff is, "I can feel self-righteous self-pity." It's the narcissism of pain. The issue is really how you integrate the trauma into your life—how you make peace with it, come to terms with it. Al-Anon teaches people to do this in a very slow, thoughtful way, working the Twelve Steps. But I feel there will be a sorting-out process. There already is. There has to be. Because if people go on systematically retraumatizing themselves, they will burn out and drop out. They'll either go to Al-Anon and work its program, or they won't go anywhere.

She quoted one of her colleagues, a family therapist named Philip Oliver-Diaz, who is on the board of NACOA. "If we don't watch out," he said, "the next movement will be the Children of Adult Children of Alcoholics."

# 8

## THE DISEASE

Who hath woe? Who hath sorrow? Who hath contentions?
Who hath babbling?
Who hath wounds without cause? Who hath redness of eyes?
They that tarry long at the wine; they that go to seek mixed wine. . . .
At the last, it biteth like a serpent, and stingeth like an adder.

—*Proverbs, Chapter Twenty-three*

Imagine a terrible disease striking America, a disease of unknown cause. Suppose that this disease is so harmful to the nervous system that eighteen million people go insane for periods lasting from a few hours to weeks or months, with the madness recurring and getting worse over periods ranging from fifteen to thirty years. If untreated, the victims go permanently insane, or die. They commit suicide at a rate up to seventy-five times higher than that of the general population. Imagine that those afflicted by the disease itself and the other illnesses it causes already occupy more than half the hospital beds in the United States on any given day, and that last year the illness killed nearly 100,000 Americans. Suppose further that those out of hospital, during their spells of insanity, commit acts so destructive that the material and spiritual lives of whole families are in jeopardy, leaving many millions of other people cruelly affected. Work in business, industry and professions is faulty, sabotaged or left undone. Finally, imagine that this disease so alters its victims' judgment, so brainwashes them, that they cannot see that they are sick at all: Their view of life has become so distorted that they try with all their might to go on being ill.

This dread disease is already among us. It has been with us for centuries. It is, of course, alcoholism.

Most of the above words were written in the 1970's by Dr. Ruth Fox, who treated and saved as many compulsive drunks as any other single person in this nation. She was a president of the American Medical Society on Alcoholism and medical director of the National Council on Alcoholism. Soon after the founding of Alcoholics Anonymous and well before the establishment of the Yale School of Alcohol Studies or any government agency, she was researching and treating and writing voluminously about the disease.

A nonalcoholic, this great and modest psychiatrist tried everything to help her patients: aversion therapy, mind-altering drugs, hypnosis, psychoanalysis, Alcoholics Anonymous and disulfiram, whose trade name is Antabuse. She experimented on herself. She introduced Antabuse—the nearest thing to a "magic pill" ever found to stop drunks from drinking—to the United States in 1950. She believed there was no such animal as a "hopeless alcoholic." Finally, she decided that nothing worked with so many for so long as Alcoholics Anonymous. She sent all of her alcoholics into A.A. Those who stayed, she noted, often got sober for good; those who dropped out did not.

A plain, thin, bony-faced woman with a jutting jaw and a tight hairdo, she was slightly forbidding on first sight. Her manner was so mild and unjudging, however, that this impression soon faded.

She loved alcoholics and understood their suffering. No story ever disgusted her. No case was ever turned away. She treated an unending stream of alcoholics in her office-apartment on Manhattan's Upper East Side until she was into her eighties, twisted and bent by arthritis and in constant pain.

The idea of alcoholism as an illness is a central concept of A.A., but it did not originate there. Nor did it start with Elvin Morton (E. M.) Jellinek, Dr. Fox's contemporary, whose great work, *The Disease Concept of Alcoholism*, was published in 1960, the culmination of years of research, writing and teaching. It did not begin with the American Medical Association, which declared alcoholism a disease in 1956. The roots of the disease concept go back at least to ancient Rome—to Seneca, who distinguished a drunken man from one who has no control over his accustomed drunkenness, and to Ulpian, the first to suggest that habitual drunkenness might be a disease.

The history of alcohol itself, its use and abuse, is as old as the history of man. Alcohol, the cup of joy and sorrow. Alcohol, the comforter, the seducer, the destroyer. The earliest known records of alcohol consumption date back to the Mesopotamians: Clay tablets from 4,000 years before Christ chronicle the amount drunk by the populace and record recipes for using alcohol as a solvent in medicines. The Code of Hammurabi of Babylonia, from 1700 B.C., includes restrictions on the sale and consumption of alcohol. Equally old records from the reign of China's Emperor Chung K'iang show that drunkards were executed. The aristocratic classes in ancient Persia drank enormous amounts; in response, the rising Islamic culture adopted a total, permanent ban on alcohol to fight widespread health problems. Buddhist sects in India, from the fifth century B.C. to this day, also prohibit all alcohol consumption.

Euripedes, with Aeschylus and Sophocles one of the great triad of Greek tragic writers, was the first person in literature to describe a drunken blackout. In his play *The Bacchae*, the mother of Pentheus, king of Thebes, tears her son to pieces in a drunken frenzy, thinking him to be a lion. Then she triumphantly bears his head to Cadmus, her father, before the ghastly reality dawns on her.

Temperance movements date to ancient times and are described in the records of China and dynastic Egypt, among other cultures. The single most important and influential temperance document in all history is the Bible. *The Encyclopedia of Alcoholism* notes that the Bible contains more than 150 references to alcohol. This carefully researched volume, edited by Robert O'Brien and Dr. Morris Chafetz, a physician who was the founding director of the National Institute on Alcohol Abuse and Alcoholism in 1970, offers some opinions on why alcoholism had not been—until recently—a serious problem among Jews. The authors focused on the Old Testament as one reason. "Although alcohol is deeply rooted in Jewish culture and granted an important role in religious celebrations," they wrote, "the Hebrew people have enjoyed a relative freedom from alcoholism that must in part be attributed to the many warnings about excess found in the Old Testament." The Book of Proverbs is singled out for its strictures, such as "Wine is a mocker, strong drink is raging: and whosoever is deceived thereby is not wise." The chilling quotation from Proverbs that begins this chapter, "Who hath woe? Who hath sorrow?" is a startlingly apt description of alcoholism, as applicable today as it was when it was written 3,000 years ago. O'Brien and Chafetz contended, "These sorts of warnings about the dangers of excess, deeply ingrained in the society's behavior patterns, created such effective cultural controls that carefully regulated consumption could be condoned and even encouraged without great danger of alcohol abuse."

This is no longer true among Jews in America. They are assimilating more and more into mainstream society. They are adapting to non-Jewish ways of behavior and ethics. They are drinking more, coming in large numbers into Alcoholics Anonymous and being served by new agencies springing up to meet their needs. For generations, Jews comforted themselves with the notion that only Gentiles were drunks. Now, a drunk can also be Jewish: painful news for many, particularly those who are religious.

The idea of drunkenness as sinful and a disgrace permeates many civilizations and is far more strongly entrenched than the idea that alcoholism is an illness. From the sons of Noah, who looked with shame upon their drunken father, naked in his tent, to Increase Mather, the Puritan preacher and scholar who in 1673 wrote *Wo [sic] to Drunkards,* the concept persists. "Drink is in itself a good creature of God ..." Mather declared, "but the abuse of drink is from Satan ... the Drunkard is from the Devil."

It was not until 1849 that the word *alcoholism* was coined. A celebrated Swedish physician, Magnus Huss, wrote volumes called *Alcoholismus Chronicus* ("Chronic Alcoholism") and *Chronische Alkohols-Krankheit* ("Chronic Alcohol-Sickness"), which introduced the term to the world.

More than half a century earlier, another doctor was the first American to define what we now call alcoholism as a disease and a pathological process. In 1784, Dr. Benjamin Rush of Philadelphia wrote an influential tract called *An Inquiry into the Effects of Ardent Spirits on the Human Mind and Body.* It challenged previous thinking in hard-drinking America—that alcohol, and plenty of it, was a good thing.

Rush identified alcohol as a drug, an addictive agent. He described "habitual drunkenness" as involuntary and said total abstinence was the only cure. The doctor claimed that once an "appetite" for spirits took hold in a person, he was helpless to resist. "In these cases," wrote Mark Lender and James Kirby Martin in *Drinking in America,* explaining Rush's approach,

> drunkenness was no longer a vice or a personal failing, for the imbiber had no more control over his drinking—the alcohol now controlled him. ... In Rush's view, the old colonial idea that drunkenness was the fault of the drinker was valid only in the early stages of the disease, when a tippler might still pull back; once addicted, even a saint would have a hard time controlling himself.

Before his death in 1813, Rush had thousands of reprints of the *Inquiry* distributed nationally, attaching a list that he called "A Moral and Physical Thermometer." That list came strikingly close to modern medicine's ideas of alcoholism and its inexorable progress in the alcoholic. The "thermometer" of diseases ran as follows:

Sickness,
Tremors of the hands in the morning, puking, bloatedness,
Inflamed eyes, red nose and face,
Sore and swelled legs, jaundice,
Pains in the hands, burning in the hands, and feet,
Dropsy, Epilepsy
Melancholy, palsy, appoplexy [sic], Madness, Despair.

Lender and Martin wrote that the real impact of Rush's work was years ahead: "He lamented that his generation would not see a change in popular drinking habits or attitudes and that it would probably be a hundred years before people really got upset about the social and medical consequences of drunkenness. Rush's attitudes on the entire subject of drinking marked him . . . as a man of the future."

Rush's own time was the heaviest drinking era in American history. From 1800 through the 1830's, the consumption of pure alcohol by the drinking-age population of the United States kept moving upward until it reached 7.10 gallons per person per year. Consumption of alcoholic beverages in this nation has never been as high since. By the 1840's, as temperance movements flourished, it plummeted to 3.10 gallons per person of drinking age per year, and kept falling. In 1980 and 1981, the annual consumption of pure alcohol for the population fourteen years of age and older was 2.76 gallons per person, or about one ounce of pure alcohol per person per day. Three one-ounce drinks of 100-proof whiskey or four eight-ounce glasses of beer or half a bottle of wine all contain about the same amount of pure alcohol: one and a half ounces. It takes the body of a 150-pound adult one hour to metabolize three quarters of an ounce.

Those figures on the diminishing intake of Americans are not as heartening as they may seem. The reason is that the alcoholics and alcohol abusers among us—eighteen million in 1986, according to what the National Institute on Alcohol Abuse and Alcoholism told Congress—drink up half of all the liquor, beer and wine consumed every year. It must also be remembered that 30 percent of our drinking-age population doesn't drink at all, for religious or other reasons. America may have been "born wet," as Lender and Martin suggested, and there might be huge amounts of liquor gulped on the East and West coasts and in Washington, D.C., the heaviest drinking metropolis in the nation. But there are millions of abstainers among American adults, concentrated mainly in the South and Midwest. America is two nations—one third dry, two thirds wet. The majority of us drink, and drink moderately. At least one twelfth of our citizens, however, have lost all control over booze.

There is hope. There is more help available for alcoholics now than there ever has been in our history. But despite the enormous growth of Alcoholics Anonymous and inpatient and outpatient alcoholism treatment centers in the past fifteen years, only a fraction of the country's sufferers are being served. And although the disease concept of alcoholism has become implanted ever more firmly in the past half century in America, the stigma remains. Even *recovered* alcoholics who have been truthful about their past alcoholism can be branded forever because of a moralizing or ignorant attitude. Many have been rejected for jobs, insurance coverage or drivers' licenses.

Between the death of Benjamin Rush in 1813 and the rebirth of the disease concept in the 1930's and 1940's, Americans wobbled between the notions that alcoholism was either a sin or an illness. Early in the development of the nineteenth-century temperance movements, alcoholic individuals were approached with sympathy and concern. Dr. Sheila B. Blume, in her excellent booklet put out by the Johnson Institute, *The Disease Concept of Alcoholism Today*, wrote,

> It was not only the well-known Society of Washington (Washingtonians), but many temperance fraternal groups which followed that also attempted to rehabilitate alcoholics. . . . It was toward the close of the nineteenth century, when the temperance movement began to focus single-mindedly on prohibition, that this concern for the alcoholic was lost and the disease concept

faded in the public mind. Interestingly enough, the concept of addiction was increasingly applied to other drugs during that same period.

The generations of temperance reformers who toiled to build a dry America achieved their "final victory" when the Eighteenth Amendment went into effect in January 1920, outlawing booze. The reasoning appeared sound: If people could not get alcohol, they could not become drunkards. National Prohibition, which Herbert Hoover called "a great social and economic experiment, noble in motive and far-reaching in purpose," lasted fourteen years. The law was flouted on a national scale, and the most controversial of all amendments to the U.S. Constitution became the only one ever repealed. With the end of Prohibition in 1933, the disease concept of alcoholism was reborn. In 1935, two years after repeal, Alcoholics Anonymous, with its central philosophy that alcoholics were sick, not sinful, was founded.

That same year at Bellevue Hospital in New York, Dr. Norman Jolliffe became convinced that treating the complications of alcoholism was useless without treating alcoholism itself as a primary disease. He conceived the idea of organizing a distinguished research group on alcoholism and a review of the literature about the biological effects of alcohol on man. This work was funded by the Carnegie Foundation and carried out by E. M. Jellinek. Not a physician but a physiologist and biostatistician, Jellinek pulled together the most advanced knowledge of his time and became the world's greatest authority on alcoholism. He served as the first director of the Yale School of Alcohol Studies, which he founded in 1943; first editor of the *Quarterly Journal of Studies on Alcohol*; and alcoholism consultant to the World Health Organization. Of his many works, *The Disease Concept of Alcoholism* became the most famous. That book and the school at Yale—the first formal school in the history of the United States to study the consequences of alcohol—became his enduring legacies.

He was born in New York, the son of Rose Jacobsen and Ervin Marcell Jellinek, and from high school on, from 1908 until 1930, he traveled the world, studying at the universities of Berlin, Grenoble and Leipzig. He became a biometrician, making statistical analyses of biological observations, at the Government School for Nervous Children in Budapest. He studied plant growth in West Africa and directed research for the United Fruit company in Honduras. In 1931 he went to the Worcester State Hospital in Massachusetts, and eight years later began heading that hospital's studies into the effects of alcohol. He became a professor of applied physiology at Yale University in 1941.

Jellinek, whose rather formal appearance was offset by a rakish lock of hair shaped like a question mark over his high forehead, had a knack for spotting and attracting talent. He made the School of Alcohol Studies, its summer school and its free clinic for alcoholics irresistible magnets for experts in the field. Some of the lecturers were recovered alcoholics themselves, among them Bill Wilson and Marty Mann.

"[Jellinek] considered the . . . impaired ability of the individual to control his or her drinking to be one of the central aspects of alcoholism as a disease," Dr. Blume wrote in 1983 in *The Disease Concept of Alcoholism Today:*

> Indeed, involuntariness is a critical element in our thinking about disease in general. Diseases happen to people, although, of course, much individual and group behavior can either prevent disease or encourage its likelihood. Jellinek's concept differs from that of the early temperance movement in an important way. The temperance spokesmen (including Rush) saw alcoholism as a disease caused by alcohol, an addictive substance, particularly in the form of hard liquor. Jellinek's . . . approach places the hypothesized cause more in the individual . . . in the interaction of alcohol with individual physical, psychological, and social factors.

In other words: Nobody *wants* to become an alcoholic. Once a person becomes alcoholic, that individual cannot control the compulsion. If alcohol were the only thing that caused alcoholism, all drinkers could become drunkards. Alcoholism is not just physical; it also becomes an emotional sickness that can be worsened by a person's environment. Alcoholics Anonymous holds the same point of view. It is a belief based on the personal experiences of almost two million members currently in A.A., the millions more whom A.A. has helped but who are no longer attending meetings, and further millions whom A.A. members tried to assist but who are still out there drinking.

Jellinek died in 1963. The year before, Yale University had discontinued certain types of applied research programs, including its School of Alcohol Studies, which was transferred to Rutgers, the State University of New Jersey in New Brunswick. Rutgers remains the most prestigious multidisciplinary alcoholism center anywhere, with a matchless library, and a staff and visiting lecturers who have included everybody who is anybody in the fields of alcoholism treatment and research. Both Yale and Rutgers popularized the modern disease concept of alcoholism.

There are few people among those experts at Rutgers and across the country who do not share the firm conviction that Alcoholics Anonymous has consistently produced more impressive, long-term results than any other treatment approach.

Almost all of them also believe that recovery cannot occur without total abstention from alcohol. That is why the Rand Report of 1976 shook A.A. to its foundations and shocked the entire alcoholism treatment establishment. The findings suggested that some alcoholics could return to moderate drinking. The research, conducted by the Rand Corporation of California, was sponsored and funded by the U.S. government's National Institute on Alcohol Abuse and Alcoholism. The critics charged that the report would cruelly delude compulsive, addicted alcoholics into thinking that they could return safely to social drinking. The second Rand Report, in 1980, was more cautious and did not stir up such a fuss. It was not a complete retraction, but few people seemed to notice. "Scientifically, the first Rand Report was a disaster," said Dr. Enoch Gordis, the NIAAA's director, when questioned about it in 1987. "On the other hand, the alcoholism field reacted as if heresy had been spoken in church, rather than treating the report as what it really was—a mistake in science."

The alcoholism establishment generally approves of A.A.'s Twelve-

Step program for recovery. In some scientific circles, however, the Twelve Steps are viewed as going beyond mystery into a cult that is "antiscience." "Some scientists and psychotherapists wrongly perceive A.A. as a kind of magic," said Robert J. Pandina, a neuropsychologist at Rutgers who has worked with thousands of alcoholics and drug addicts over twenty years:

> They are baffled by A.A.'s success because the first thing you have to accept in A.A. is the notion that you're powerless—helpless—over a drug. And that's antiscience, antireason, antilogic. My belief is that A.A. principles—applied not just to alcoholism but to addiction in general—hold up very well. It's also my opinion that A.A. principles are not antithetical to the basic principles of psychology. But there's another problem. I don't know of a more emotion-laden, more value-laden field than the field of alcoholism. People come to it with baggage, and that baggage gets in the way. Why should this be? Because we're both subject and object. Alcohol is part of society. It's part of our daily lives. It's like religion and politics—we become emotionally involved, no matter how objective our profession trains us to be. Even doctors often seem to feel they are making an accusation, not a valid diagnosis, when telling their patients they might be alcoholic.

Worse, many physicians have not been taught how to detect it. "It is tragic but true that most medical schools have offered very little training in the disease of alcoholism over the years," wrote Dr. William C. Van Ost, a pediatrician, in *Al-Anon Faces Alcoholism* in the 1960's. "Today, with around 120 schools in existence, only forty offer courses that would remotely prepare a doctor for the disastrous physical, psychological and social results of alcohol abuse. In these schools only a few precious hours are devoted to a disease that claims more than ten million victims 'hooked' on a socially acceptable but addictive drug. With so little training, what role can we ask a family physician to assume when he encounters the active alcoholic or the damaged family?"

Medical training is better now than it was when Dr. Max Schneider, the immediate past president of the American Medical Society on Alcoholism and Other Drug Dependencies, went to medical school. He said:

When I went to the University of Buffalo School of Medicine from 1944 to 1949, I got two lectures on alcoholism. One professor in psychiatry told us there was a linked triad of homosexuality, paranoia and alcoholism—"And we don't know how to treat it, and so let's go on to the next subject." The other professor said: "Alcoholism is the outward manifestation of an underlying psychiatric problem, and if we cure the underlying psychiatric problem, the alcoholism goes away. But we don't have much luck with it."

That was going on in the city where Dr. Marvin Block was screaming and raving and ranting and cajoling and preaching and teaching that alcoholism was a primary disease—a disease unto itself, not a symptom of something else. Doctor Block was then chairman of the American Medical Association's committee on alcoholism. It was Block who finally got the powers-that-be and the American Hospital Association to declare alcoholism a disease in 1956. It was Block who taught me personally that alcoholism was both primary and treatable—I used to help cover his patients in Buffalo when he was away. I am a gastroenterologist and an internist. I am in this field for no other reason than that I like to see people get well.

Today, Dr. Schneider, a cheerful, outspoken man who is the educational consultant of Family Recovery Services at St. Joseph Hospital in Orange, California, sees signs of hope. "Most of the country's 127 medical schools have established programs on alcoholism," he said. "Some very minor, however." In the past two years, he added, "There has been a huge increase in the membership of the American Medical Society on Alcoholism." It now totals 2,600 members, with new recruits coming in at a rapid rate. The society has also just established the first national certification test in the field of chemical dependency. It does not test competency, as in a board examination. It does test knowledge about alcoholism and other addictions. "In other words," Schneider said, "it tests how much you know, not how well you carry it out."

Of the medical schools teaching about alcoholism in his region, Schneider singled out the University of California at Irvine. There, almost half the medical students choose the course on alcoholism and other drug dependencies among seven possibilities in psychiatry; they get a minimum of five hours of teaching lectures, are exposed to the psychopathology of alcoholism (how it affects the physical systems, such as the liver, brain and pancreas), spend four weeks on a hospital alcoholism unit, and must attend at least eight meetings of Alcoholics Anonymous, Narcotics Anonymous or Cocaine Anonymous.

"Despite the growth in awareness, there are still people teaching in America's medical schools who regard the study of alcoholism as a questionable science and a questionable disease," Dr. Schneider said. "It's a disgrace."

No one has set forth the arguments for and against the disease concept of alcoholism more clearly than Dr. Blume, who, like Schneider, has worked with thousands of alcoholics and addicts. A forceful, articulate, politically astute woman who clearly does not suffer fools gladly, she now runs a treatment program for alcoholics at South Oaks Hospital on Long Island, near New York City. A psychiatrist with many interests, including alcoholism among women, she was one of the most effective and visible directors ever to head the New York State Division of Alcoholism and Alcohol Abuse. This is, in paraphrase, how she sums up the advantages of the disease concept:

• It is useful in treatment. It lifts a large burden of guilt from both patient and family. "Involuntariness" is a characteristic of all diseases—they happen to you, you don't cause them. The alcoholic's guilt is not focused on having failed to take preventive steps before the alcoholism developed, but on not being able to control the drinking now. If the alcoholic and the family dwell on the past, if they blame themselves or each other, they will get nowhere: "If I had more willpower . . .", "If I had tried harder . . .", "If I were a better child to my mother . . .", "If he really loved me . . .", "If she were any kind of wife . . ." are typical. These guilt-provoking accusations can be put to rest by accepting the disease concept, allowing recovery to begin. "The alcoholic patient may realistically feel guilty about things he/she did or failed to do," Blume wrote, "but not about being an alcoholic. That was unintentional. Family members may regret certain actions, words and attitudes, but they will understand that they themselves did not cause the alcoholism."

• It is socially useful. Making the disease concept the official view encourages the establishment of treatment centers, rather than jails, to deal with alcoholism. It puts the civil rights of alcoholics on a par with those of other disabled people. It also encourages health insurance coverage for alcoholism services, research into the causes and treatment of alcoholism, and the training of doctors, psychologists and social workers in professional schools. It prompts mechanisms such as "employee assistance programs" to spring up in corporations, through which an employee who develops alcoholism is helped instead of fired.

"That the debate over the disease concept goes on interminably should not surprise us," Blume wrote, "considering the complexity of alcohol problems, the incomplete state of our knowledge, the ambivalent attitude of society toward alcohol, and the political, legal and economic forces involved." She went on to state the major arguments against the disease concept:

• Moral and social objections. A fellow physician accused Dr. Blume of "glamorizing" alcohol addiction by calling it a disease. "Can the habit of opening one's mouth and pouring alcohol down one's throat be called a disease?" he asked her. Blume answered, "The disease concept does, in fact, absolve the sufferer from responsibility for *becoming* an alcoholic, with all the consequent guilt. It should not be extended to exempt all people, or even all alcoholics, from responsibility for alcohol-related acts [such as drunk driving]." She cited Jellinek of Yale, who in 1952 wrote: "The lay public uses the term *alcoholism* as a designation for any form of excessive drinking instead of as a label for a limited and well-defined area of excessive drinking behavior [where there is a] physical and psychological pathology involved. Such an unwarranted extension of the disease concept can only be harmful, because, sooner or later, the misapplication will reflect on the legitimate use, too, and, more importantly, it will tend to weaken the ethical basis of social sanctions against drunkenness."

Blume remarked, "This confusion may be expressed in questions such as, 'If alcoholism is a disease, why do you want to increase penalties for driving while intoxicated?' It is the responsibility of professionals to clarify this point."

- Objections that the disease concept interferes with recovery. Some argue that the concept places patients in a passive, irresponsible role, providing them with a ready-made excuse for their drinking: "Don't blame me, I'm sick." "Nothing could be further from the reality of accepted medical practice," said Dr. Blume. "Relieving guilt feelings about having become an alcoholic does not relieve the patient of responsibility for following the treatment regimen and taking the steps necessary for recovery. . . . Alcoholism differs very little from other chronic diseases where following a diet, doing prescribed exercises, taking medication, attending therapy sessions, avoiding certain environmental hazards [such as bars, cocktail parties and heavy-drinking friends] are the clear responsibility of the patient."
- Political and social objections. If alcoholism is a disease, then doctors and health agencies should be in charge of trying to solve the problem, rather than the clergy, the social welfare and criminal justice systems, or agencies that regulate taxes and industry. "This argument reveals an exceedingly narrow view of public health. Was any disease ever wiped out by treatment?" Dr. Blume asked. "Surely, techniques of prevention are required." Smallpox was conquered through preventive measures, although no effective treatment was ever developed. Public education, sanitation, and regulations establishing standards of

purity for foods and safety and effectiveness for drugs have accomplished a great deal in preventing illnesses. Further, alcoholism, the disease, is far from the single cause of alcohol-related problems. Many such problems, such as accidents caused by driving while drunk and alcohol-related birth defects, can be prevented through public education and policy. Fetal alcohol syndrome—the third most common cause of mental retardation in newborns after spina bifida and Down's syndrome—is the only one that can be prevented. If the mother drinks, the baby drinks too; that is a powerful argument for abstinence during pregnancy.

"If such public policies turn out to lower the incidence of alcoholism, does this disprove the disease concept?" asked Blume. Hardly, she replied. "No one would deny that social custom has a profound influence on the incidence of gonorrhea. Is gonorrhea therefore not a disease?"

She concluded that until a better model comes along—one that adequately serves the public interest and has no serious disadvantages—"We ought to stick with Seneca, Benjamin Rush . . . [and] E. M. Jellinek. We ought to continue to regard alcoholism as a disease."

Alcoholism fits almost every definition of a disease that science can come up with. Rare is the medical journal that does not publish new evidence of its physical results: inflammation of the pancreas, cirrhosis of the liver, anemia, heart disease, malnutrition, nerve damage, muscle damage, impotence and a host of other bodily ills. Few experts these days consider alcoholism as just a symptom of a deeper psychological malady. Most agree that the profound psychological problems often characteristic of alcoholics are a result, rather than a cause, of the disease. In time, alcohol abuse alters brain-cell function, shrinks the cerebral cortex and throws the hormonal system so out of balance that, some doctors think, it induces the body to shut off the production of natural euphoriants. Without these euphoriants, the theory goes, drinkers fall into mental distress.

It is definitely a disease that runs in families. People have suspected this at least since Plutarch, the prolific and perceptive Greek essayist who said, "Drunkards beget drunkards." Plutarch was born in A.D. 46; his wisdom has been confirmed by many scientists in the last quarter of the twentieth century. Drunkard parents do indeed tend to have drunkard children. They have them about four times more often than do parents who are not alcoholic. By 1979, there were more than one hundred studies that proved beyond any doubt that alcoholism was a family disease.

It is not just that parents are a child's first teachers, and from them a child learns how to drink, and how to abuse drink. There is also a genetic reason. In recent years, studies have shown vividly that alcoholism is inheritable. When the child of alcoholic parents is separated from them as an infant and is raised by nonalcoholic adoptive parents, the infant remains likelier to grow up to be an alcoholic, too. Studies of twins also point to the genes. There is even recent persuasive evidence that the electrical brain waves of small children of alcoholics, decoded and seen as pictures on television screens, look and react differently from those of the brains of children of nonalcoholics—long before the children have touched a drop of liquor.

One of the experts who is sick and tired of people asking, "Is alcoholism a disease?" is Dr. Donald Goodwin, head of the Department of Psychiatry at the University of Kansas Medical Center. Dr. Goodwin is responsible for a series of landmark studies on the genetics of alcoholism in the 1970's. He was an inspirational teacher at Washington University in St. Louis, which has produced a generation of brilliant explorers into the genetic role in alcoholism. He also wrote a book called *Is Alcoholism Hereditary?*, which is exemplary for its wit and clear writing about a terribly complicated subject.

The short answer to the question posed by the title of Dr. Goodwin's book is no, not exactly. Alcoholism is not purely hereditary, not a mathematical certainty as are hemophilia and Huntington's disease. But the heightened risk of alcoholism in the offspring of alcoholics has been firmly established. Goodwin is one of those who has succeeded in separating inheritance, or nature, from environment, or nurture.

To the other question, "Is alcoholism a disease?" Dr. Goodwin answered:

Is lead poisoning a disease? Chronic lead intoxication is diagnosed by a specific set of symptoms: abdominal pain, headaches, convulsion, coma. Alcoholism is also diagnosed by a specific set of signs and symptoms, a more or less predictable course and certain complications. Both lead poisoning and alcoholism are "medical" problems, meaning that doctors are supposed to know something about them and possibly be of help.

Treatment is less than perfect, the best being abstinence from lead or alcohol. The point is this: Why or how a person "catches" a disease is not relevant. If some people *enjoyed* lead and ate it like popcorn, this would not change the diagnosis of lead intoxication. Diseases are known by their manifestations as well as their causes, and why alcoholics drink is irrelevant to the diagnosis of alcoholism.

To the frequent question "What is the 'alcoholic personality'?" Goodwin has a short and realistic answer: "There is none." Alcoholism, like death, strikes people without discrimination—short and tall, thin and fat, the tense and the placid, the timid and the bold, the successful and the failed and everybody in between. It may be condoned by the culture, as among the Irish, or frowned upon, as among Jews. Its inroads may be frustrated by a built-in physiological inability to drink, as among many Orientals. It seems to run in a few professions, some of which can be lonely and self-regulated, as that of writers, and others of which can be intensely pressured and gregarious, as those of newspaper people and doctors. But then again, most journalists and physicians are not drunks, and the alcoholics among them don't show up in disproportionate numbers in A.A.

At a recent A.A. meeting in New York, the speaker of the evening was expanding on the perils of his profession. It was pressured hard work, he said, with awful demands, ups and downs, frequent disappointments, a few triumphs, and incessant deadlines. "I've never seen so many people drinking to keep going," he said. "My profession is riddled with alcoholics."

After the meeting, another A.A. member approached the speaker, thinking, "He must be an advertising man. Or maybe a doctor, or an actor." A little curious, he asked the man, "What line of work are you in?"

"I," said the speaker, "am an upholsterer."

Alcoholism does seem to run in some cultures and not in others. Take two groups of Americans, one at very high risk, one low. The first is the Irish Americans and the second, Americans of Oriental extraction. Irish Americans have the highest rate of heavy drinking—31 percent—in the nation. They tend to drink hard liquor and to drink in bars. Drinking to excess is done often and is encouraged or condoned as a property of manliness. Their tolerance to alcohol appears to be low. Sober Irishmen are found in huge and disproportionate numbers in Alcoholics Anonymous. By contrast there are the Orientals. Here, cultural displeasure with heavy drinking is reinforced by a dramatic physical inhibitor: the "flushing" reaction. "Roughly two thirds to three quarters of Orientals experience a cutaneous [skin] flush, mainly of the face and body, after drinking a small amount of alcohol (for example, one or two beers)," said Dr. Goodwin. "The flush is usually accompanied by unpleasant subjective reactions, including feelings of warmth and queasiness, as well as an increase in heart rate and decrease in blood pressure. The Oriental flushing phenomenon is undoubtedly genetic in origin. Oriental infants have been given tiny amounts of alcohol, and they too have flushed." The reason may be, he said, that the livers of many Orientals cannot metabolize alcohol with normal speed and efficiency.

To date, there is only one proven predictor of alcoholism, the strongest of all—a family history of alcoholism. It does not mean the children of alcoholics are doomed to get the disease. It does mean they should be told about the danger and be on the alert.

The discovery of a genetic predisposition to alcoholism has opened a new era in alcoholism research. How useful is this information for doing something about the disease now? "The implications of the latest discoveries are profound," said Dr. Boris Tabakoff, scientific director of the National Institute on Alcohol Abuse and Alcoholism. "We are very close to unraveling the biological enigmas of the disease. Even if we do not find a cure for alcoholism, we will probably be able to prevent and arrest it in the future."

Alcoholism research is going on all over the country, but the medical school that has long been at the cutting edge—the genetics of the disease—is Washington University. Among the professors and students who have taught and trained there are Dr. Goodwin, Dr. Robert Cloninger and Dr. Marc Schuckit. Dr. Schuckit, now a world-famous genetics researcher, is a psychiatrist at the University of California and the San Diego Veterans Administration Medical Center at La Jolla, California. Born and raised in Wisconsin, he entered Washington University in 1964 as a medical student and was immediately inspired by its energetic, questing and compassionate teachers. "The men and women there taught me that you don't mess with people's lives and minds until you have data that tells you what you're doing does more good than harm," he recalled. During his medical school years, he began interviewing alcoholic families in the inner city of St. Louis for one of his professors. His career has been in the alcoholism research field ever since.

Dr. Schuckit is tall and thin, with dark eyes that seem to burn with intensity. He has spent years studying young men at future high risk for alcoholism: sons and other close relatives of alcoholics: He matched each of these men, age eighteen to twenty-five, with a "control," another male who has no family history of alcoholism. In each pair, the two men were closely similar in age, religion, race, education, drinking history and height-to-weight ratio. All the subjects were in college. Partly because of their youth, none of them had yet developed alcohol addiction—the disease of alcoholism. On several occasions they were fed various amounts of pure alcohol masked by nonalcoholic mixers. They showed identical blood-level concentrations; yet the results from Schuckit's laboratories showed three dramatic differences between the sons-of-alcoholics group and the controls:

1. The sons of alcoholics, as they reported sensations such as euphoria or dizziness, did not *feel* as drunk as those from non-alcoholic families.

2. The sons of alcoholics did not *look or act* as drunk; they were less impaired at performing certain tasks.
3. The sons of alcoholics *experienced less intense hormonal changes* after they drank alcohol.

Dr. Schuckit and other researchers coming up with the same results found three immediate implications for doctors in the daily practice of medicine. According to Dr. Schuckit:

First, the evidence supporting the importance of genetic factors in this disorder, combined with clinical experience, underscores the importance of recognizing that alcoholism is a biologically influenced problem, not a moral weakness. Many physicians may need to change their stereotype of alcoholics or they will continue to misdiagnose the average middle-class alcoholic who needs help.

Second, the genetic factors can help us begin to work on preventing this illness. It makes sense that children of alcoholics should be educated about their risk, taught that they may not react to alcohol the way their peers do, and informed that attempting to drink like others could be a dangerous undertaking.

Finally, the implications for the future of prevention and treatment of alcoholism are even more marked. Identifying factors that actually increase the risk could help us to pinpoint those children of alcoholics who are most likely to become alcoholic themselves.

On the East Coast, another researcher, Dr. Henri Begleiter of the State University of New York Health Science Center, Brooklyn, has come up with equally startling discoveries about the sons of alcoholics. Studying subjects between seven and fourteen years old, he has found that sons of alcoholics, *long before* drinking age, display abnormal brain waves. "Even more striking," said Dr. Begleiter, "is that these same abnormalities seen in little kids also show up in adult alcoholics I have studied who have been abstinent in Alcoholics Anonymous at least five years." Those adults were also sons of alcoholics.

The brains of these children, as well as adults long sober in A.A., even look different from those of people with no alcoholic family history. On television screens in his laboratory, Begleiter showed brightly colored computerized images of the two types: On the right was the brain of a child of an alcoholic; on the left, the brain of a child from the control group. Multicolored circles in the brains of the sons of alcoholics were much smaller than those in the normal brains. What does this mean psychologically? Begleiter said those differing images mean that the sons of alcoholics have some memory and learning problems when they are presented with significant stimuli and that their emotional reactions are more bland than the norm. "If you ask me, 'Is there a biological marker—a reliable biological difference—between these kids?' I can answer unequivocally—yes." He added, "Unfortunately, we don't yet have a foolproof way of predicting whether the kid will become an alcoholic when he grows up."

The explorers in the genetics of alcoholism have gone along many paths in their search. Two of the most rewarding are studies of twins and of adoptees.

Studies of twins take advantage of an accident of nature. Twin pairs are born at the same time and are likely to experience major childhood events at the same time, such as the death of a parent. "Therefore," said Dr. Schuckit, "if childhood environment is important in the development of alcoholism, the risk [of becoming alcoholic] should be greater in the twin of an alcoholic, whether the twins are identical or fraternal."

Identical twins share 100 percent of their genes. Fraternal twins share only 50 percent, the same as any brothers and sisters born at different times. As a result, if genetics influence alcoholism, the identical twin of an alcoholic should be twice as likely to become alcoholic as a fraternal twin. And that is exactly what has been shown. The closer the genetic tie, the higher the risk. Most of the studies done on twins show that the risk of becoming alcoholic is 60 percent or higher for the identical twin of an alcoholic and 30 percent or less for a fraternal twin.

Some of the most compelling evidence supporting the genetic predisposition for alcoholism comes from adoption research. The studies of Dr. Goodwin and, more recently, of Dr. Cloninger of Washington University, are important. Both men have attempted to separate "nature," or inherited genes from "nurture," or the environment. Their approach was to study individuals who had been separated from their biological parents soon after birth and raised by nonrelated foster parents.

Goodwin's research was done in Denmark in the early 1970's and analyzed at Washington University. He chose Denmark because in the United States, getting access to adoption agency records can be hard; most agencies have little information about the parents of infants who are placed for adoption. Among highly mobile populations such that in the United States, locating subjects is difficult. In Denmark, few of these barriers exist. Centralized national registries are available for scientific purposes, and there is little population movement in or out of that small, racially homogeneous country.

Goodwin picked his subjects from a pool of 5,000 nonfamily adoption cases—all that had taken place in the city and county of Copenhagen between 1924 and 1947. He selected men with a biological parent—mostly the father—who had been hospitalized for alcoholism. All had been separated from their biological parents in early infancy, all had been adopted by nonrelatives and none had any known contact thereafter with their biological mothers and fathers.

Then Goodwin matched them with a control group of men of the same ages who were different from the first group in only one respect: They had not had a biological parent hospitalized for alcoholism. The study was "blind" from beginning to end: No subject knew what the Danish psychiatrist was interviewing them about, and the Dane who took their life histories did not know which group any subject was from. More than 60 percent of the subjects were still in their twenties at the time of the interviews. Not one mentioned a parent with a drinking problem. This is what Goodwin found:

By their late twenties at the latest, the offspring of alcoholics adopted soon after birth by nonrelatives had nearly *twice* the rate of alcohol problems and *four times* the rate of alcoholism as the children of nonalcoholics similarly adopted away in infancy. Goodwin separated the alcoholics in these two groups from the "heavy, problem drinkers" by using the following criteria, at least three out of four of which the subject had to meet to be considered a true alcoholic:

1. Social disapproval of drinking by friends, parents; marital problems.
2. Job trouble, traffic arrests or other police trouble because of drinking.
3. Frequent blackouts, tremor, withdrawal hallucinations, withdrawal convulsions, delirium tremens.
4. Loss of control (compulsive drinking); morning drinking.

Previous studies suggested that the highest period of risk for developing alcoholism is roughly from the age of twenty through forty-five. Therefore, Goodwin concluded, the alcoholism rate in his two predominantly young groups might continue to increase "over the next two decades." He could not predict whether the gap would widen between the adopted-out sons of alcoholics and their controls.

Other researchers into the genetics of alcoholism have made some additionally surprising findings. In sum, they are:

1. Children of alcoholics are no more likely to become drunks if they are raised by an alcoholic parent than if they are separated from that parent soon after birth and brought up by a nonalcoholic.
2. Children of nonalcoholics, adopted and raised by alcoholics, are no more likely to become drunks.

However, Dr. Cloninger has found that environment *can* have an impact on children of alcoholics adopted away as babies. In his recent landmark studies, based on voluminous Swedish data, he threw a wider net than Goodwin and brought the research a step further: He included women in his research. He sorted the adoptees into two types of alcoholics and found that in the more common type, there *was* an environmental as well as a genetic influence.

All of these studies strike a serious blow against purely environmental explanations of alcoholism. Nonetheless, Dr. Begleiter warned, "Nobody—absolutely no one—is saying that alcoholism can be accounted for one hundred percent by genetic factors. But we *are* saying that there is a sizeable proportion of the alcoholic population in which genetics plays a role. Hemophilia and Huntington's disease are truly hereditary, truly homogeneous diseases. Alcoholism is an extremely heterogeneous disease. It's like a symphony in four movements, with many variations on a theme."

Why are there so few studies on the genetics of alcoholism in women? Leading researchers, virtually all of them male, were asked this question. Their explanations were as follows: They believe there are fewer women alcoholics than men—about 3 to 5 percent as against 12 to 15 percent of the general population. The results of previous studies on women—and there are very few studies so far—are vague, inconclusive and conflicting. The inherited predisposition to alcoholism is much more striking and prevalent in men than it is in women. Women are more biologically complicated; they undergo hormonal changes, triggered by such things as menstruation and pregnancy, which have tremendous influences on the brain and throughout their bodies; therefore it's too daunting to study them. One researcher remarked, somewhat defensively, "You can't study everybody."

One man who is daring to scout this terra incognita is Dr. Sean O'Connor, a psychiatrist at the University of Connecticut's medical school in Farmington. In 1987, his research team embarked on a five-year plan to study alcoholism in women. "There *was* a perception that there were fewer women alcoholics than men," he said. "That is changing. We at the University of Connecticut believe that the perception is incorrect. Women alcoholics were 'hidden' alcoholics—their drinking was hidden from society because of the extra stigma, they were not seen as much in treatment and therefore have not been studied. We are going to spend the next five years testing our notion that the genetic predisposition for alcoholism is just as strong in women as it is in men. For the next two years, we will study the effect of the menstrual cycle on brain waves. We will spend the three years after that applying our knowledge to the study of women at risk for alcoholism."

In all research on alcoholism, there is no true "animal model," no laboratory rat or frog, dog or cat that can be tested and whose reactions can then be translated into human terms. The reason is that no animal except the human voluntarily drinks a lot of alcohol, gets into serious trouble because of it and goes on drinking anyhow. No dog would take "the hair of a dog" to cure itself.

Alcoholism is not just a disease. It is also the number one drug threat in the nation today. Adam Paul Weisman, who wrote a wittily devastating article in the *New Republic* magazine called "I Was a Drug-Hype Junkie," pointed out that cocaine and crack and heroin were trivial menaces compared to alcohol, despite the hysteria in the press in 1986. That was the Year of the Drug Crisis in America, the year of one of the fastest bills ever passed in Congress—the Anti-Drug Abuse Act. Only a relative trickle of the $1.7 billion in new funds went to alcoholism prevention, treatment and research.

"While public concern about alcoholism, drunk driving and teenage drinking has been rising, the press still tends toward separate discussion of drugs and alcohol," Weisman wrote. "Ostensibly, the difference is that alcohol is legal, but really it is because alcohol use and abuse gets people too close to where they live: the corner tavern, the Super Bowl party, the 19th hole."

He reiterated for the umpteenth time what everybody should know by now: that the figures for alcohol abuse not only dwarf those of all illicit drugs but "reduce to high comedy the flap over 'legal' designer drugs. Alcohol is truly legal, and nothing could be more 'designer' than a tall, frosty glass topped with a pink parasol. And talk about a threat to society!" He then went on to enumerate the toll in lives and suffering.

The repository of this country's most complete statistics on alcoholism is the National Institute on Alcohol Abuse and Alcoholism, based in Washington, D.C. In 1986, its officials told Congress that eighteen million American adults were alcohol abusers or alcoholics, and 4.6 million more—teenagers under the age of eighteen—were in trouble at school, with their parents or the law because they drank to excess. The NIAAA divided the eighteen million into 10.6 million "alcoholics" and 7.3 million "alcohol abusers" who had been arrested or involved in an accident or whose health or job performance had been impaired because of out-of-control drinking. Loren Archer, the modest and experienced deputy director of NIAAA, was asked what the difference was between the two groups. He laughed and used the "cucumber-into-pickle" analogy. "The alcoholics are certifiable pickles, addicted to drink and showing symptoms of total dependence on it," he said. "The alcohol abusers are cucumbers turning into pickles. And once you're a pickle, there's no way you can go back to being a cucumber again."

Yet the prospects for overcoming alcoholism are immensely hopeful. Yes, hopeful. That is the word Archer uses. He knows, like everybody in the field, that as godawful as these statistics are, alcoholism is treatable. Perfectly treatable. There is still no cure, no "magic bullet," but it can be arrested permanently. The treatment starts with a breathtakingly simple notion: A person can *not* take the next drink. Alcoholics Anonymous has grown and flourished on an even more breathtakingly simple idea: A person can *not* take a drink one day at a time.

# 9

▼

# THE DRUNK TANKS

"This place is a drunk tank—and everybody in it is angry."

—Dr. LeClair Bissell, founding director
  of Smithers Alcoholism Treatment and Training Center, New York

"Patients ask how important it is that they go to A.A. after they're through here. I say, 'I can give you a guarantee. When you leave here, if you don't go to A.A., you won't make it.' "

—John T. Schwarzlose, program director of
  the Betty Ford Center, Rancho Mirage, California

Lowell's heart was thudding with apprehension. A tall, broad-shouldered man of fifty, nattily dressed, he looked as if he might have been handsome once, but now he was slightly moth-eaten in appearance, with wisps of gray hair sticking to a damp forehead and a hectic, purplish flush darkening his face. He had taken a couple of belts of vodka to get up his courage before coming to this place; he didn't like vodka, but of course nobody could smell it. Now he was seated beside a desk being interviewed by a motherly nurse named Mary. Mary ignored the whiffs of vodka coming her way and said in her thick Irish brogue, "Welcome to Smithers, Lowell. We're glad you've come. I just need to ask you a few questions. We'll take your medical history and your blood pressure and then someone will come to get you settled. This will be your home for the next twenty-eight days."

Lowell felt a little better. He liked Mary's manner and the genteel, old-world looks of the lobby, with the carved marble fireplace and the grand staircase spiraling up a curved wall to the upper floors. Somebody had told him it had been Billy Rose's mansion once. He liked the idea that Rose, a great show-business entrepreneur, had lived there, since Lowell was in the entertainment business, too. The Smithers Rehabilitation Unit was a quick taxi ride uptown from Lowell's apartment in mid-Manhattan, where he had kissed his wife good-bye just twenty minutes before. "I'll make it this time, kid," he told her. Nancy had said, "If you don't, I don't know what I'll do." There were tears in her eyes. She was Lowell's second wife, thirty-one years old. The gap in their ages sometimes frightened him.

Mary the nurse jotted down Lowell's vital statistics and queried him about his past illnesses, medical complaints and drinking history. She took his temperature and blood pressure and said the doctor would give him a complete physical examination later in the day. She asked him how he had come there. His wife had threatened to leave him several times, Lowell said, but he couldn't seem to stop. He drank wine, beer, about three quarts of Scotch a week. "I took a week's script [prescription] of Valium in twenty-four hours," he said. "I smoke real good hash, too—you know, high-class marijuana. Look, in my business, everybody drinks and drugs." He was talking faster. "My wife told me I went to the Metropolitan Opera the other night with only one shoe on, and I didn't even know it!" He gave a forced laugh, and then subsided. Mary smiled benignly. "Nancy didn't think it was funny. Well, the thing that got me here was—I have a great staff, terrific young kids—I love 'em. Last Tuesday, I had kind of a liquid lunch with an old client, and I got back to the office and I was talking about the great times in the sixties. One of the kids looked at me and said, 'Lowell, it'll never be 1969 for you ever again. If you don't get help right away, I'm looking for another job. You're ruining the business. We're all ready to quit.' A friend of mine who doesn't drink anymore had told me about Smithers. I called Tuesday night, and somebody said there'd be a bed for me today."

While Lowell and Mary were talking, one of the security guards was riffling through Lowell's suitcase in another room off the lobby. He removed a bottle of mouthwash, a bottle of after-shave lotion, some cough syrup, a packet of aspirin and two capsules of Valium. Drugs of any kind and lotions and medicines with alcohol in them are forbidden in an intensive rehabilitation center. Any necessary medications are given by staff physicians and nurses. Mary explained this to Lowell. She took a Polaroid snapshot of him "for staff recognition" and attached it to his file. "It's almost lunchtime," she said. "Someone will take you to your room. Meals are in the second-floor dining room, cafeteria style. Your first lecture is at one-thirty. Here's your patient's handbook. It gives your schedule and the rehab rules."

Lowell's bedroom, a large, airy chamber on the third floor, had six neatly made beds in it. Three young roommates were already there to say hello. Other patients drifted about the landings, the library and the lecture hall, all carrying notebooks, chatting, smoking, sipping from coffee containers. Lowell noticed there were lots of young people and quite a few blacks. Suddenly he felt old, worn out. The universal uniform for both men and women seemed to be sweats and jeans. He had just a few minutes to skim through his handbook.

"All patients," he read, "are expected to be up and out of bed by 7 A.M. daily. You are expected to attend all lectures and [therapy] groups and to arrive on time. You must attend all meals. Those patients receiving medication are expected to arrive at the nursing station according to the schedules given to them. All patients are expected to be in bed with the lights out by 11:30 P.M."

The warning about medication was especially important. Rehabs use tranquilizers to withdraw patients from alcohol gradually and safely. Medically supervised withdrawal is advisable. Alcoholics who attempt to stop drinking cold turkey run a risk of medical complications and even death.

The handbook warned against excessive card-playing, telephone calls, napping and any form of gambling. Cigarette-smoking, radios and television sets were prohibited in the bedrooms. The center's one television set, in the lecture hall, could be watched only between six and eleven o'clock at night. "A major obstacle to recovery," Lowell read, "involves being distracted from taking a serious look at yourself and your disease." All packages received by patients were to be inspected by the security guards. Visitors were permitted on Sundays and holidays only, from 1:30 to 5 P.M., and, the handbook said, "No visitors will be admitted who have alcohol on their breaths or appear to be high on drugs." There was a section on fraternizing: "The development of 'romantic' or emotionally dependent feelings between two patients while in treatment here," the handbook said, "is a sure way of staying sick." Lowell read about the reasons for immediate discharge from treatment: any use of alcohol or other mood-changing drugs; sexual activity between two patients; physically violent or threatening behavior; smoking in a patient's room or other restricted areas. There were no passes to the outside. He thought, "Well, at least there aren't any bars on the windows, and the front door isn't locked."

So began Lowell's first hour in the place Dr. LeClair Bissell, who founded Smithers, had once called, despite its elegance and amenities, a "drunk tank" full of angry people. "Very rarely do we get someone who says, 'I'm an alcoholic—Eureka! I want to stop drinking,'" she said. "Usually, there's a definite footprint on the seat of the pants."

Lowell's name has been changed and his physical description slightly altered to protect his identity, but his drinking story and what he went through at Smithers is true. It could happen at any good rehab, in settings as different as Hazelden's motel-like brick buildings scattered across 250 acres of Minnesota farmland to the

Betty Ford Center's dazzling white stucco cubes among Technicolor grass and palm trees in a California desert oasis.

In the days and weeks that followed Lowell's admission to Smithers, the experience sometimes reminded him of Marine boot camp, or a total immersion course, or a religious conversion. At first he felt fury, shame, resentment, depression. Then, increasingly, there were bursts of relief or gratitude or a feeling of being safe at last, alone no more. He was inundated with information about his illness and what he must do if he wanted to get well, stuffed to bursting with lectures, films, small-group therapy, "rehab community" meetings, A.A. meetings, counseling, physical and psychological tests, reading, homework assignments. Lowell liked the food, which was plentiful and nutritious. His appetite, sated before by alcohol's empty calories, became ravenous. Between meals, he could go to the kitchen, where the refrigerator was stocked with milk, juices, fruit and light snacks. The flush faded from his face. His eyes looked clearer. His energy was coming back.

Lowell made his bed, tidied his room, helped set and clear tables when he was on dining-room duty. He was required to study many books and pamphlets, among them A.A.'s Big Book and its *Twelve Steps and Twelve Traditions*. He kept a daily diary. He wrote a letter of farewell to chemicals. A twenty-year-old roommate named Eddie, pale, skinny and earnest, helped him with the letter and showed him his own. It was titled "Breaking Up Is Hard to Do," and began, "Dear Chemicals: The time has come for Eddie W. to make his first great step toward accepting life on its own terms. . . . This is truly the most painful experience that I have ever known, for I loved you, my chemicals, more than life itself. . . . This place has given me the opportunity to love other people. To love myself for what I am and not for what I wish I was."

Lowell soon learned that the other forty-three patients were a key part of his treatment. He made friends among them and spent hours in bull sessions. He realized after a while that a single, manipulating person could wreck the morale of an entire rehab, but he also found that the intensity and closeness of the Smithers experience could bring out a strength and sweetness neither he nor the others had known they possessed.

During his first few days, Lowell had felt almost too confused and lost to function. The first lecture he attended, in a huge, wood-paneled room with French doors at one end leading to a tiny garden, was about anger. A staff member told how alcoholics and addicts deal with it. "We put it down. We stuff it," Renee said. "We put it off. We put it on somebody else. We dilute it, we try to rationalize it away, get rid of it rather than feeling it in the gut. We create a slush fund of poisonous anger. We say, 'To hell with it' and reach for a drink or a drug. We overeat. We feel anxiety. Anger doesn't go away just because we're unaware of it. We get depressed, we have headaches, insomnia, high blood pressure, skin disorders, ulcers. We turn to sex. Sex will never fill up the emptiness. We have been anesthetized for years. We can't drink, we can't drug at Smithers. We can't use sleep as a narcotic. You *can* deal with yourself here, and with your emotions—with the help of other people."

At the end of the lecture, Lowell raised his hand. "Yes, Lowell?" asked Renee.

Lowell looked confused. "I . . . I don't remember what I wanted to ask," he said, smiling sheepishly. "I guess I'm still in a fog."

At his first small group therapy meeting, Lowell had appeared hopeful but nervous. He smiled at the other seven people seated in a tight circle and, when his turn came to speak, proceeded to tell about his business and drop the names of some famous entertainers he had known and managed. "My wife is even more successful than I am," he said with an ingratiating grin. The others gazed at him, stone-faced.

Finally David spoke up. "Who gives a fuck what you do or who you know? You're a drunk and a drug abuser, like the rest of us." Lowell looked stunned, and stared at the floor.

The others began talking about their feelings. Near the end of the ninety-minute session, the counselor, a quiet black man named Bob, turned to Lowell. "How's your marriage?" he asked.

"How about perfect?" shot back Lowell with a self-confident smirk. Then he muttered, "I guess it wouldn't have been if I hadn't come in here. She read the riot act to me about my drinking."

As the weeks wore on, the group learned or suspected what the staff already knew from interviewing Lowell's young wife. She felt neglected. She felt frustrated, empty. Her appetite was gone. She was depressed, anxious, irritable, numb. She had been embarrassed by Lowell's drinking behavior. She was enraged. She had scolded, nagged and bribed; avoided going to parties; hidden or thrown away his bottles and drugs. She had never, however, carried out her threats to leave him.

"How's your marriage?" Bob asked again, almost four weeks later.

"How about awful?" Lowell answered. "I hope to God I can make it up to her. I can start by not drinking or drugging."

Some of the patients held tight to their delusions throughout their treatment. "I've got eight wonderful kids," Georgia kept saying to anyone who would listen. A tiny, energetic woman who looked fifteen years younger than her thirty-eight years, she displayed some of their photos on her bedside table. It turned out that six of them were in foster care, two others with Georgia's estranged husband.

"It's impossible for me to go to aftercare therapy group meetings every week in New York after I get out of here," said Peter, a brawny fireman sitting at one lecture. "I've got to go to Florida to exterminate my sister's house. She's got termites."

The patients howled with laughter. "Aren't there any exterminators in Florida?" somebody asked with an air of wonderment. More howls.

Dan, the lecturer, explained, "You can find time to do anything you must do. After you finish here, you've got to find time for A.A.—it's as necessary as inhaling and exhaling. In addition, there is aftercare. When you leave Smithers, you're not a well man by a long shot. Everybody needs at least three to six months of therapy in a recovery group, plus lots and lots of A.A. meetings from here on out. You've got to stay sober, a day at a time, forever. You want to live? Or you want to kill your sister's termites?"

Although the staffs in the best of the rehabs care deeply about their charges, they are very tough. "This is a life-and-death situation—your life and your death," a Smithers counselor told his patients. "About half of the people in this room will go out of here and drink again. Up to now your life has been abuse. What it *can* be is recovery."

The staff members work far harder than the patients. It is a revelation to sit in on daily staff briefings, which last from an hour to ninety minutes before the working day begins. The entire rehab team of alcoholism counselors, social workers, nurses and psychologists discuss each patient, his or her medical, emotional and family background, progress or lack of it. Soon, they know so much, and tell each other so much, that whole human beings rise up in flesh and bone and spirit, complete with the life they led outside and the life they may be going to once they leave the rehab.

The staff urges family members or "significant others," such as close friends or lovers, to come for their own treatment during the final days of a patient's stay at Smithers. Lowell's wife, pleading an urgent business conference on the West Coast, was not there as his twenty-eight days drew to a close. The staff's final prognosis on Lowell was, "Cautious. Probable risk of drinking again."

Members of the four families who did come were exposed to a three-day crash course including films, lectures and small discussion groups on alcoholism, how it distorted their own lives and behavior, and how they could help themselves to get well. "If you're living with an alcoholic, no way you're not going to be sick yourself," one of the family therapists told them. "You've got all the symptoms without the glass in your hand." The mothers, wives, sisters and sons listening to her gasped with surprise.

On the final afternoon, the day before their discharge, four patients joined their families in the library. Each family acted out in improvised dramas what life had been like at home. In each case there had been a pattern of fights and shouting, withdrawn or absent fathers. All said, "Nobody talks to anybody in our family about anything that matters." The hours together in the library were often moving, full of pride and hope for the graduating patients. There were harrowing moments. By the end of the day, Marian, the mother of a twenty-eight-year-old patient named Paul, had been confronted by her son and two daughters and forced to admit that she was an alcoholic, too. At one point, a handsome woman patient called Carol told her lover of thirteen years, sitting beside her on a sofa, "I have grown up in this place. You have controlled and dominated me for years. Please, let's be equal partners." As she said this, Carol gazed with a look of deep love into her friend's eyes, which began to fill with tears. The next morning, the patients left Smithers to begin new lives without alcohol.

When it was founded in 1973, Smithers was one of only several dozen intensive alcoholism rehabilitation centers scattered across the United States. Now there are between 6,000 and 10,000, with more being opened almost every day. Inpatient and outpatient, hospital-based or "freestanding," they have given an enormous propulsive thrust to the care and saving of alcoholics. Not many years ago, drunks whose families had given up on them would have been consigned to jail, or an insane asylum.

Daniel J. Anderson remembers those times. "When I went to work at Willmar State Hospital in Minnesota in 1950," he said,

> it was just the beginning of the end of the "snake pit" era for alcoholics. We didn't call them alcoholics then. The nicest word for them was "inebriates," "ineebs" for short. They were thrown into locked wards with schizophrenics, psychopaths, terminal syphilitics and the senile-demented. At Willmar, we fed each of them slop for thirty-eight cents a day. Drunks weren't accepted in general hospitals. They were the lowest of the low. The public attitude was either "Shoot 'em all" or "Let God decide." Few people knew about Alcoholics Anonymous. It was still young, and the biggest, strongest groups, with experience dating back to 1935, were in Ohio and New York. People thought it smelled like some kind of religion, like the Salvation Army. Nobody knew if it did any good.

Anderson was reminiscing in the Renewal Center, a quiet retreat for recovered alcoholics, many sober for years, on the grassy campus of Hazelden near Center City, Minnesota. Around it were low, modern, rosy-brick buildings surrounding a lake where other alcoholics were undergoing treatment. A psychologist, Anderson is a jolly butterball of a man who speaks in the flat accents of the Midwest. He was the longest-serving director of Hazelden, the great prototype of alcoholism rehabs. Both Smithers and the newer Betty Ford Center, among many, modeled their treatment programs on Hazelden's.

Anderson recalled the sinister look of Willmar State Hospital as he first saw it, built of dark-red brick and stone like hundreds of other asylums and orphanages soon after the turn of the century; it might as well have had "Abandon Hope, All Ye Who Enter Here" over its front door. He began to talk about his earliest mentor, Dr. Nelson J. Bradley, who had just come to Willmar as its superintendent in 1950. "I was young, right out of college, with some part-time experience at another asylum," he said. "Bradley was a Canadian doctor, a humane man with enlightened ideas. He separated the 'ineebs' from the insane, unlocked the doors for everybody but the violently crazed—and the escape rate for all patients fell from twenty-five percent to six percent. Some early members of A.A. in a nearby town needed some drunks to sober up, and so they came out to convince Bradley that they could work with our alcoholics. Over endless cups of coffee, they made us see that Alcoholics Anonymous made sense. By 1953, we had begun to believe that maybe alcoholism was a complex illness."

Bradley and Anderson began to do what had not been done before: They put together teams of physicians, psychologists, family counselors, clergymen and members of A.A. to work on alcoholics in a coordinated way. "At that time, people thought we were crazy to hire somebody whose only qualification was that he had been a drunkard," Anderson said.

In 1949, the year before Bradley and Anderson began to transform Willmar State Hospital, a group of rich Minnesotans, all recovered alcoholics in A.A., bought a little white farmhouse northeast of Minneapolis as a refuge and treatment center for other alcoholics. It was called Hazelden Farm. One of the first patients was Patrick B., a wealthy contractor. During the 1950's, the work going on at Willmar fascinated Pat and his friends, and there was an interchange of information between the hospital and Hazelden.

It was Pat who paid for Dan Anderson's training in clinical psychology and then sent him on to the Yale School of Alcohol Studies to learn from giants in the field such as E. M. Jellinek, Selden Bacon and Marty Mann. In 1961, Anderson came to Hazelden as its director, where he was to serve for a quarter of a century. He is still active as Hazelden's president emeritus.

From Willmar and Hazelden to the present day, A.A. has had an enormous impact on the rehabs. No treatment center worth its name would dream of not familiarizing its patients with the precepts of A.A. and then encouraging them to use the organization as a follow-up that must go on for years. The typical rehab gives its drunks about twenty-eight days to turn around; after that, it is the patients' own desire to stay well that keeps them going to meetings.

As important as the impact of A.A. has been on the rehabs, however, the reverse is also true: The rehabs are channeling recovering drunks by the tens of thousands into A.A. The nature of A.A. is changing because of them. And they have become big—very big—business. The double boom, in A.A. membership and in treatment centers, has been parallel and "mutually reinforcing," according to a major survey conducted in 1985 by the National Institute on Alcohol Abuse and Alcoholism. In A.A.'s own 1983 sampling, almost one third of the members named alcoholism counseling and rehabs as the single most important factor in bringing them into Alcoholics Anonymous—an enormous jump over the proportion having received outside treatment in the previous poll taken three years before. The numbers continue to rise.

The torrent from the rehabs has created problems for A.A. Historically, A.A. has always seemed to be infinitely expandable and accommodating. Although timidly at first, and despite the resentment of some hard-line old-timers, it opened its arms to women, homosexuals, the very young and those dually addicted to alcohol and other mood-changing chemicals. The conventional and the odd and all those who seek solace for their suffering are welcomed. Yet now A.A. headquarters is worried. It fears that it might be drowning in its own success.

"It's a big problem," said Cathy B., a staff member at head-quarters. "Take Jaffrey, New Hampshire, where a big rehab is located. Each of the little towns and villages around Jaffrey has at least one well-established A.A. group with several weekly meet-ings. All of a sudden a meeting with eight people is inundated by forty patients who don't care much yet about A.A. Coffee costs money. The rent for the hall costs money. Those eight people want to get on with their sobriety, their A.A. life. I think the answer should be to start another, beginners' meeting for the rehab people. Some old-timers get really disturbed when the patients come in and only talk about drugs. But the rehabs need us. They desperately need us. There's no doubt about it."

Staffers at headquarters said that many people go to alcoholism treatment centers before coming into A.A. because a rehab is "someplace nice" to recover—nicer, at any rate, than the typical A.A. meeting is thought be. (The public image of A.A.'s as a bunch of skid row bums, or, at best, people one wouldn't invite to dinner, dies hard. And it is true those church basements seem dreary, until a newcomer is comforted and strengthened by what goes on inside them.) Alcoholics who go to treatment also are covered by medical insurance; A.A., of course, is free. Finally, employers by the thou-sands are sending their workers into treatment rather than pun-ishing them. James S. Kemper, Jr., a recovered alcoholic and founder of the Kemper Group of insurance companies in Illinois, has shown the compassion typical of managers who understand the unnec-essary suffering that alcoholism causes, as well as its cost to busi-ness. "The most expensive way to handle alcoholics," he said, "is to fire or ignore them. The most profitable and effective way is to help them recover." Kemper, who established an early Employee Assistance Program for his alcoholic workers in 1962, also pi-oneered in insuring recovered alcoholics. Until recently, they were rejected by life insurance companies until they had gone five years without drinking. Even after that proof of solid recovery, alco-holics were charged higher premiums.

In the last decade, Employee Assistance Programs (called EAPs) have multiplied into the thousands. Most of the Fortune 500 list of major corporations now have them. They dealt at first only with alcoholic employees, but now those who run them also counsel workers on family and emotional problems and drug abuse. The Stanford Research group has estimated that by treating workers with drinking problems, industry saves about $6,000 a year for each alcoholic employee. Labor unions, once suspicious that companies were trying to "spy" on their members, now manage some of the most effective EAPs in the nation. Robert O'Brien and Dr. Sidney Cohen, writing in *The Encyclopedia of Drug Abuse,* pointed out: "Perhaps EAPs have greater leverage because while problem drinkers are generally not intimidated by threats of losing family, possessions, reputations or pride, they are usually deeply concerned about losing their jobs."

The costs of structured treatment can be steep. The minimum charge for an excellent rehab in 1987 was about $6,000 for twenty-eight days in residence. Outpatient treatment costs much less than even the cheapest of rehabs. Some rehabs, particularly those in hospitals, charge up to $24,000 for a month's treatment. The nonprofit Betty Ford and Smithers centers fell in the $6,000 range in 1987; Hazelden cost less than $4,000. Hazelden can charge less because its services are subsidized by its gigantic publishing empire: It is the world's biggest publisher and distributor of literature about alcoholism and drug abuse. Not only does it create and sell its own books and pamphlets; it also orders from other publishers and is one of the most important single outside customers for A.A.'s "official" literature. The seventeen million books and pamphlets Hazelden mailed out in 1986 included 168,000 of A.A.'s Big Book and 120,000 of its *Twelve Steps and Twelve Traditions.* Treatment centers everywhere put both Hazelden and A.A. literature on their "must" reading lists for patients.

Four weeks seems to be the minimum for residential treatment. Some patients, more seriously damaged physically and emotionally, may be sent on for further months of recovery in "halfway houses." The number of patients on any given day at a typical freestanding rehab—that is, one not located within a hospital—falls between forty and 125. At the best rehabs the ratio of professional staff to patients is high; at Hazelden, for example, it is four to one.

Some alcoholics can be propelled into treatment by a process called intervention. It was developed by Vernon Johnson, who in 1962 founded the Johnson Institute in Minneapolis for training in alcoholism treatment. His 1973 book, *I'll Quit Tomorrow,* describing the process, has sold more than 300,000 copies, and his booklet, *Intervention: How to Help Someone Who Doesn't Want Help,* has also been immensely popular. Betty Ford was one of those catapulted into treatment by the Johnson method. It consists of a "loving intervention" that family members, friends or employers carefully rehearse beforehand with an alcoholism expert.

There is another, even more recent development. Saving drunks has become big business. For many years, private philanthropists, most notably Leonard Firestone, Joan Kroc and J. Brinkley Smithers, have poured millions of dollars into rehabs and other forms of alcoholism treatment and education. Now the giants of industry are becoming involved, from the huge medical-hospital-insurance complex of CompCare to Avon, the door-to-door purveyor of beauty products. Alongside this is the hectic growth of smaller, for-profit rehabs. Some are as posh and overpriced as country clubs, others as seedy and overstuffed as hot-bed hotels. In the worst of them, rules are shockingly lax, conditions unsafe, staffs poorly trained, medical supplies short. For all the good they do, they might as well be revolving doors back to the bottle. They are proliferating like kudzu grass, unchecked and uncontrolled. They are ignorant of A.A., or give it only lip service. They are licensed by the states, but are not required to obtain accreditation from the Joint Commission on Accreditation of Hospitals, the national agency charged with ensuring quality of care.

It is true that America is thinking more and doing more about its alcoholics than any other nation in the world. Yet only one out of fifteen of alcoholism's adult victims is getting some kind of help, in or outside A.A. The plight of the school-age children of alcoholics is even more tragic: There are millions of them, living and suffering in the homes of drunken parents. "No one is paying that population the slightest attention," wrote Charles Deutsch, the author of *Broken Bottles, Broken Dreams,* who was an education specialist at CASPAR, a successful school-community program on alcoholism in Cambridge, Massachusetts. "Do we really need more data to believe that many children of alcoholics are seriously damaged by their parents' illness—or to believe that it would make all the difference in the world if they could be helped when still young to understand the illness and throw off the feelings of shame, guilt and hatred it engenders?"

Some people say that alcoholism carries no stigma any longer, that almost everybody knows it is a disease that can be treated. If that were true, it would not be "the secret that everybody knows," a secret that active alcoholics and their families invariably attempt to hide from outsiders. Most recovered alcoholics also shield their A.A. affiliation from public view, although usually they tell close friends. And as far as this nation has come from the 1950's world described by Hazelden's Dan Anderson, punishment for alcoholism can still be severe.

Consider the case of Kathleen Neal. In October of 1986, Neal —a thirty-four-year old white woman from Rockland, Massachusetts, mother of three, who had committed no crime, abused no child, struck no other human being while drunk at the wheel of a car—"just dropped through the cracks" of Massachusetts law, a judge said. For being rowdily drunk in public one night, she was arrested and brought before a district court in Taunton. Court officials had tried to get her into several treatment centers: They refused her either because they were full, or because her treatment would not be covered by Medicaid. The judge committed her to what he thought was a state hospital in Framingham for thirty days, where he said she would be helped to overcome her eight years of worsening addiction to alcohol. Neither the judge nor Neal's court-appointed lawyer knew that there was not, and never had been, an alcoholism treatment unit at Framingham, the state's only prison for women. When Neal got there, handcuffed and shackled around the waist, she was strip-searched "in unbelievable places," she later said, and thrown in a cell with four other women, one of whom had been imprisoned for attempted murder. Neal said she was preyed upon, slapped and sexually fondled by other prisoners.

When her lawyer and Maureen Rose, a clerk in Taunton District Court, discovered six days later that there was no hospital or treatment for women alcoholics at Framingham, they alerted judges, the press and several state legislators. The Massachusetts secretary of human services commented, "It's outrageous. If a woman hasn't committed a crime she shouldn't be locked up." Neal, who had no criminal record, was not the only alcoholic to suffer such a fate in recent years. Since 1973, when Massachusetts decriminalized public drunkenness and declared alcoholism a disease, at least sixty women like her had been jailed with criminals. When Neal was freed, unrehabilitated, "I drank even more," she said.

That is the true story of what happened in America, in 1986, to an alcoholic.

# 10

## NAN'S STORY

This is not the story of my life. It is the story of how I got drunk, and how I got sober. I have told it before, many times: at A.A. meetings, and to my A.A. sponsor, and to other close A.A. friends gathered in coffee shops—what we in A.A. call "the meeting after the meeting." But I have never before told it in full. By tradition, no speaker leading an A.A. meeting runs over thirty minutes. I will tell it as I would at an A.A. meeting, in the same spirit.

My name is Nan, and I am an alcoholic.

I haven't got a single excuse for being one. I come from a stable, affectionate, middle-class, middle-western family where drinking was considered a civilized, graceful accompaniment to social occasions, always done in moderation. There are no alcoholics in my family. I am not shy. I have had a fulfilling career, many friends and, in my second marriage, a great love.

But I became an alcoholic anyway.

I was a boring drunk. I never wept, or got sick all over people, or threw things. I rarely became ugly or maudlin. I did not undergo any truly dramatic personality changes. I became another, blunted self. I went to sleep a lot. Sometimes I would wander off from a party for a refreshing hour's nap in the guest bedroom and then return, wondering why the other guests were looking so embarrassed. I withdrew in other, more subtle ways. My husband used to say, "When Nan gets bombed, she goes off into some little room in her mind, and pulls down the shade."

When I was young I could drink anybody under the table. I was always the one who drove friends home, held their heads when they threw up and put them to bed. I began drinking seriously when I was twenty-two, just out of college and beginning my career as a newspaperwoman. My generation of newspaper people consisted of two-fisted drinkers. In the circles I moved in, drinking was not just socially acceptable; it was an emblem of maturity. If you drank hard and long and well, you had earned the badge that set off the men from the boys and the women from the girls. If you drank hard and long and not well, your exploits became part of newspaper legend and the subject of endless funny stories.

Looking back on my drinking career, I believe I crossed the invisible line into alcoholism when I was about thirty-three years old. Shortly afterward I married my second husband, Stanley Levey, a man of moderation in almost all things. Because I loved him, I could not bear for him to think badly of me. I tried to control my drinking, or to hide it by sneaking drinks. By the time we married, I was using any pretext to take a drink: when I was happy, when I was sad or frustrated, when I was on the road and lonely, when

I was surrounded by friends in familiar places. And I always needed that extra Scotch—the glass of whiskey and soda that got darker with every passing year—to send me off to sleep at night. When Stan died, after ten years of marriage, a part of me was fatally wounded. And with his death, the last control on my drinking was off. His traumatic heart attack and subsequent deterioration had already accelerated my drinking. For several months after his death I drove suicidally while drunk. One day, I realized with horror that if I went on, I would kill or maim somebody else. I stopped driving while drunk. But I didn't stop drinking. I took taxis, or had friends drive me home, or stayed with them overnight.

One morning in August 1971, about five months after Stan's death, I was at work in the Washington bureau of my newspaper when I began to develop the worst bellyache of my life. Within the hour, I was doubled over with pain. Laura, the extremely proper secretary of one of our famous columnists, offered to take me to the doctor. Our family doctor was on vacation. A physician I had never seen before, Dr. Charles Thompson, was covering for him. The waiting room was jammed. Dr. Thompson, a baldish man with a blunt, pugnacious manner that I instinctively felt masked great compassion, put me on the table in the examining cubicle. The door was wide open. He took up my hands and began scrutinizing the palms. In the center of each was a deep red rash about the size and shape of a quarter. He gazed intensely at me, questioned me and stared again at the palms, thoughtfully running a thumb over the rash. He asked me if the pain in my belly had begun to travel up my right side. Yes, it had.

Then Dr. Thompson put me on my back on the table and poked and prodded around my abdomen and looked at my reddened palms once more. He bent over with his nose almost on mine and asked in a husky whisper, "Do you know what's wrong with you, my dear?"

I looked up meekly, nose to nose, and said, "No, Dr. Thompson, I don't."

"BOOZE!!!" he bellowed. "BOOOOOOZE!!!"

The sound boomed out through the open door and echoed around the crowded waiting room, where all those people, including Laura, my very proper colleague, were hearing the ghastly truth about me. I was rigid with mortification.

"STOP IT!" roared Dr. Thompson.

Having captured my total attention, he proceeded to tell me that I had acute pancreatitis—an inflammation of the pancreas—and that my deeply reddened palms were a serious early warning sign of alcoholic damage. I would have to stop drinking at once and entirely. I promised.

Dr. Thompson had frightened me. I kept the promise for one month, while relaxing on vacation. The rash cleared up. I felt full of energy. And then I came back to the pressure of the Washington office. I thought, "Well, I'm in good shape again. What harm would it do to have a drink or two?" Soon I had resumed my double martini and two beers at lunch, with lots of coffee afterward, which I thought would sober me up for the deadline sprint at the end of the afternoon. Nights were reserved for oblivion drinking.

My newspaper sent me to Paris in January 1973: a wonderful advance in my career. Professionally, it was exciting. Personally, I was achingly lonely so far from friends and home. Soon, however, I fell in with a terrific bunch of drinking buddies. I was writing and reporting well, I thought, but it was becoming harder. I was struggling at the typewriter, taking hours to do stories that I used to finish in forty-five minutes. I often lunched alone at a little restaurant near the office called Le Sportsman, so that I could read all the Paris newspapers, and drink, in peace.

One day, deep in my newspapers, gently glowing after my usual two double Scotches and a carafe of wine, I heard the varnished blonde who ran the place talking in French to another customer. "She gets drunk here, very nicely, every day," the woman said. "And then, very nicely, she goes away."

I never went to Le Sportsman again. I got drunk elsewhere.

Being a drunk in a good job in a beautiful city was as sordid and shaming as it would have been in squalid surroundings. I began taking a whiskey or two in the morning, rationalizing that it would get me through the day's tensions. I bought bottles at different shops in my neighborhood, so nobody would know my true intake. I felt utterly alone with my guilty secret. The rash on my palms reappeared. I remembered Dr. Thompson's warning. Finally, late in 1974, loathing my obsession and terrified that it might cost me my job, I went to my doctor at the American Hospital of Paris. "I think I am becoming an alcoholic," I told him, "and it is beginning to damage my life and my work."

He offered to put me in the hospital for a week, "to dry out," and added, "I'd like to send some people up from A.A. to see you." I gratefully agreed, because I had heard over the years that those A.A. people could perform miracles.

The next morning, a friendly, attractive young American couple entered my hospital room. They were from Alcoholics Anonymous. I do not remember a word they said, except that there was a meeting twice a week at 8 P.M. at the American Church of Paris on the Quai d'Orsay. I attended several A.A. meetings, sitting with a dozen others around a table to tell my story. I did not find it strange in that sympathetic company to say, for the first time, "My name is Nan, and I am an alcoholic." But I was not ready. Soon I began to make excuses, the most powerful being that 8 P.M. was my deadline hour for filing stories to New York. I would not admit to myself that I could have written most of my pieces by early evening.

The months that followed were full of remorse and confusion. I did not go again to A.A. "I have the willpower to stop myself," I thought. I swore off drinking repeatedly. I could not keep my resolve for more than a week. I was so depressed I was almost incapable of action. The morning drinking got worse. I needed booze to still my trembling hands and give me the impetus to get out of bed and to the office. My doctor at the American Hospital recommended a French psychiatrist who had impressed him. I went to the psychiatrist and ran through my drinking and depression story. After fifty minutes, he ended the session by saying, "If you continue, you will destroy yourself." I went straight to the nearest café and gulped down two double Scotches. Fuck him, the self-righteous bastard.

In April 1975 my newspaper sent me to Lisbon to cover the first free election in Portugal in forty years. I hired an interpreter and went about the city and the surrounding countryside for two days, interviewing everybody in sight and taking notes. At night I drank heavily with my foreign-correspondent friends in the bar of the Hotel Tivoli. On the third morning, having cabled the New York office to expect a long descriptive article that day, I sat down at my typewriter. I read and reread my notebooks, underlining important passages. I read the lines over and over. They were chaos. Or rather, my mind was chaos. I could not write a single sentence. For the first time, I could not summon at will almost thirty years of discipline and experience as a professional reporter.

I paced that hotel room, drenched in sweat, for eight hours. I sat and shook and stared at the typewriter. The words in my notebooks bounced out and jumbled together. I thought of throwing myself in the River Tagus. I had never—never—not met a deadline.

Late that afternoon, I called my bureau chief in Paris. "Flora," I said, "I'm at the end of the line. I can't read my notes. I can't write a word."

"Don't worry, dear," she said. "I'll call New York and explain. Get the next plane back to Paris and come straight from the airport to my apartment."

Back in Flora's apartment, I faced a friend who was all sympathy. It was nervous tension, she said. It was exhaustion. I had been working myself to the ragged edge.

"It isn't any of that, Flora," I said. "It's booze."

She didn't believe me. "I want you to talk to Dr. Fred Plum tomorrow," she said. Flora explained that he was a family friend, a brilliant diagnostician, the chief neurologist at New York Hospital, who, as it happened, had just arrived in Paris for a medical convention. "He'll know what's wrong with you," Flora said.

I met Fred Plum in the Tuileries gardens the next morning. He was a dapper man with a resonant voice and a self-confident, cordial air. He loved Flora and her children. He put me at ease. We sat on spidery little chairs in front of the Jeu de Paume museum, gazing at the gray clouds scudding over the Place de la Concorde.

I talked for almost an hour—about Stan, my grief, the onset of menopause that had coincided with his illness and death, my drinking, the crisis in Lisbon. I told him I enjoyed nothing any longer, that I slept constantly when not working or drinking, and that the world looked unrelievedly grim to me. I had been by nature a sunny and optimistic creature; now I loathed even getting up in the morning. I felt numb, anesthetized.

Very quietly, Dr. Plum said, "You are clinically depressed." He told me that the chemical effects of menopause could be profound and could go on for years after onset: "And your drinking reinforces your grief . . . and your loneliness . . . and your depression." He confided that he was the son of a wonderful man who had died an active alcoholic, irreparably damaging the family. He was convinced I could not get well in Paris. "I know your French is fluent, but you must be treated by a psychiatrist whose culture and frames of reference are your own," he said. "You've got to be in a place where you already have friends and family."

Then he said, "You must do three things. You must go home to New York. You must stop drinking. You must enter psychotherapy."

For the first time, I believed all of it. Yet it brought me no relief. In agony, I thought, "This is the end of me, and of my career as a foreign correspondent." I felt I had betrayed Flora, my boss. She was the first woman bureau chief in my newspaper's long history; I was her number two. There had been battles among the male executives at the highest levels of the paper over whether a woman could run a bureau, and later, whether another woman correspondent should join her. We had showed them that two women reporters could perform very well together, and had become close friends in the process. Now I would be going home, I believed, in disgrace.

That conversation with Dr. Plum in the Tuileries was not the end of the road for me. It was the beginning of the way back. I did believe him, I was convinced he was right, but I could not bring myself to do what he was asking. Without Stan, my work had become my life. Yet I could not stop drinking. I drank to smother my remorse and my indecision, my sense of failure. I was wallowing in what the French call *la nostalgie de la boue,* a yearning for self-degradation. The bottle had become my best friend. It had become my only friend.

Flora came back to Paris after a long working trip out of the country and found I had been neglecting assignments, cowering at home in bed. "You are very, very sick," she told me, her patience finally exhausted. "You are far sicker than I thought you were." I know now that I was desperate for her to believe that. I was ill with lying, sick to death with covering up. She could no longer ignore my erratic behavior. I learned much later that the way I was recklessly squandering my Paris assignment, almost inviting disaster, was really a final cry for help.

I went home to New York in August 1975. Dr. Plum was waiting with his daughter, Carol, at the airport. He recommended a psychiatrist. I rented a room in an acquaintance's apartment while looking for a place of my own. I stayed miserably sober for weeks at a time, and then went on secret two- or three-day benders, smuggling bottles into my room and locking the door behind me. My editors, notably the executive editor, Abe Rosenthal, were sensitive and understanding. They saw me teetering on the verge of a nervous breakdown. They could sense I was close to cracking up, but they did not know the drinking part of it.

Early in November 1975, Dr. Howard R. Brown, the director of my newspaper's medical clinic for employees, told me as authoritatively and as kindly as Dr. Plum that I was an alcoholic. By this time, I was almost certain that I was, but my shame was such that I denied it. Dr. Brown suggested that he put me into Smithers, an intensive rehabilitation center in Manhattan that had achieved a remarkable record of success with alcoholics. He gave me a brochure showing some shots of the center, in a beautiful mansion just off Park Avenue on Ninety-third Street. The treatment inside the residence would last one month. My gloom and despair lightened. It looked like a lovely place. I said I would go to Smithers.

The next Monday, the morning of November 10, 1975, I sat on the edge of my unmade bed surrounded by packing cases from Paris, in a bare apartment I had rented days before. I was due to enter Smithers at three o'clock that afternoon. I toasted myself from a soggy paper cup brimming with Scotch, luxuriating in self-pity. I was on my way to a fancy drunk tank. "So, Nan," I said to myself. "You have come to *this*."

I must say I took my last drink in style. I went to Sardi's with my editor, Joan Whitman, and one of my closest friends, Ruth Adler. Lying to the end, I told them that Dr. Brown had recommended that I have a couple of vodka martinis before going to Smithers, to boost my resolve. Then I rolled off uptown in a taxi and landed, half bombed, in the elegant lobby on Ninety-third Street.

"Are you an alcoholic?" asked the kind nurse who admitted me.

"Probably," I said airily.

"Have you ever had memory blackouts?" she went on, smiling encouragingly. "Have you ever sneaked drinks?" There was nothing judging about her. "Do you find it difficult to discuss your drinking? Do you take a drink in the morning to stop tremors? Do you think about drinking a lot? Do you sometimes neglect to have a meal?"

I answered yes to all her questions. The truth dawned that I was *really* an alcoholic. I did not feel shattered. I grinned at the nurse. "Yep," I said, "I sure am an alcoholic." There, I had said it. I was overwhelmed with relief.

I sat down to supper at Smithers soon thereafter, swinging up to the sky on a trapeze of wild exhilaration. I was genuinely intoxicated, not just from Sardi's martinis but from the knowledge that at last I was not alone. I went through the cafeteria line and sat down at a round table in the stately dining room with three women and a skinny young man named Tom. I barely noticed what they looked like; I was too busy congratulating myself on my decision to come to that place. Here were alcoholics just like me, forking in the meat and potatoes, all of us being saved together. I loved those strangers. I knew I would love the staff of doctors, nurses, psychologists and social workers, most of whom were recovered alcoholics. They had been there. They knew what it was all about. I was insufferably happy.

Tom told me he was a doctor. I was astonished, but his news made me feel more ebullient. I thought, "Even doctors can be alcoholics." Days later, when we had become friends, Tom said to me, "The night you came in here, you were babbling like a maniac. You couldn't stop smiling. You made a little castle of your mashed potatoes with a gravy moat all around it and you hardly ate a thing. You must have been bombed out of your mind."

I was assigned to a bedroom, a room of noble proportions with a huge carved fireplace and French doors opening out onto a balcony overlooking a back garden. My roommates were two welfare mothers, an eighteen-year-old ballet dancer burned out on drugs and booze, and a chirpy, middle-aged society matron who had lived for years at the Delmonico Hotel on Park Avenue. I lay awake all that night in a state of sober euphoria. I thought, "I have been given a gift, the gift of writing. I have abused that gift." I also thought, "I have been given a chance to change my life."

We were up at seven to make our beds and go down the curving grand staircase to breakfast. The rest of the day was tightly structured, packed with lectures, films and meetings with our counselors. I was asked to fill out a Blue Cross hospitalization form for my employers, to cover the expensive month's stay at Smithers. I came to the line that said "Reason for hospitalization." I could not bring myself to write "Alcoholism." "Now everybody at the office will know," I thought. I left the line blank. Ashamed, I told myself, "Let somebody else fill it in."

I was quickly back in a manic mood. I phoned all my close friends and told them where I was, and why. I was making what I thought was a major disclosure. "I am an alcoholic!" I cried joyously. It came as no surprise to any of them. But without exception, they responded with hope, pleasure and support. Rob, my stepson, took the news in his usual calm and loving way. However, I detected skepticism in his tone. He knew me intimately, and he had seen me drink my way through some of the major crises of my life.

I kept putting off my toughest decision at Smithers: how to tell my eighty-three-year-old mother. My counselor and the patients in my therapy group insisted that I be candid with her and tell her the real reason that I could not be at home with her in Illinois for the Thanksgiving weekend. Finally I telephoned her, burbling on with false enthusiasm about the wonderful place I was in. Mother cut through my effusions and told me how happy I had made her by finally facing my drinking problem. On Thanksgiving Day, I called her again from Smithers to apologize for not being with her. "Nan, dearest," she said, "you have given me the greatest Thanksgiving gift of my life."

On that Thanksgiving weekend in 1975, a quarter of the forty-four patients in residence at Smithers defected, dribbling away prematurely, one by one, to the outside world. The rest of us were immensely upset. We knew what was waiting for them, and for us, out there. Temptation. We thought, "There, but for the grace of God, go I." The staff tried to reassure us; they said that on the Thanksgiving and Christmas weekends, always a time of memory and emotional turbulence, there was usually an exodus.

I considered myself a model Smithers patient. I met every challenge seriously. I did not shirk my homework, I threw myself into my first encounters with group therapy, I made friends with almost all the other patients. In a foretaste of my future experience with fellow alcoholics in A.A., the patients proved to be my most effective therapy and support.

I made a plan for living on the outside that, I hoped, would protect me from the pitfalls that I correctly imagined would lie ahead. I was proud of myself, and very confident. I had been told that Smithers graduates had a better chance of succeeding in their sobriety than those who struggled on their own directly into A.A., simply because of their month-long total immersion course on how to stay sober.

The day before I was released, I asked to see my medical record, which contained the staff's prognosis on my chances of making it. I read their conclusions in private.

They thought I would drink again.

One counselor wrote that it was likely that I was treating the Smithers experience as "just another assignment" and that I would leave it behind me, as I had so many reportorial adventures, to go on to fresh excitement.

I was gripped with rage. I raved to myself that what I had regarded as the most courageous act of my life had been greeted with disbelief and contempt. When I was able to control myself, I thought, "I'll show them. I'll show them, the ungrateful sons of bitches. I *won't* drink again."

I will never know whether the staff gambled that because I was a reporter, I would be one of the rare patients to know that I had the right to see my confidential medical record. They may also have gambled that my enormous resentment at their prognosis would pay off the right way, fueled by my obvious will to win. Smithers had taught me that resentment was one of the alcoholic's worst enemies. Without their teaching, I could just as well have said: "I'll show them—I *will* drink again." I am convinced now that the final kick in the teeth that Smithers gave me was the healthiest graduation present I could have gotten.

On the morning of December 8, 1975, I said good-bye to Smithers. As usual, there were hugs and kisses from the other patients, the counselors and the nurses. "I *know* you'll make it, Nan," said Donna, a patient. I thought, "It's a good thing she hasn't read the staff report on me." I pushed open the heavy glass and iron front door and went out into the noisy streets of Manhattan. I passed Nodeldini's, a restaurant-bar around the corner, where so many patients who had bolted Smithers had gone to tie one on. I hailed a taxi to take me home. I was nervous and disoriented but hopeful.

That night, armed with the meeting book that lists the days, times and places of hundreds of A.A. meetings every week in Manhattan, I went to the group that met each Monday in the parish house of an imposing Gothic church on Upper Fifth Avenue. Despite Smithers, I was not prepared for what I saw. I somehow expected a gathering of shabby depressives, yet there before me was a quintessentially Upper East Side Episcopalian congregation, some men in pinstripes, many women shod in low-heeled, perfect Ferragamo pumps, with bits of discreet family jewelry at the throat and wrists.

The hospitality committee of my fellow drunks welcomed me

at the door with smiles and handshakes. Their warmth swept away my timidity. The meeting was as impeccably ordered as any Sunday service at my own church, St. James, a mile down Madison Avenue.

During the weeks that followed, I went table-hopping every night to a different meeting, each featuring a slice of New York life. There were blocked writers expressing their angst on the Upper West Side and blue-collar workers in Brooklyn recalling bars they had loved. The beginners' meetings everywhere were charged with raw emotion, close to the edge. The people in them, only days or weeks away from their last drink, could be on pink clouds of jubilation or jittery, unstrung and sullen. In distinct contrast to the group I had gone to my first night out of Smithers, the dress code was universally casual.

Soon, I began to see why A.A. members kept going to meetings. They comforted and centered me. The people in them steadied and supported me in ways as small but crucial as an arm around my shoulder. Sometimes my attention wandered for stretches of time while I retreated into my own thoughts. Sometimes I was bored. But a speaker, or even a sentence uttered from the floor, would get through to me. At one meeting, a man said, "I began coming to these basements and I discovered that I was right about myself —I am a decent person." I thought with surprise, "So am I." I helped make coffee, unfolded chairs, cleaned ashtrays when the meetings were over. Veterans asked me to come with them to nearby coffee shops afterward, and in these little clusters I enjoyed their stories, told my own, made friends, swapped telephone numbers.

But I was afraid to speak up in meetings. A shyness foreign to me stopped me every time I wanted to open my mouth. Finally, after four months in A.A., I raised my hand in a group that gathered near my apartment, six floors up in the parish house of a Presbyterian church. The group was small, and after attending several meetings there I felt at home. Overwhelmed with nervousness, I said, "My name is Nan, and I am an alcoholic. I have been sober four months, and I am so grateful to be here." I could not go on. My voice trembled, and I knew that if I said anything more, I would burst into tears. Everybody in the little group turned to me, smiling and applauding. They knew that the beginners are the bravest ones, enduring the hardest times. They knew that as you go on, it gets easier.

Those first months, I simply put one foot ahead of another. I took everything the old-timers told me on faith. They told me not to take that first drink, and to go to meetings every night. Simpleminded as the advice seemed to me, I had nothing else to hold on to. I was often depressed. I disliked much of the A.A. official literature and its "onward and upward with Babbitt" tone. I was convinced I could never again enjoy life with my old gusto, never have fun at a party again. My work did not interest me. I was struggling in a fog of ennui and blunted feelings. I believed I would never again experience life with the intensity that had been natural to me in my best years.

In the winter of 1976, just two months out of Smithers, I experienced my first strong compulsion to have a drink. I had thrown out all the liquor in my apartment, and so, when three friends asked me to go to a theater matinee with them, I suggested that I fix them lunch at home and that they bring their own wine to accompany it. They arrived with two bottles of white wine but drank only one. I put the other in my refrigerator, and we went off to the theater. My mood darkened during the play. I could not concentrate. I went home and opened the refrigerator door. There was the bottle of wine, dewy and inviting. My mouth watered. I reached for it. Then I slammed the refrigerator door and rushed to telephone an A.A. friend. She told me: "Get that bottle of wine and pour it right now down the sink. *Now.* I'll hang on." I did as she asked. We talked for thirty minutes, and by then my obsession with the wine had dissipated.

In the early spring of 1976, I began to be swept along in a manic rush like that on my first night in Smithers. One day I awoke at dawn in what I can only describe as a state of exaltation. I was weeping with wonder and gratitude, alone in my bed. I felt a terrific need to telephone the psychiatrist who had been treating me for depression, or to rush into my church and pray. It was much too early to do either. And then I thought, "My soul is my church."

I read the Twenty-third Psalm, over and over. I hunted for a poem that had haunted me for years; why, I had not known. I found it—Francis Thompson's *The Hound of Heaven*—in an anthology on my bookshelf. I memorized the opening lines:

> I fled Him, down the nights and down the days;
> I fled Him, down the arches of the years;
> I fled Him, down the labyrinthine ways
> Of my own mind; and in the mist of tears
> I hid from Him, and under running laughter."

My psychiatrist had sensed for weeks that the ice jam inside me was beginning to break up. Early on in my treatment, he had remarked that I was telling the story of my life to him "in perfectly edited paragraphs." He had been intimating that what I had been leaving out of it was the only thing that mattered—my feelings. When it was late enough to reach him that extraordinary morning, I telephoned and blurted out what was happening to me. "Now," said the doctor, "we can begin." What he said comforted me at the time. But a tiny alarm bell in my mind went "Ting!" Months later I remembered. He was paraphrasing the shrink's last line in *Portnoy's Complaint*.

Soon thereafter, on the way to Washington, D.C., I stopped for a weekend at at the house of two friends. For years, their love and support had sustained me in the best and the worst of times. One afternoon they left me alone in the house while they did some errands. A neighbor's son came to the door. Some guests had dropped in unexpectedly on his parents, and they wondered if they could borrow a bottle of white wine from my friends' exceptionally good stock. I remembered I had seen a bottle in the refrigerator. I gave it to the boy and replenished it with another kind of white wine from their cellar so they would have some already chilled to sip at dinner.

I forgot to tell them that evening about the visit from the neighbors' son. The next morning, my hostess appeared in my bedroom with breakfast coffee. Something was obviously troubling her, and she was struggling to get it out. Finally, I understood that she was suggesting that I take an earlier train to Washington. Then she said, "I wouldn't have minded, except for the wine. . . . I think it would be better if you left."

I stared at her. "It was the wine!" I thought. "They thought I stole the wine and drank it!" My heart constricted. I explained what had happened, and we laughed about the misunderstanding. But I was overwhelmed with such pain and anger that I felt physically ill. I packed and fled that house within the hour.

In Washington later that day, another close friend, Patricia Herman, welcomed me at her front door. She took one look at my wretched face and said, "My God, what's wrong?" I told her. "Of course you're shattered," Patty said. "They didn't trust you. You haven't had a drink for eight months, but people still don't trust you." If it had not been for Patty, I might have drunk again.

Gradually, I came to realize that I could not resent or dispel the suspicions of even my most unjudging friends by the simple announcement that I had stopped drinking. For years they had watched me drinking and getting drunk and denying what alcohol was doing to me. It was a year or two after I left Smithers before everyone close to me outside A.A. was convinced I was serious: that the glass of bubbling liquid I was drinking with them in increasing comfort was plain tonic or club soda.

My last and most terrible compulsion to drink gripped me in September 1976. My newspaper sent me to a far corner of northern Maine for an interview with a family of authors. Helen and Jose Yglesias, their son Raphael, and Lewis Cole, Helen's son by a previous marriage, were all writing books in various corners of an old farmhouse near Brooklin. The interview proceeded smoothly with this lively, articulate and amusing family. I stayed for lunch, and Helen brought out the white wine to accompany it. Without warning, I began to come apart. I wanted to drink that wine, with the kind of sickening urgency only an addict knows. My concentration was going; I could not sustain the conversation. I abruptly terminated the interview.

I drove like a madwoman, heading for the Bangor airport an hour and a half away, where I had reserved a room at the airport hotel for that night. By this time, the obsession to drink had seized me and was shaking me like some great dog. I could barely see the road. Every bar along the way seemed to be beckoning to me. I wanted to drink, but I could not drink. I had been taking a little white Antabuse pill every morning for several months, prescribed by a doctor who worked with alcoholics. With Antabuse in me, one ounce of liquor—or less—would make me dangerously ill.

I pulled up to the Bangor airport sweating with fear. I telephoned my A.A. sponsor, Anna L., in New York. She was not there. I called another close A.A. friend in New York. Jerry said, instantly, "Don't stay there overnight. Take the next plane here." He told me to come straight from La Guardia to his apartment and to stay and talk with him until I felt better. "Stay overnight with me and my wife if you need to," Jerry said. "We'd love to have you."

Jerry's calm assurance, the unhesitating willingness to help that is typical in A.A., catapulted me onto the next plane to New York and through the hours that followed. After an hour or so with Jerry, I went serenely home to bed. I am convinced that without Antabuse in me, I would have pulled in at one of the bars on the road to the Bangor airport. In those early months and years of sobriety, I was deeply grateful to the drug, because it protected me from even the most overwhelming urge to drink.

I had begun taking a daily dose of Antabuse several months before the Bangor episode under the supervision of Dr. Ruth Fox, an elderly psychiatrist who had introduced the drug into the United States from Denmark in 1950 and who had been doing research and treatment in the field of alcoholism since the 1930's. My psychiatrist, a friend of Dr. Fox's, had suggested I join her small therapy group for alcoholics, which met every Wednesday night at her office-apartment in midtown Manhattan. I loved the group, which had a nucleus of about eight regulars, all in A.A. I immediately took to Dr. Fox and her accepting ways. She was utterly unlike my own psychiatrist, a tall, weedy and self-satisfied man who patronized me. That doctor had lectured me about how I managed my money. He had suggested I assuage my grief over Stan's death by picking up men at concerts. I sensed he did not respect women. He made me angry, although I was too intimidated by his intelligence and the air of command he exuded to say so. But he did send me to Dr. Fox. She was then in her early eighties, twisted with arthritis but never complaining of her pain. She would sit crumpled in a deep chair in her living room, nodding benignly as her circle of tortured patients struggled their way toward recovery. She prescribed Antabuse for most of us.

Antabuse meant that I made one decision a day not to drink, instead of dozens. Some people call it a crutch, but I call it blessed insurance that strengthened my determination to stay sober a day at a time. Is insulin a crutch for a diabetic?

Dr. Fox, the world authority on the drug, told me that when you are saturated with Antabuse, you know you cannot drink safely after the last dose for the next four or five days, or even longer. If you do drink on Antabuse, you become violently ill. She called it "a time bomb that will never go off unless you trigger it with alcohol." It was dispensed by prescription in a white, 250-milligram tablet the size of an aspirin. "The drug makes you sick if you drink on it," Dr. Fox said, "because it blocks a vital enzyme that helps the body to metabolize alcohol." Since 1950, she had treated thousands of alcoholics with a combination of psychotherapy and advice to stick with A.A. I came to her therapy group as a supplement to my A.A. meetings and while continuing individual sessions with my male psychiatrist.

She warned me to avoid cough medicines, fruit compotes in wine and desserts such as rum cake containing uncooked alcohol, but she said I need not avoid dishes in which wine or other alcohol had been evaporated through boiling, baking or simmering. She told me that I should suffer no side effects as long as I stayed off alcohol. Then she told me what would happen if I did drink on Antabuse: shocklike symptoms including a drop in blood pressure, rapid heartbeat, flushing, vomiting and fainting, and the necessity to be rushed to a hospital for emergency care. She gave me a card to carry in my purse, saying I was on Antabuse and giving instructions for treatment. I was suitably frightened. She told me that the medicine would really be a comfort and a support to me in my resolve. "You know that, from now on, alcohol can't make you feel better; it can only make you feel very ill," she said. "You will find something else to do, the impulse will pass, you will feel relieved." She said that as the weeks and months went by, in therapy and in A.A., I would find that my urges to drink would come less often and not as insistently. "Eventually, and it may take several years," she said, "you will feel strong enough in your sobriety to do without Antabuse altogether."

I had one close call with Antabuse. I was dining out one night with a friend who knew I was on the drug and what its side effects could be. He ordered a Bloody Mary, so I ordered a Virgin Mary. I was bored with the endless succession of plain tonics I had been drinking and thought, "Why not a spicy tomato juice for a change?" I gulped it down (like most alcoholics, I was a gulper, not a sipper). Within ten minutes, my face began to flush, my heart was pounding madly and I felt woozy. Bob said, "My God, they must have put some vodka in your drink by mistake." He rushed me to the restaurant bathroom, taking Dr. Fox's telephone number from me as I lurched through the door.

"Yes, she is having a mild toxic reaction," Dr. Fox told Bob. "There was probably not much vodka in her drink, so she won't have to be hospitalized." She instructed Bob to take me home at once, put me to bed, and stay with me until I fell asleep. "She will sleep peacefully for about eight hours and then awake refreshed and feeling normal," she said. That is what happened.

At Dr. Fox's, I found Anna L. A clinical psychologist, Anna was co-leader of the doctor's Wednesday night therapy group. She became my sponsor. A sponsor in A.A. is not someone who recommends you for entrance; it is a big sister or big brother who has a longer experience of sobriety and, under the best of circumstances, becomes your closest friend and adviser. Some people call their sponsors every day, if only to say hello. I called and saw mine frequently. We loved each other. The last service I was able to perform for her and her husband seven years later was to write her obituary after her death from cancer.

Anna was a tall, bony, aristocratic southerner who wore chic, expensive clothes and was witty and well educated. No human failing seemed to surprise or disgust her. She was an original and a maverick, the extreme opposite of the kind of A.A. member I came to call "the hard-nosed, square-assed fundamentalists." She was an atheist, and yet the most spiritual person I have known. She stood silent while others recited the Lord's Prayer at the close of A.A. meetings we attended together. When the choice was the Serenity Prayer, A.A.'s other favorite, she would not begin it by saying, "God grant me . . ." but "Grant me. . . ." She did not like rules or formulas. She told me that the Twelve Steps boiled down to three suggestions: "Be honest. Change yourself. Help others." She was always available for me in every joy and every crisis. "The trouble with life," she would drawl, with that chuckling laugh of hers, "is that it's just one damn thing after another." I learned from her that being in A.A. went far beyond staying sober, and that if you stuck with it, you might learn how to cope with life without losing your balance, common sense or humor. Anna did not lecture. She showed me the way by what she did and was. She represented in her own life and actions the essence of what makes A.A. work.

Several months after I joined Dr. Fox's group, a new man arrived who was clearly in terrible trouble. Rotund and prosperous-looking, dressed in a pin-striped suit, he introduced himself as Frank, a lawyer. He was a graduate of Ivy League schools. As he told his story, perspiration dribbled down his deeply flushed face. He wrung his hands, he jittered. He told us his colleagues knew about his drinking and that they had warned him he would lose his job if he did not stop. When he had finished his tale of inexorably progressing degradation, he began to pound his knee, slowly and rhythmically. And then, in a voice cracking with desperation, he cried out, "I . . . want a drink! I . . . want a drink! I . . . want a drink!"

A thrill of horror went through me. The other members of the group seemed as stunned as I was. Anna was not present that night, and Dr. Fox simply looked on, waiting for one of us to make a move. I blurted out, "Frank, can I take you to a meeting with me tonight?" He glared around him, radiating danger and intense need. Finally he said yes.

Outside on the corner, waiting for a taxi, Frank said tensely,

"I'm not a lawyer, I'm a judge. I'll be ruined if I don't stop drinking."
He told me his real name, and I recognized it immediately. I was
truly frightened now. But I dragged him off to a meeting up Park
Avenue and sat beside him while he sweated and fussed through
most of it. I found the speaker exceptionally honest and eloquent.
But I knew there was only one thought in Frank's mind: getting
the next drink. And so, as we stood outside afterward, I asked
him to walk me the short distance home.

Frank, a suburbanite, was staying in town that night at his club.
The club has a bar. Once I got him inside my apartment, I plied
him with plain tonic and talked tough to him. Among other things,
I told him that he was lying about taking the Antabuse Dr. Fox
had given him, because I could smell liquor on his breath. I told
him parts of my own story. I tried, I must confess, to impress him
with my own background and to find every kind of intellectual
and social connection with him that I could so that he would not
feel that alcoholism was somehow a moral lapse in a man of his
quality. I told him about Smithers. By then he was incapable of
concentrating and I was running out of steam. He rushed from
the apartment, straight for his next drink.

I called Dr. Fox, knowing that I had gone against A.A.'s very
strong suggestions that Twelve-Steppers—the A.A. members who
try to save active drinkers in crisis—should be of the same sex as
the drinker. Dr. Fox assured me that I had done everything I
should. A week later Frank was in Smithers. I visited him after
three days and could hardly believe the improvement in his appearance and manner. That was eleven years ago. From time to
time Frank and I, two friends with a special bond, have dinner at
his club.

After two years in Dr. Fox's group, despite its special attractions
of intimacy and intensity, I began to feel that A.A. meetings alone
would suffice. So I said good-bye to the doctor and to the patients
whom I had come to know so well.

The diversity of A.A. meetings astonished me. In fact, I discovered that Alcoholics Anonymous reflected not only nationalities
but regions, cities, even neighborhoods. For this reason—the end-

less variety—I have always done a lot of moving around in A.A.: in New York, across the country and overseas. At home or on the road, I know I will not be a stranger in any room where there are alcoholics to greet me. On two extraordinary occasions, I could not help but think of the particular aptness of St. Crysostom's prayer. It is a kind of welcome or verbal embrace, spoken by Episcopal ministers soon after a service begins, and it says in part that "when two or three are gathered together" in Jesus's name, God "will be in the midst of them."

Once, while visiting London, I was going through a severe emotional crisis and felt the need for a meeting every day. I got the London meeting schedule from A.A. headquarters and ranged across the city, from the West End to Notting Hill Gate and the Tower. There was a noon meeting one weekday in a Catholic Church near Covent Garden. I arrived while a mass was going on. The dark, ancient building was packed with worshipers. I peered around in vain for some clue that A.A. was also in that place. I crept up to an aged beadle standing in the rear. "Where's the A.A. meeting?" I whispered.

In a hoarse croak—audible, I was sure, throughout half the church—the beadle said, "The A.A. meeting? It's right through that door back there," as he hitched himself around and pointed.

I slunk through an old oaken door and found myself mounting a narrow, spiral stone staircase twisting up and up into darkness. After a moment, I heard footsteps echoing behind me. My heart began to pound.

I kept going upward; I quickened my pace; the footfalls followed. Finally I could bear it no longer. I stopped and turned. A thin, dark man came around the curve and I thought, "Oh, God, I'm trapped."

He said, "Are you going to the meeting?"

Feeling humbled and relieved, I nodded and went ahead. I pushed open a door at the top, and there was a little whitewashed room with a thick rope dangling down through a hole in the boarded ceiling. This was the belfry. There was no one in it. There were some folding chairs, an electric heating ring with a kettle on it, thick white china cups, a box of tea, a sink, and several framed A.A. slogans hanging on the walls: ONE DAY AT A TIME . . . KEEP IT SIMPLE. The man and I sat down facing each other and waited. Then I said, "Well, as long as there are two of us alcoholics gathered together, I guess we have a meeting. Do you want to go first?"

The man smiled, and began, "My name is John, and I am an alcoholic." We told our stories to each other, alone there in the belfry high above London. We talked for an hour and parted on the street below.

The only other meeting I ever went to where there were only two of us took place in the Palm Court of the Plaza Hotel in New York. The man I was meeting was a European friend I had not seen for years. I had learned just that afternoon that he had become an alcoholic, had finally found his way into A.A. in Germany, and wished to go to his first New York meeting with me that evening. But by the time we had rushed into our first hug in years in the Plaza lobby, it was streaming rain outside. I said to Horst, as I had to John, the stranger in the London belfry, "As long as there are two of us, we have a meeting." We had a late supper in the Edwardian elegance of the Palm Court while Horst told me his story of horror and salvation and I told him mine. A violinist played Viennese waltzes.

Once, in Nairobi, Kenya, I noticed an advertisement for A.A. in the local newspaper, announcing that there were three English-language meetings and two in Swahili every week. That evening, a taxi deposited me in a dusty alley behind a theater on the outskirts of the city. I went into a nondescript brick building. There was not a sign anywhere to tell me what the building was, or whether A.A. was meeting inside it. Then I saw a young woman lugging a big coffee urn—a universal tipoff to the presence of a group of alcoholics—up the stairs. "Is this the way to the A.A. meeting?" I said. She grinned and greeted me, and I fell into step behind her.

Of course, the settings were seldom so exotic. The hard work of my recovery was done in hundreds of church basements, many of them drab and some of them forbidding, most of them in my home city of New York. But wherever I went across this country, on business or pleasure, I looked up the "Alcoholics Anonymous" listing in the local telephone book, and called to say, "My name is Nan. I'm from New York. Is there a meeting tonight?" The voice on the line was invariably helpful and always asked, "Can we give you transportation?"

In Helena, Montana, I was reading the daily events column in the newspaper and discovered that there were four A.A. meetings that night, listed with the Helena Symphony Orchestra rehearsal, a get-together of the Helena Senior Citizens and a meeting of the Home Ec Graduates Club. A.A. was accepted there like any other daily event. In Peterborough, New Hampshire, population 10,000, I found four big meetings a week. I used to go to a coffee shop on Peterborough's main street where they baked meltingly light doughnuts starting every morning at four o'clock. This was the unofficial hangout for A.A. members throughout the area; I kept seeing familiar faces from local meetings as soon as I walked in the door. We would spend hours there, drinking coffee, smoking, eating doughnuts and talking about everything in the world. No Viennese coffeehouse could have been more gemütlich, although I did find New Englanders slightly reserved in meetings.

The most uninhibited A.A. groups I have ever encountered have been in New York City and in Marin County, California. While visiting a friend in Marin one summer, I hobnobbed with hairy-chested, open-shirted, gold-chained recovering alcoholics. The A.A.s' conversations sometimes seemed to run to pop-psych jargon. At the trendier meetings there in the 1970's, I would find them discussing creative divorce classes, granola, macramé, vaginal orgasms and the wine-tripping they had done before joining A.A. "I'm in a bad space right now," one member told me. "I don't know where your head is, but like, wow, I can really relate to you." I shouldn't have been surprised. Whether it's Marin County or New Hampshire, the people in A.A. meetings look and sound like the people outside.

As I got better, many problems I had pushed down or pushed away by drinking began to surface. The therapy I had begun with the psychiatrist in New York only shortly before joining A.A. was forcing me to examine my most negative and deeply repressed memories for the first time. Sober, I could not run away from the grief I had felt ever since Stan's death. Sober, I had to come face to face with my anger, confusion and depression.

"Of course you are angry," my psychiatrist said. "You are angry because Stan went and died on you and left you a widow at the age of forty-four."

"How could you?" I protested. "It wasn't Stan's fault."

"This has nothing to do with reason," the psychiatrist answered. "Everybody is angry. We are all like a bunch of teakettles, simmering and bubbling away, with only the rattling of the lids to tell us something is going on underneath." The idea had never occurred to me. In my family, spectacular displays of anger were not only rare but considered unseemly. Anger itself was unseemly. Then the psychiatrist told me of the classic psychoanalytical maxim: "Depression is anger turned inward." I have never heard a better description.

Despite the psychiatrist, the A.A. meetings every week and Dr. Fox's therapy group for alcoholics on Wednesdays, my black moods persisted into 1977. I was struggling to get better; there were good days, but then a kind of hopelessness, a bottomless sadness, would sweep over me. During our many telephone conversations my mother would ask me, "Nan, *why* are you depressed? You are successful, you have friends, you're not drinking anymore."

I would attempt to make light of my condition. "Oh, Mother," I'd say, "there isn't any logic about why people feel depressed. I just am. I can't seem to shake it off."

At times I contemplated suicide. I knew how I would do it. I got up some mornings at dawn to sit on the window ledge of my bedroom. I would gaze long moments, fascinated, unable to tear myself away, at the courtyard ten floors below. I would open the window and lean out, and say to myself, "It's ten stories down, it's quick and it's certain. A flash of pain, and darkness." Then I would shrink back, moving away from the window, hating myself. I could not leave those I loved with a legacy of guilt, asking themselves questions they would never be able to answer.

In the spring of 1977, I found myself becoming increasingly confused and frightened. It was a horrible ordeal to go to the office, and even more agonizing to try to write. I felt as if I were breaking in pieces. On my days off, I would lie in bed, the curtains drawn, never answering the telephone. Finally, I could not function at all. I called my psychiatrist.

"I want to go to a hospital," I said.

"Do you think you might do harm to yourself or others?" he asked.

I said yes.

I committed myself to the Payne Whitney Psychiatric Clinic of New York Hospital that night. When the nurse brought me off the elevator on the seventh floor and locked the door behind me, and I saw the disoriented patients roaming the hall, I was terrified. I had made a ghastly mistake. I was trapped. I had signed away my freedom. I rushed to the pay phone for patients.

"Get me out of here," I told my psychiatrist. "I don't belong in here."

The doctor laughed scornfully. "Oh, baby," he said, "yes you do."

I frantically dialed my internist and friend of more than twenty years, Dr. Ira Cohen. "Ira, for God's sake, get me out of here," I said, sobbing. "I don't belong here."

"Nan, dear," said Ira, "this is the sanest act of your life. You could have thrown yourself out the window. You could have taken a drink. Instead, you asked to be put in a safe place. I am proud of you."

I told myself, "That is the way a doctor should talk to someone in trouble."

Within a day or two, I calmed down and began to realize that I really did belong in a mental hospital. The diagnosis was acute depression. I remained for five weeks, until I was discharged with the doctors' approval.

After about four weeks there, the Payne Whitney staff had begun to indicate in their conversations, subtly but persistently, that my own psychiatrist was wrong for me. They suggested I try another, a young psychiatrist at Payne Whitney named Margaret Gilmore, whom everyone seemed to admire. With her help in the years that followed, I began to heal. My work went better. I fell in love for the first time since Stan's death.

And then I was struck with a nearly fatal attack of toxic shock syndrome.

It hit me on Thanksgiving night 1981, while I was visiting my family in Rockford, Illinois. That grisly and still mysterious disease is caused by a deadly strain of a common bacterium, *Staphylococcus aureus,* and is found most commonly in menstruating women who are wearing tampons. A blood-filled tampon provides a perfect culture for the bacterium.

Almost every major organ of my body, including my heart, lungs and liver, was deeply poisoned. The doctors at St. Anthony Hospital in Rockford told me there had also been "almost inconceivable muscle damage." By measuring an enzyme that the disease had released into my bloodstream, they could measure that destruction. Anything over 100 units is considered abnormally high; I showed 21,000 units. At first the doctors thought they would have to amputate my right leg and the toes of my left foot. Because the treatment had been swift and correct, my leg and toes were saved. But the dry gangrene on my fingers persisted, caused by the collapse of my circulatory system on Thanksgiving night. Before I slipped into a coma at dawn the next day, I had been awake and aware enough to tell the emergency room doctors that I was a recovered alcoholic, in A.A. for years. That warned them not to give me addictive drugs or medicine with alcohol as a base. I had been told at Smithers to do that with every new physician. The information went into my hospital record.

When the critical phase was over, I had eight partially dead and gangrenous fingers, a form of paralysis in both feet that could have left me with a permanent limp, and severely poison-damaged muscles all over my body. Shirley Katzander, a close friend from New York, came to see me. "Your hands were a mummy's hands," she told me long afterward. "The fingers were black and shriveled, with small, perfect black nails. I almost fainted when I saw them."

It was clear by then that the end joints of all eight fingers would have to be amputated. The day the surgeon told me he would have to operate, I was filled with horror. I was certain I would never be able to write again. I was certain that nobody would ever love me again. After ten dark, troubled years, I had finally emerged the previous summer onto what Winston Churchill had called the "broad, sunlit uplands" of life. Now fate had once again struck me down.

As soon as they took me off the respirator and I could speak again, I began to heap my anger onto my family, the doctors and nurses. I reviled everyone who entered the room. I became imperious, demanding, argumentative, impossible. One day, when my sister materialized at the foot of the bed, I looked at her with hatred. "Go home," I said icily.

For at least ten days I was possessed by fury, at everyone. Then one afternoon two strange women appeared in the doorway of my room. I turned to the nurse, saying, "Who are these people?"

There was a little silence, and then one of the women said, very gently, "We are friends of Bill Wilson."

I welcomed them in.

# AFTERWORD:

## WHO IS
## AN ALCOHOLIC?

Q. What is the difference between a problem drinker and an alcoholic?
A. A problem drinker is an alcoholic you care about.

—*A.A. saying*

When the *Encyclopedia of Alcoholism* was being planned in the early 1980's, an official of a major government agency in Washington dealing with alcoholism research suggested only half-jokingly that it be published in one hundred volumes. One volume would contain basic information about alcoholism. The other ninety-nine volumes would contain the caveats, disclaimers, qualifications, special cases and contradictions about the disease.

Alcoholism is complicated, especially because it is a disease of denial—the disease that tells you, "You don't have a disease." Or it can tell you that you're sick, or crazy, but from some other cause. Alcoholism is insidious, baffling, powerful, progressive. It only gets worse, never better. And you can't count on your doctor to tell you what's wrong with you: Often your own physician may not detect the cause because you are lying about your drinking, or because he or she knows little more about alcoholism than you do. To this day, no more than several hours of instruction about the disease are given to students in most of America's medical schools.

There are, however, strong clues to help you, guideposts built by recovered alcoholics who have been there, who know every lie and excuse and rationalization because they have used them; and other signs familiar to knowledgeable physicians and experts on the disease.

And then there are your own secret fears. Ask yourself, "Am I worried about my drinking?" If you are, chances are you have reason and do have a drinking problem. But you are not weak-willed; you are not mentally unbalanced; you are not a bad person. You may be ill, with the disease of alcoholism.

How can you tell if you are an alcoholic? Only you can make that decision.

Sit down, alone and in a quiet place, and try to answer yes or no to the following twenty-six questions. Your responses are nobody's business but your own. You won't learn immediately how many questions you have to "flunk" before you're considered an alcoholic. The answers follow this list; don't sneak a look before you have answered all of them. Be honest with yourself, with the decent person you know yourself to be. The questions, drawn from more than forty years of experience, were put together by the National Council on Alcoholism, the first nationwide volunteer agency in the field of this disease. They should help you decide whether you need help. Remember, answer yes or no to each:

1. Do you occasionally drink heavily after a disappointment, a quarrel, or when the boss gives you a hard time?

256

2. When you have trouble or feel under pressure, do you always drink more heavily than usual?

3. Have you noticed that you are able to handle more liquor than you did when you were first drinking?

4. Did you ever wake up on the morning after and discover that you could not remember part of the evening before, even though your friends tell you that you did not pass out?

5. When drinking with other people, do you try to have a few extra drinks when others will not know it?

6. Are there certain occasions when you feel uncomfortable if alcohol is not available?

7. Have you recently noticed that when you begin drinking you are in more of a hurry to get the first drink than you used to be?

8. Do you sometimes feel a little guilty about your drinking?

9. Are you secretly irritated when your family or friends discuss your drinking?

10. Have you recently noticed an increase in the frequency of your memory "blackouts"?

11. Do you often find that you wish to continue drinking after your friends say they have had enough?

12. Do you usually have a reason for the occasions when you drink heavily?

13. When you are sober, do you often regret things you have done or said while drinking?

14. Have you tried switching brands or following different plans for controlling your drinking?

15. Have you often failed to keep the promises you have made to yourself about controlling or cutting down on your drinking?

16. Have you ever tried to control your drinking by making a change of jobs, or moving to a new location?

17. Do you try to avoid family or close friends while you are drinking?

18. Are you having an increasing number of financial and work problems?

19. Do more people seem to be treating you unfairly without good reason?

20. Do you eat very little or irregularly when you are drinking?
21. Do you sometimes have the shakes in the morning and find that it helps to have a little drink?
22. Have you recently noticed that you cannot drink as much as you once did?
23. Do you sometimes stay drunk for several days at a time?
24. Do you sometimes feel very depressed and wonder whether life is worth living?
25. Sometimes after periods of drinking, do you see or hear things that aren't there?
26. Do you get terribly frightened after you have been drinking heavily?

The National Council on Alcoholism says: If you answered yes to *any* of the questions, you have some symptoms that may indicate alcoholism. Yes answers to several of the questions indicate the following stages of alcoholism:

Questions 1 through 8—Early Stage. The NCA put the average duration of this period at ten to fifteen years. An exception would be people who seem to leap into problem drinking from almost their first drinking days, weeks or months.

Questions 9 through 21—Middle Stage. The average duration of this period is two to five years.

Questions 22 through 26—The beginning of the Final Stage of alcoholism.

One general question that any reader can ask himself or herself is "Is my drinking causing a *continuing* problem in *any* department of my life—my inner life, home life, social life, physical life, business, professional or financial life?"

Or you could ask yourself this, the first question of twelve in the National Alcoholism Test, developed by researchers at Johns Hopkins University in Baltimore: Do you tell yourself you can stop drinking anytime you want to, even though you keep getting drunk? A question often put to teenagers, who are flooding into A.A. at an ever-increasing rate, asks them whether they consider it a virtue to be able to drink a lot without passing out.

Women are often forced to drink in secret because society continues to judge female drunks more harshly than male. Ann Landers, who has done as much to help people with alcohol problems as anyone else in America, wrote a column with questions addressed to women but applicable to men as well:

1. Do you buy liquor at different places so no one will know how much you purchase?
2. Do you hide the empties and dispose of them secretly?
3. Do you plan in advance to "reward" yourself with a little drinking bout after you've worked very hard in the house?
4. Are you often permissive with your children because you feel guilty about the way you behaved when you were drinking?
5. Do you have "blackout" periods about which you remember nothing?
6. Do you ever phone the hostess of a party the next day and ask if you hurt anyone's feelings or made a fool of yourself?
7. Do you take an extra drink or two before leaving for a party when you know liquor will be served there?
8. Do you feel panicky when faced with nondrinking days, such as visits to relatives?
9. Do you invent social occasions for drinking, such as inviting friends for luncheons, cocktails or dinner?
10. When others are present, do you avoid reading articles or seeing movies or TV shows about women alcoholics, but read and watch when no one is around?
11. Do you ever carry liquor in your purse?
12. Do you become defensive when someone mentions your drinking?
13. Do you drink when under pressure or after an argument?
14. Do you drive even though you've been drinking, but feel certain you are in complete control of yourself?

If you've answered yes to any one of these questions, you have a drinking problem.

Finally—and again, often overlapping the above tests—there are the guidelines given by doctors to other doctors. Here are excerpts from the American Medical Association's *Manual on Alcoholism*, first published in 1968 and updated regularly since. Informed at every turn by the experience of recovered alcoholics as well as empirical medical knowledge, the following paragraphs give a history of the relentless progress of the disease:

The onset of alcoholism is usually sufficiently insidious and gradual to make it difficult to distinguish the alcoholic from the heavy drinker, although the distinction between the two might be evident from the beginning. The alcoholic, as compared with the non-alcoholic, has greater emotional response to alcohol and often attaches inordinate significance to it, often at the time of the first drink and then progressively so as the illness develops.

One of the earliest signs of alcoholism may be that the use of alcohol precedes, rather than accompanies, a person's having a good time, and that social events become occasions for him to continue to drink and to excess. Alcohol gradually seems required for real pleasure and enjoyment, and the alcoholic ensures having enough by "fortifying" himself with it before leaving for a party. . . . Soon he finds other reasons for using it, such as coping with stress and anxiety. The frequency and degree of his intoxication increase and are at times highly inappropriate to the circumstances. He may become severely intoxicated quite unintentionally, but with greater and greater frequency. He is likely to show irritation and annoyance with those commenting on his intake and associated behavior, especially if they express concern.

In the second major phase of advancement the alcoholic begins drinking surreptitiously, faster and earlier, and becomes intoxicated regularly. Drinks are gulped down, while more (but less valid) reasons are given for having a few. Along with his growing preoccupation with alcohol he starts to feel unmistakable guilt, leading him to make excuses and to "justify" his drinking. He typically becomes even more defensive about his drinking pattern and often is openly hostile and angry when it is so much as alluded to. Not infrequently his own concern will have reached the point where he tries to regain control by changing brands or types of beverage, seeking other company, rationing his in-take, or limiting his drinking to specific times of the day. He may even "swear off" to prove he can "take it or leave it." Unfortunately at about this time he may try to achieve abstinence by substituting other drugs for alcohol such as barbiturates or amphetamines. These he may take alone, concurrently or com-bined with alcohol.

The alcoholic next loses control over his drinking and fre-quently drinks to a point of serious intoxication and stupor. Drinking no longer serves its original purposes but now grad-ually becomes an instrument of destruction. He begins to plan his life around alcohol, taking pains to guarantee a supply, seek-ing excuses to leave work or escape others in order to maintain his intake. Supplementation with other drugs increases.

Not uncommonly he drops old friends or quits employers, perhaps sensing their impending rejection. He softens the blows by abandoning them first, and replacing them with inferior sub-stitutes. Marital and family problems are compounded; arrests for drunkenness or drunken driving may occur; and social, oc-cupational, mental and moral disintegration commonly take place, as the alcoholic seeks greater isolation. Tolerance to alcohol is usually lost progressively, and the more serious physical com-plications of the disease often begin to predominate over the psychiatric and social ones. Finally he "reaches bottom."

The American Medical Association then provides a checklist for doctors, summing up when a patient should be suspected as an alcoholic. The list of thirteen points grows ever more serious as it reflects the progression of the disease and the increasing disruption of the alcoholic's life.

1. Increasing consumption of alcohol, whether on a regular or sporadic basis, with frequent and perhaps unintended episodes of intoxication.
2. Drinking as a means of handling problems or relieving symp-toms.
3. Obvious preoccupation with alcohol and the expressed need to have a drink, especially if habitually repeated.

4. Surreptitious drinking or gulping of drinks.
5. Tendency toward making alibis and weak excuses for drinking.
6. Refusal to concede what is obviously excessive consumption and expressing annoyance when the subject is mentioned.
7. Frequent absenteeism from the job, especially if occurring in a pattern, such as following weekends and holidays (Monday morning "flu").
8. Repeated changes in jobs, particularly if to successively lower levels, or employment in a capacity beneath ability, education and background.
9. Shabby appearance, poor hygiene, and behavior and social adjustment inconsistent with previous levels or expectations.
10. Persistent vague somatic complaints without apparent cause, particularly those of insomnia, gastrointestinal difficulties, headaches, anorexia.
11. Multiple contacts with the health care system with disorders that are alcohol caused or related.
12. Persistent marital and family problems, perhaps with multiple marriages.
13. History of arrests for drunkenness or drunken driving.

Every person who is worried about his or her drinking has tried to control it—tried, in short, to drink like other people. As set forth in A.A.'s Big Book, these are some of the most popular methods tried: drinking beer or wine only, limiting the number of drinks, never drinking alone, never drinking in the morning, drinking only at home, never having it in the house, never drinking during business hours, drinking only at parties, switching from Scotch to brandy, agreeing to resign if ever drunk on the job, taking a trip, not taking a trip, swearing off forever, taking more physical exercise, reading inspirational books, going to health farms and sanitariums, accepting voluntary commitment to psychiatric hospitals . . . the list could go on forever.

In 1958, in her *New Primer on Alcoholism,* Marty Mann set forth a classic test on controlled drinking. It is as revealing today as it was a generation ago. Here is an excerpt from the passage about what is commonly known among alcoholism experts as The Test:

It has been my experience, working in the field of alcoholism, that many heavy drinkers, and even social drinkers, are sometimes concerned about their own drinking. To such people, and to any alcoholics who may exist among them, I would say only this: Try your control against your drinking. If you are not an alcoholic, you are bound to win. Many people do this for the assurance it gives them that they are safe to continue enjoying a drink when they want one. Don't make the mistake of testing yourself by "going on the wagon." That is no test, because even the most advanced alcoholic can do that for quite a considerable time.

She went on to say that "even an extremely heavy drinker" should have no trouble in passing the test, "whereas an alcoholic, if able to complete it at all, could do so only under such heavy pressure that his life would be more miserable than he thinks it would be if he stopped drinking altogether. The chances are a hundred to one, however, against a true alcoholic's being either willing or able to undertake the test." Nonetheless, thousands of worried drinkers have tried it.

The Test: Select any time at all for starting. Now is the best time. For the next six months *at least,* decide that you will stick to a certain number of drinks a day, that number to be not less than one and not more than three.

If you are not a daily drinker, then the test should be the stated number of drinks from one to three, on those days when you do drink. Some heavy drinkers confine their drinking to weekends but still worry about the amount they consume then.

Whatever number of drinks you choose—from one to three, remember—must not be exceeded under any circumstances whatever, and this includes weddings, births, funerals, occasions of sudden death and disaster, unexpected or long-awaited inheritance, promotion, or other happy events, reunions or meetings with old friends or good customers, or just sheer boredom.

There must also be no special occasions on which you feel justified adding to your quota of the stated number of drinks, such as a severe emotional upset, or the appointment to close the biggest deal of your career, or the audition you've been waiting for all your life, or the meeting with someone who is crucial to your future and of whom you are terrified.

Absolutely no exceptions, or the test has been failed.

This is not an easy test, but it has been passed handily by many, many drinkers who wished to show themselves, or their family and friends, that they were not compulsive drinkers. As Mann wrote:

If by any chance they failed the test, showing that they were alcoholics, they showed themselves, too, that they were, whether they were then ready to admit it openly or not. At least it prepared them for such an admission, and for the constructive action which normally follows that admission.

It is important to add that observers of such tests should not use them to try to force a flunkee to premature action. This may well backfire and produce a stubborn determination on the part of the one who has been unable to pass the test to prove that it is not alcoholism that caused the failure. He can and does do this in several ways: by stopping drinking altogether for a self-specified time (when this is over he usually breaks out in even worse form than before, and with an added resentment toward those who "drove" him to it); by instituting a rigid control over his own drinking, which produces a constant irritability that makes him impossible to be with . . . or by giving himself a very large quota and insisting that he has remained within it, even when he was obviously too drunk to remember how many drinks he had. . . .

The backfiring from too great outside pressure may also cause a complete collapse: Knowing and admitting that he cannot pass the test and is therefore an alcoholic, he will resist efforts to force him to take action by saying in effect, "So I'm an alcoholic, so I can't control my drinking, so I'll drink as I must, and go all out for perdition." This last, despite the expressed concern of some people (who believe that admitting alcoholism to be a disease, and alcoholic drinking to be uncontrollable drinking, is simply to give alcoholics a good excuse to continue), very rarely happens. Nevertheless the possibility must be taken into account by those who are trying to help an alcoholic to recognize his trouble and take constructive action on it. If he [the alcoholic] is left alone after failing such a self-taken test, the failure will begin to work on him—it has planted a seed of knowledge which may well grow into action.

But before anything happens, the alcoholic must admit that drinking is ruining his life—not just his health, as in cigarette-smoking, but his life, and the quality of that life. He will deny it to the end, until desperate enough to seek help. That is the reason that alcoholism is so often called the disease of denial. Denial means lying—to yourself and to others.

Dr. Le Clair Bissell, a medical doctor who is a leading authority on treating alcoholics, broke down the mental, physical and social process of denial that prevents the alcoholic from recognizing that he or she is sick. She listed nine kinds of denial. They are:

1. The simple lie about your drinking—to get people off your back. You'll never admit how much you drank last night if you think you're going to be bawled out about it.
2. Unconscious denial—a psychological defense mechanism. Suppose you had done something terribly painful, like making a sexual advance to your child or a pass at your boss's wife while drunk. You just repress it utterly; it didn't happen.
3. Rationalization and wishful thinking: You must have mixed wine with rye last night; or, you took antihistamines with alcohol. That's why you pissed on your neighbor's lawn.
4. Blackouts—forgetting all or parts of conversations or actions the night before while drinking. You might not have looked or acted drunk. This kind of forgetting should not be confused with passing out, which most people associate with the word *blackout*.

5. Euphoric recall—the accurate remembering, while sober, of an inaccurate perception, while drunk. For example: You were telling a story at the party. You were the life of the party. Actually, you were making an ass of yourself. You saw yourself as charming, and nobody will tell you anything different. What you remember is absolutely accurate—that you told a story. But your perception is wrong.

6. Inaccurate feedback: The rest of the world won't tell you that you were drunk, that you made an ass of yourself. If a drunk is told that, his response may well be, "You're the only one who criticized me."

7. Interference with recent memory: Alcohol causes brain damage, usually temporary, sometimes permanent. It impairs both the ability to concentrate and to analyze.

8. Learning impairment: You do not learn well when you are tranquilized. The reverse happens during a highly emotionally charged event. Where were you when John Kennedy was shot? Everybody remembers; they were traumatized. But if you're full of booze or Valium, there is no emotional zing to real-life events; your feelings are muffled.

9. Simple ignorance about the disease of alcoholism: You believe such widespread myths as "A nun cannot be an alcoholic"; "A Jew cannot be an alcoholic."

Dr. Bissell pointed out, "You've got to break through all those kinds of denials to get somebody to admit that he's an alcoholic. Plus, you've got the family's denial. Plus society's denial. Society is doing the same kind of enabling that the nuclear family is doing. Society is already quarantining smokers. But society won't touch an alcoholic except when he's a drunk driver, or he's under eighteen years old."

What can people who think they may be alcoholic do for themselves?

They can talk to somebody—break out of that prison of loneliness and fear and shame. They are lucky that their disease happens to be alcoholism because there is so much help out there.

They are lucky also that it can be arrested—at once—by stopping drinking.

Pick up the phone and call Alcoholics Anonymous. It is listed in the telephone directory of every big city in America. The man or woman on the other end of the phone, a recovered alcoholic, will listen carefully and then reach another recovered alcoholic who can talk to you within minutes or hours by phone, or, this very day, in person.

If you are not comfortable with the thought of going directly to A.A., talk with a trusted member of the clergy; with your doctor or psychotherapist; with a social worker; with a friend you feel will not judge you but is likely to be honest with you; with your husband, wife or lover. The point is, you *must* talk about it; your burden is too great to be borne alone.

Talk to someone without a drink in you. If you are high or drunk, it will be the bottle talking, not you, and you will not clearly absorb what someone else is saying.

If you are in therapy, your aim should not be to discover *why* you drink. You drink, and you have used alcohol to blunt and cover up your problems, to run away from them, to anesthetize yourself. First, you get sober. Then you confront your problems with a clear mind.

Listen to the doctors in the American Medical Association's *Manual on Alcoholism:*

> In the achievement of abstinence, there needs to be a here and now, goal-directed, no-nonsense approach. The patient, in his need to protect his drinking style, may try to lead the psychotherapy into endless pursuit of neurotic roots which provide him with a cover for his continued drinking. The psychotherapist, acknowledging that there may be neurotic roots worthy of pursuit, gives these a later time for attention—after abstinence has been accomplished.

Friends and family can help, particularly if they are informed. But in the end, the decision to stop drinking is up to the alcoholic.

Of course you are afraid. You are afraid that you cannot live without alcohol. You are afraid that you will never have fun anymore, never enjoy a party, never be comfortable with yourself or with others who can drink socially. You are afraid you will be thought "different" if you take drinks that do not have booze in them. None of this is true for long. First, remember that *nobody* at the party is interested in what you have in your glass. Other people are interested only in what they have in their own glass. This is sharply different from attitudes about what people eat, as any dieter can attest. If you turn down any part of a meal served at home, many hosts perceive this abstention as a slur on their cooking.

Are you afraid that your friends may pity you or laugh at you or urge you to have just one drink? In this case, they are not your friends—these are cruel and hostile reactions to a recovering alcoholic. Also, the chances are good that such "friends" have a drinking problem themselves.

Are you afraid that you are weak? Ashamed that your willpower is not strong enough for you to stop drinking by yourself? Try feeling the reverse. Try being ashamed that you are not seeking help for your illness. Are you afraid that you are insane? Many alcoholics have secretly feared that they are mentally disturbed. They can go for years, masking their growing fears by drinking even more. Remember that alcohol affects the central nervous system—it distorts personality, perception, intelligence, common sense. No wonder you think you may be crazy; certainly your brain is impaired by drinking—and that means everybody, no matter how well you think you hold your liquor.

Have you told yourself: "Okay, it's a disease, I can't help myself, so I'll keep on drinking"? Or are you asking yourself: "Am I sick and tired of being sick and tired?"

If you are an alcoholic, or suspect you may be one, turn to another human being. You cannot hope to solve your problem alone. The sooner you seek help, the better for you, and for those you love. There are people out there who want to help you. They are listed in the section called "Where to Find Help" on page 271.

All it takes is one step, one telephone call, one conversation to begin the process of healing. You need never be alone again. You will be free.

# APPENDICES

WHERE TO FIND HELP

NOTES AND SOURCES

ACKNOWLEDGMENTS

# WHERE
# TO FIND HELP

You will find "Alcoholics Anonymous" listed in the telephone books of almost every city and town in the United Kingdom and in every major foreign city. The person at the other end of the line will be a recovered alcoholic in A.A. He or she can tell you the times and places of the meetings nearest your home or office—or hotel, if you are an out-of-town visitor.

If it is an emergency, the A.A. member on the phone will make every attempt to find another member who can call you back or talk to you in person and take you to an A.A. meeting. This service is for alcoholics only, both those still drinking and those sober in A.A.

For information and literature about what Alcoholics Anonymous is and does, write to A.A.'s world headquarters at this address:

**Alcoholics Anonymous**
Post Office Box 459
Grand Central Station
New York, N.Y. 10163-1100

Families and friends of alcoholics should look for "Al-Anon Family Groups" in their local telephone directories. If only "Alcoholics Anonymous" is listed, call that number; the A.A. member who answers should have the telephone numbers of Al-Anon contacts.

Al-Anon, like A.A., also runs citywide telephone centers. Members will offer information on the phone about local Al-Anon meetings and, in an emergency, attempt to find help for the caller. This service is solely for the families and friends of alcoholics, not for alcoholics themselves.

# APPENDICES

For information and literature about Al-Anon and Alateen (its auxiliary for adolescent children of alcoholics), what they are and what they do, write to Al-Anon's world headquarters at:

**Al-Anon Family Group Headquarters**
Post Office Box 862
Midtown Station
New York, N.Y. 10018-0862

Or you can reach Al-Anon in almost any place in the world by writing to Al-Anon Family Group Headquarters or telephoning 010 1 212 302-7240 to request its worldwide directory, *Getting in Touch with Al-Anon/Alateen*.

Below are listed addresses and telephone numbers of self-help groups and agencies throughout the world. By the time you are reading this book, some of them may have changed. If so, simply look in the phone book or call Directory Enquiries for the new number.

## Great Britain

**Alcoholics Anonymous**, PO Box 1, Stonebow House, Stonebow, York YO1 2NJ. Tel: 0904 644026/7/8/9. A.A. is for anybody who wants to stop drinking. There are local offices in many areas, so consult your local phone book.

**Al-Anon Family Groups**, 61 Great Dover Street, London SE1 4YF. Tel: 01-403 0888. Al-Anon is for anybody who has a relative or friend with a drinking problem. It can help those adults who grew up in an alcoholic home. Alateen, its branch for teenagers, helps young people whose parents or relatives have a drinking problem. Local phone books may have a number. A.A. offices usually will pass this on, if it is not in the book.

**Narcotics Anonymous**, PO Box 246, London SW10. Tel: 01-351 6794. N.A. is for anybody who wants to stop using drugs—no matter who they are or what drug they are using, including legally prescribed drugs like tranquillisers and sleeping pills.

**Families Anonymous**, 88 Caledonian Road, London N1 9DN. Tel: 01-278 8805. F.A. is for anybody with a relative or friend who is using drugs, including prescribed drugs and glue sniffing. F.A. will help those who are not yet sure if the problem is one of drugs.

**St Bernard's Hospital**, Ealing Health Authority, Uxbridge Road, Southall UB1 3EU. NHS hospital.

**Warlingham Park Hospital**, Warlingham, Surrey. NHS hospital.

**Farm Place**, Ockley, Surrey RH5 5NG. Tel: 030679 742 (in-patients); 39 Upper Grosvenor Street, London W1. Tel: 01-491 8409 (out-patients). Alcoholism and addiction treatment.

## Other agencies

**Standing Conference on Drug Abuse**, 1–4 Hatton Place, Hatton Garden, London EC1N 8ND. Tel: 01-430 2341. SCODA can supply a list of hospitals which provide a service for drug users, a list of residential rehabilitation places for drug users, and a list of advisory services and day projects for drug users. Send a large stamped addressed envelope for these.

# APPENDICES

### Republic of Ireland

**Alcoholics Anonymous,** 109 South Circular Road, Dublin 8. Tel: Dublin 538998 (9a.m.–5p.m. Mon.–Fri.); at other times 774809/714050.

**Al-Anon,** 61 Great Dover Street, London SE1 4YF. Tel: 01-403 0888. The London office deals with enquiries about meetings in Eire.

**Narcotics Anonymous,** PO Box 1368, Sherriff Street, Dublin 1. No Dublin phone number was available in 1985. Phone London N.A. office on 01-351 6794 for details of local meetings.

**Families Anonymous,** 88 Caledonian Road, London N1 9DN. Tel: 01-278 8805 for details of meetings in Eire. In 1985 there were F.A. meetings in Dublin, though the central office was in London.

### Australia

**Narcotics Anonymous:** PO Box 440, Leichandt, New South Wales 2040. Tel: 02-810 2020. There are also other N.A. offices in other major cities, so check your phone directory to see if there is one near you.

**Alcoholics Anonymous,** PO Box 5321, Sydney, New South Wales 2001. Tel: 02-290 2210. Also many local A.A. offices.

**Families Anonymous.** There is no general office, but in 1985 there was an F.A. meeting being held in Melbourne. Up-to-date information from Families Anonymous, PO Box 528, Van Nuys, California 91408.

**Nar Anon,** PO Box Q108, Queen Victoria Building, Sydney, New South Wales 2000. Tel: 02-300 9736. Nar-Anon is another organisation for the families of those addicted to drugs.

**Al-Anon Family Groups,** PO Box 1002H, Melbourne, Victoria 3001. Tel: 03-62 4933.

*Other agencies*

In so far as there is a national organisation, it is the **Alcohol and Drug Foundation,** PO Box 477, Canberra City, ACT 2601. There are plans for an emergency phone service in all capital cities in the future with a national (008) number.

In addition there are the following state organisations:

*New South Wales*
**Alcohol and Drug Information Service,** St Vincent's Hospital, Sydney. Tel: 02-331 2111. 24-hour service of advice and referral.
**New South Wales Drug and Alcohol Authority,** Level 14, McKell Building, Rawson Place, Sydney, New South Wales 2000.

*Victoria*
**Victorian Foundation on Alcohol and Drug Dependence,** PO Box 529, South Melbourne 3205.

*Queensland*
**Alcohol and Drug Dependence Services,** "Biala", 270 Roma Street, Brisbane, Queensland 4000.

# APPENDICES

*South Australia*
**Drug and Alcohol Services Council**, 161 Greenhill Road, Parkside, South Australia 5063.

*Western Australia*
**Western Australian Alcohol and Drug Authority**, Salvatori House, 36 Outram Street, West Perth 6005.

*Northern Territory*
**Northern Territory Drug and Alcohol Bureau**, PO Box 1701, Darwin 5794.

## New Zealand

**Narcotics Anonymous.** PO Box 2858, Christchurch. No fixed telephone number at the time of this book's publication in 1986. Check in your local phone book. Sometimes A.A. offices have an N.A. contact number. Or get in touch with the Narcotics Anonymous head office, 16155 Wyandotte Street, Van Nuys, California 91406. Or telephone the N.A. Australasian region head office in Australia: 02-810 2020.

**Alcoholics Anonymous,** PO Box 6458, Wellington, NI. Tel: 859 455.

**Families Anonymous.** In 1985 there were not yet meetings of F.A. in New Zealand. For up-to-date information write to Families Anonymous, PO box 528, Van Nuys, California 91408. If your addict uses alcohol (and most do) you can get help from Al-Anon.

**Al-Anon,** Suite no 4, Charter House, 56 Customs Street, Auckland. Tel: Auckland 794–871.

*Other agencies*

**The Drugs Advisory Committee,** Department of Health, Macarthy Trust Building, Lambton Quay, Wellington. Tel: 727 627. This committee advises the Minister of Health on drug abuse. It has a list of treatment and rehabilitation centres.

## South Africa

**Narcotics Anonymous.** In 1986 there were reports of a very small N.A. community in South Africa, but without an office. The main office of Alcoholics Anonymous may have a contact. If not, contact the N.A. World Service Office, 16155 Wyandotte Street, Van Nuys, California 91406.

**Alcoholics Anonymous,** PO Box 23005. Joubert Park 2044. Tel: 23 7219.

**Families Anonymous.** In 1985 there were no F.A. meetings yet in South Africa. For up-to-date information write to Families Anonymous, PO Box 528, Van Nuys, California 91408. If your addict uses alcohol (and most do) you can get help from Al-Anon.

**Al-Anon,** PO Box 2077, Johannesburg, Transvaal 2000. Tel: 011 29 6696.

*Other agencies*
**South African National Council on Alcoholism and Drug Dependence,** Happiness House, corner Loveday and Wolmarans Street, Johannesburg 2001. Tel: 011 725-5810.

# NOTES AND SOURCES

This book is largely based on my direct observation and experience, first as a recovered alcoholic, a member and meeting-goer in Alcoholics Anonymous since 1975, and then, since I began my research four years ago, as a reporter. It is a peculiarity of the book and a sadness for me that I cannot properly credit nearly as many people as I would like among the hundreds that I interviewed during the last four years. Those I am not able to thank as I would wish in public are members of A.A. and their families in Al-Anon.

In accordance with a tradition of the two societies, these sources have remained anonymous. The nonalcoholics I have thanked in print with their full names in the "Acknowledgments" section are only a fraction of those who gave me their thoughts, trust and experience. To all of them, both named and unnamed, I am everlastingly grateful.

The archives of Alcoholics Anonymous were opened to me and proved very useful in the research for my history chapters: "Two Men" and "The Early Christians." The two authorized biographies of A.A.'s founders, Bill Wilson and Dr. Bob Smith, were excellent resources.

A.A. and Al-Anon literature is usually not available in outside bookstores. The "conference-approved" books, booklets, and pamphlets of these two organizations may be ordered from their New York headquarters. The headquarters addresses are listed in the "Where to Find Help" section.

A.A.'s authorized books were crucial to my research. All were published by A.A. World Services, Inc., which keeps its authors anonymous. The conference-approved books are:

*Alcoholics Anonymous* (the Big Book), the basic text of A.A., first published in 1939. More than five million copies have been sold to A.A. members, about 800,000 of them in 1986. All but the "Personal Stories" chapters were written by Bill Wilson.

*Twelve Steps and Twelve Traditions* ("the 12 and 12"), 1953. Also by Wilson, this book of interpretative essays on the A.A. program for recovery is the second most-read volume within A.A., often discussed point by point in "Step" meetings. A total of 400,000 copies was sold last year.

*Alcoholics Anonymous Comes of Age*, 1957. Wilson was the author of this brief history of A.A. up to 1955.

*As Bill Sees It*, 1967, a selection of Wilson's musings in print on topics ranging from hatred to sex.

*Dr. Bob and the Good Oldtimers*, 1980. The conference-approved biography of A.A.'s co-founder, Dr. Robert Holbrook Smith.

*Best of the Grapevine*, 1985, a sampling of more than forty years of A.A.'s monthly magazine, which its editors call "a meeting in print."

A.A.'s conference-approved booklets are:

*Living Sober*, 1975. A practical and deservedly popular volume, it sets forth some methods A.A. members have used for not drinking and for learning to enjoy a sober life of quality.
*Came to Believe . . .*, 1973. Spiritual experiences of seventy-five A.A. members.

In addition, A.A. publishes more than forty pamphlets, most of them helpful to me in my research. They offer the reader information on many aspects of alcoholism and A.A. Titles include: *A.A. and the Armed Services, A.A. for the Woman, A.A. in Your Community, A.A. in Prisons, A.A. in Treatment Centers, The A.A. Member—Medication and Other Drugs, A Brief Guide to Alcoholics Anonymous, A Clergyman Asks About A.A., The Co-Founders of Alcoholics Anonymous, Do You Think You're Different?, 44 Questions, How It Works, Inside A.A., Is A.A. for You?, Member's-Eye View of A.A., A Newcomer Asks, Problems Other Than Alcohol, This Is A.A., Time to Start Living* (for older alcoholics), and *Too Young?* (for younger alcoholics).

I found the following nonauthorized books on A.A. of use:

Kurtz, Ernest, *Not-God: A History of Alcoholics Anonymous*, 1979, Hazelden Educational Materials, Center City, Minn.
Maxwell, Milton A. *The AA Experience: An Inside View for Professionals*, 1980, 1984, McGraw-Hill Book Company, New York.
Thomsen, Robert. *Bill W.*, 1975, Harper & Row, New York.

Conference-approved books for Al-Anons and Alateens were also important for my research in printed materials. They are all published by and available from Al-Anon Family Group Headquarters in New York. (The address is in "Where to Find Help" section.) The books are:

*Al-Anon Family Groups*, formerly titled *Living with an Alcoholic*.

Al-Anon's Big Book, its central text, it was first published in 1966 by Al-Anon Family Group Headquarters.

*Al-Anon Faces Alcoholism*, 1965. Essays on Al-Anon by its members and by professionals who work in the family and alcoholism treatment fields.

*The Dilemma of the Alcoholic Marriage*, 1971. How alcoholism distorts the life of an alcoholic's spouse, and what to do about it.

*One Day at a Time in Al-Anon* (called ODAT.) Twentieth printing, April 1986. A pocket-sized volume of daily readings, ODAT is unquestionably the best-selling, best-loved text in Al-Anon.

*Forum Favorites*, 1970, selections from Al-Anon's monthly magazine.

*Lois Remembers*, 1979, the autobiography of Lois Wilson, co-founder of Al-Anon and wife of the co-founder of A.A., Bill Wilson.

*Al-Anon's Twelve Steps and Twelve Traditions*. (The Al-Anon "12 and 12," adapted from A.A.'s model.)

*First Steps: Al-Anon . . . 35 Years of Beginnings*, 1986, Al-Anon's official history book.

*Alateen—Hope for Children of Alcoholics*, 1973.

*Alateen—A Day at a Time*, 1983.

There are two cassettes available from Al-Anon, one video, one audio. They are:

*Al-Anon Speaks for Itself*, 1986 (video).
*Alateens Tell It Like It Is*, 1984 (audio).

Al-Anon publishes about fifty excellent conference-approved or "official" pamphlets, many very useful in my research. The titles include: *Alcoholism: A Merry-Go-Round Named Denial, A Guide for the Family of the Alcoholic, Al-Anon: Is It for You?, Alcoholism: The Family Disease, Al-Anon: Family Treatment Tool in Alcoholism, Freedom from Despair, So You Love an Alcoholic, Al-Anon Is for Men, Information for the Newcomer, My Wife Drinks Too Much, Facts About Alateen, How Can I Help My Children?* and *Did You Grow Up with a Problem Drinker?*

I found the following books pertinent to the Children of Alcoholics Movement and helpful in my research:

Ackerman, Robert J., *Children of Alcoholics: A Bibliography and Resource Guide,* 1987, Health Communications, Inc., Pompano Beach, Fla.

Brooks, Cathleen, *The Secret Everyone Knows,* 1981, Joan B. Kroc Foundation, Operation Cork, San Diego, Calif.

*Children of Alcoholics: A Review of the Literature,* 1985, Children of Alcoholics Foundation, New York.

Deutsch, Charles, *Broken Bottles, Broken Dreams: Understanding and Helping the Children of Alcoholics,* 1982, Teachers College Press, New York.

Gravitz, Herbert L., *Children of Alcoholics Handbook: Who They Are, What They Experience, How They Recover,* 1985, National Association for Children of Alcoholics, South Laguna Beach, Calif.

Seixas, Judith A., and Youcha, Geraldine, *Children of Alcoholism: A Survivor's Manual,* 1985, Crown Publishers, New York.

Seixas, Judith A., *Living with a Parent Who Drinks Too Much,* 1979, Greenwillow Books, a division of William Morrow & Company, Inc., New York.

O'Gorman, Patricia, and Oliver-Diaz, Philip, *Breaking the Cycle of Addiction: A Parent's Guide to Raising Healthy Kids,* 1987, Health Communications, Inc., Pompano Beach, Fla.

Woititz, Janet Geringer, *Adult Children of Alcoholics,* 1983, Health Communications, Inc., Pompano Beach, Fla.

My shelves now contain dozens of books on the general subject of alcoholism. Those that have proved central to my research are the following:

American Medical Association, *Manual on Alcoholism,* 1968, third edition, 1977. Copies available from Order Department, American Medical Association, Monroe, Wis.

Blume, Sheila B., M.D., *The Disease Concept of Alcoholism Today,* 1983, Perganon Press. Reprinted by Johnson Institute, Minneapolis, Minn.

Goodwin, Donald, M.D., *Is Alcoholism Hereditary?*, 1976, Oxford University Press, New York.

Jellinek, E. M., *The Disease Concept of Alcoholism*, 1960, College and University Press, New Haven, Conn., in association with Hillhouse Press, New Brunswick, N.J.

Johnson, Vernon E., *I'll Quit Tomorrow: A Practical Guide to Alcoholism Treatment*, revised edition, 1980, Harper & Row, New York.

Johnson, Vernon E., *Intervention: How to Help Someone Who Doesn't Want Help*, 1986, Johnson Institute, Minneapolis, Minn.

Lender, Mark Edward, and Martin, James Kirby, *Drinking in America: A History*, 1982, The Free Press, a division of Macmillan Publishing Co., New York.

Mann, Marty, *Marty Mann Answers Your Questions about Drinking and Alcoholism*, 1970 by Marty Mann, 1981 by the Estate of Marty Mann, Holt, Rinehart and Winston, New York.

Mann, Marty, *New Primer on Alcoholism*, 1950, 1958, Holt, Rinehart and Winston, New York and Canada, Limited.

O'Brien, Robert, and Chafetz, Morris, M.D., *The Encyclopedia of Alcoholism*, 1982, Facts on File Publications, New York.

Vaillant, George E., *The Natural History of Alcoholism*, 1983, Harvard University Press, Cambridge, Mass., and London, England.

Wholey, Dennis, *The Courage to Change: Personal Conversations About Alcoholism with Dennis Wholey*, 1984, Houghton Mifflin Company, Boston.

# ACKNOWLEDGMENTS

First and always, to the memory of Anna L., my sponsor and dearest friend in A.A.

In gratitude to three physicians who gave a positive direction to my life: LeClair Bissell, Ruth Fox and Fred Plum.

My deepest thanks to Lucy Kroll, my literary agent, sensitive mentor and friend, and to Martin Garbus, my wise and humane lawyer.

As for Tom Congdon, my superb editor and teacher on the writing of a book, my thanks are mixed with awe. His intelligence and perception do honor to his craft and illuminate every page of this manuscript.

The following people and groups were particularly helpful in my research: The staffs of anonymous alcoholics at the General Service Office of A.A. and the anonymous family members at Al-Anon's World Service Office, all in New York. The staffs at A.A. and Al-Anon national headquarters in Mexico. Loren Archer, deputy director of the U.S. government's National Institute on Alcohol Abuse and Alcoholism in Washington, D.C. Dr. Henri Begleiter. Keven Bellows. Dr. Sheila Blume. Cathleen Brooks of the National Association for Children of Alcoholics.

At the Betty Ford Center in Rancho Mirage, California, my thanks to Betty Ford, John T. Schwarzlose and Susan Stevens. To Lucinda Franks. Also to Dr. Donald W. Goodwin of the University of Kansas Medical Center, and to Dr. Enoch Gordis, director of the NIAAA. At the Hazelden Foundation in Center City, Minnesota, Daniel J. Anderson, the Reverend Gordon Grimm and Damian McElrath. To the staff of High Watch in Kent, Connecticut. To Joan K. Jackson, a trustee of A.A. To Jay Lewis, editor of *The Alcoholism Report*. To Dennis Manders, former comptroller of A.A. and to his wife, Doris. To Patricia Matson.

To the staff of the National Council on Alcoholism in New York. To Dr. John Norris, former chairman of the board of A.A.; the late Robert O'Brien and his wife, Joyce. To Patricia O'Gorman. To Renah Rabinowitz, former director of the JACS Foundation in New York. At the Rutgers Center of Alcohol Studies in Piscataway, New Jersey, to Barbara McCrady, Gail Milgram, Peter Nathan and Penny Page.

To Dr. Marc A. Schuckit and Dorothy Seiberling. To the staff of the Family Treatment Center at Sharp Cabrillo Hospital in San Diego. To Dr. Max Schneider, president of the American Medical Society on Alcoholism and Other Drug Dependencies. To Robert Smith, the son of A.A.'s co-founder, Dr. Bob, and to his wife, Betty.

My deepest gratitude to the entire staff of the Rehabilitation Unit of the Smithers Alcoholism Center in New York, and to the director of the Smithers Alcoholism Treatment and Training Center, Dr. Anne Geller.

To Lois Wilson, the wife of A.A.'s co-founder, Bill Wilson. To Suzanne Windows, Dr. Bob's daughter, and to her husband, Ray. To Nell Wing, Bill Wilson's secretary and first archivist of Alcoholics Anonymous. To Geraldine Youcha.

And finally, to Nora Sayre and Rosanne Soffer, old friends and the earliest readers of this manuscript, whose unerring taste and judgment sustained and guided me.

# INDEX

A.A., *see* Alcoholics Anonymous

A.A. *Experience, The* (Maxwell), 120–123

A.A. *Grapevine,* 38, 80–81, 89–90, 102, 107–108

A.A. *Service Manual,* 102, 103

A.A. World Services, 84, 103

abstinence, 95, 120, 185, 189, 192
  pregnancy and, 198
  Rand Report view of, 192

ACAs, *see* Adult Children of Alcoholics

ACOAs, *see* Adult Children of Alcoholics

Adler, Ruth, 234

adoption, genetics of alcoholism and, 204, 206–207

Adult Children of Alcoholics (ACAs; ACOAs; COAs), 176–182
  Al-Anon's views of, 178, 179
  information sources on, 272–273
  meetings of, 177–179

*Adult Children of Alcoholics* (Woititz), 177

agnosticism, in A.A., 145–146, 148

Akron, Ohio, 29–34, 37, 38, 46–55, 58, 61–65
  A.A. in, 18, 20, 21–22
  Al-Anon in, 167–169
  City Hospital in, 21, 32, 48, 52, 54–55, 62–63

Al-Anon, 17, 23, 102, 128, 155–181
  A.A. members' suspicions about, 160–161
  credo of, 155
  enablers and, 156–157
  founding of, 159–161
  information on, 272, 273–274
  meetings of, 160–161, 164–171, 175–176
  membership changes in, 163–164
  naming of, 160
  Preamble of, 166
  publicizing of, 162–163
  publishing operation of, 171–173
  size of, 155
  Welcome of, 166
  World Service Office of, 163, 165, 172

*Al-Anon Faces Alcoholism,* 165, 172, 193

*Al-Anon Family Groups (Living with an Alcoholic),* 163, 172

Al-Anon Information Services, 165

Al-Anon International Convention (1985), 88

*Al-Anon Speaks for Itself* (videocassette), 164

Alateen (children of alcoholics), 20, 128, 163, 165, 172, 177, 178

information on, 272

*Alateen—Hope for Children of Alcoholics,* 172

alcohol:

addictiveness of, 57

history of use of, 185–186

hormones and, 198, 203

medical use of, 49

statistics on consumption of, 188–189

Alcoholic Foundation, 75, 76

founding of, 68

Union Club fundraiser for, 77–78

"alcoholic personality," Goodwin's views on, 200

"Alcoholics and God," 76

Alcoholics Anonymous (A.A.):

as anonymous program, 18, 71–72, 82, 89, 93, 105

author's experience with, 16–18, 230, 237–239, 246–249, 253

autonomy and decentralization in, 101–102

Big Book of, *see Alcoholics Anonymous*

Board of Trustees of, 103, 104

breakthroughs for, 76, 90–91

contribution restrictions and, 84, 100–101

definition of, 99

as drunk tank, 99

foreign contingents of, 18, 24–25, 88, 89, 91–93, 98–99, 101–102, 247–248

founding of, 17–21, 32–35, 54–55, 56–66, 190

growth of, 17, 38, 55, 76, 88, 90, 91

guidelines of, *see* Twelve Traditions

headquarters of, 76, 81, 82, 84, 93, 101–107

historic sites of, 21–22

information sources on, 271–274

international conferences of, 37, 83, 85, 87–88, 103

James's influence on, 60–61

leadership of, 83–85, 100–103, 104–105

love and service as essence of, 37, 131–132, 143–144

magazine of, *see A.A. Grapevine*

media support for, 75–76

meetings of, *see* meetings, A.A.

membership profile of, 89–90, 93–99

money-handling jobs in, 105–106

naming of, 38, 55, 69

nonalcoholic friends of, 21, 79, 107–108

nonrecruitment policy of, 99

as North American phenomenon, 91–92

Oxford Group's influence on, 56, 58–60, 62–67

poverty years of, 64–65

publishing empire of, 102–103

rehabilitation centers' effects on, 219–221

religion's role in, 17, 19, 55, 69–70, 81, 99–100, 138–151

Rockefeller funding of, 68, 76–78

salaried employees of, 104–106

as self-help, 112, 127–128

simplicity of, 37, 61, 109, 120

story-telling process of, 34, 125–126

structure of, 102–108
as substitute addiction, 135
success of, 38, 94–95, 112, 177, 192, 193
taboos in, 112–113
tolerance practiced in, 112–113
twenty-four-hour plan of, 120
women denied admission to, 37, 62, 158
women in, 72, 81–82, 87, 94, 135
*see also specific people and topics*
Alcoholics Anonymous (Big Book) (Wilson), 26, 28, 38, 60, 69–75, 128–129
first draft of, 69–71
foreword of, 71–72
"Personal Stories" in, 71, 73
price of, 73
radio publicity for, 74
religion and, 139, 141–143
reviews of, 73, 77
sales of, 73, 84
selection of title for, 72
"Spiritual Experience" appendix to, 141–142
"To Wives" chapter of, 70–71
"We Agnostics" chapter of, 141
alcoholism, alcoholics:
alcohol abusers vs., 209
AMA checklist on, 261–262
coining of word, 187
denial of, 265–266
detection of, 255–268
difficulty in admission of, 121–123
as disease, *see* disease concept of alcoholism
drug addiction combined with, 25–26, 94
emotional components of, 58, 81–82, 191–192, 193
enablers and, 156–157
family and, *see* family
genetic predisposition to, 95–96, 199, 201–208
heavy drinking vs., 40, 206, 263
information sources on, 271–274
involuntariness of, 191–192, 195–196
medical profession's concealment of, 52
1920s and 1930s cures for, 30–31, 43–44
number of people affected by, 156
paucity of information on, 56–57
physical results of, 198
problem drinking vs., 16, 255
progress of, 187–188, 260–262
punishment for, 224–225
risk period for development of, 206
Rush's views on, 57, 187–188
stigma of, 21, 31, 43, 185, 186–187, 189, 218, 224
treatment costs for, 221, 222
women, *see* women alcoholics
*see also specific groups*
Alcoholism, the Family Disease (Al-Anon pamphlet), 173
alcoholism rehabilitation centers, *see* rehabilitation centers
Alcoholismus Chronicus ("Chronic Alcoholism") (Huss), 187
Alexander, Jack, 90
ALMACA (Association of Labor-Management Administrators and Consultants on Alcoholism), 274
American Hospital Association, 194
American Medical Association (AMA), 91, 185, 194, 260–262, 267
American Medical Society on Alcoholism, 194–195
American Public Health Association, 90–91
Amos, Frank, 68

Anderson, Daniel J., 218–220, 224
anger, 215, 250, 253, 260
  of Adult Children of Alcoholics,
    178, 179, 181–182
Antabuse (disulfiram), 184, 242–
    244, 246
Archer, Loren, 209
*Around the Clock with A.A.*
    (pamphlet), 146–147
Association of Labor-Management
    Administrators and Con-
    sultants on Alcoholism
    (ALMACA), 274
atheists, in A.A., 144–146, 148,
    245
Auchincloss, Gordon, 77


Babylonians, alcohol records of,
    185
*Bacchae, The* (Euripedes), 185
Bacon, Selden, 220
Baron, Sheldon, 96
Begbie, Harold, 60
Begleiter, Henri, 203–204
Betty Ford Center, 25–26, 94, 219,
    222
Big Book, *see Alcoholics
    Anonymous*
biological factors in alcoholism, *see*
    genetic predisposition to
    alcoholism
Birnier, William A. H., 66–67
birth defects, alcohol-related, 198
Bissell, LeClair, 95, 210, 213
Black, Claudia, 177
blackouts, 44, 136, 185, 265
blacks, in A.A., 96–98
Blackwell, Edward, 73
Blakemore, John, 136
Block, Lawrence, 138
Block, Marvin, 194
Blume, Sheila B., 189–190,
    195–198
Board of Trustees, A.A., 103, 104

Brackett, Charles, 91
Bradley, Nelson J., 219
brain, 208
  of alcoholic vs. nonalcoholic
    children, 199, 203–204
  alcohol's damage to, 110, 198
Brazil, A.A. in, 92
Brown, Howard R., 233, 234
Buchman, Frank N. D., 58–59, 60,
    66–67
Buddhism, 185
Burnham, Dr., 42
Burnham, Lois, *see* Wilson, Lois
    Burnham
Burr and Burton Seminary, 39


Cabot, Godfrey L., 77
Caduceus group, 125
Caesar, Sid, 93
Cain, Arthur H., 105, 146
California, University of (Irvine),
    195
Canada:
  A.A. in, 92, 98–99, 101
  Al-Anon in, 156
Canty, J. W., 92
Carnegie Foundation, 190
Cathedral of St. John the Divine
    (New York City), 86–87
Central Harlem Sobering-Up
    Station, 24
Central Synagogue (New York
    City), 96
Chafetz, Morris, 186
Cherokee State Hospital, 144
children of alcoholics:
  genetic predisposition and, 95–
    96, 199, 201–208
  school-age, 223–224
  *see also* Adult Children of
    Alcoholics; Alateen
Children of Alcoholics Foundation,
    273
China, ancient, 185, 186

Chipman, A. LeRoy, 68
*Chronische Alkohols-Krankheit*
   ("Chronic Alcohol-Sickness")
   (Huss), 187
Churchill, Winston, 253
Church of the Heavenly Rest (New
   York City), 125
City Hospital (Akron, Ohio), 21,
   32, 48, 52, 54–55, 62–63
civil rights, 196
Clearing House, 161–162
Cleveland, Ohio, first international
   A.A. conference in, 37, 83
*Cleveland Plain Dealer*, 76
Cloninger, Robert, 202, 205,
   206–207
clothing, 124
COAs, *see* Adult Children of
   Alcoholics
Code of Hammurabi, 185
Cohen, Ira, 251
Cohen, Sidney, 222
"Come the Dawn" (Shoffstall), 168
Connecticut, University of,
   207–208
consciousness-raising groups, A.A
   compared to, 127
Coolidge, Calvin, 47
coordinators (staffers), 104–107
Cornwall Press, 73
corporate poverty philosophy, 101
*Courage to Change, The* (Wholey),
   93
crime, alcoholism treated as,
   224–225
"cucumber-into-pickle" analogy,
   209
cultural factors in alcoholism, 200,
   201
   *see also specific groups*

Dartmouth College, 47–48
*Days of Wine and Roses* (movie),
   91

*Days of Wine and Roses* (TV play),
   91
delirium, 44–45
denial of alcoholism, 265–266
Denmark, alcoholism research in,
   205–206
Denver, Colo., Al-Anon in, 169–
   171
Depression, Great, 42, 136, 157
Deutsch, Charles, 177, 224
*Dilemma of an Alcoholic Marriage,
   The*, 172
disease concept of alcoholism, 21,
   82, 90, 130, 183–209
   advantages of, 195–196
   "allergy" view and, 31, 43, 58,
      82
   AMA and, 91, 185, 194
   ancient view of, 185
   arguments against, 196–198
   Goodwin's views on, 200
   guilt and, 195–196, 197
   involuntariness and, 191–192,
      195–196
   Jellinek and, 185, 190–192, 196–
      197, 198
   medical training and, 193–195
   political and social objections to,
      197–198
   Rush and, 57, 187–188, 189,
      191, 198
   Silkworth's views on, 43–44, 46,
      58
   Sister Francis and, 28
   social usefulness of, 196
   temperance movement as in-
      fluence on decline of,
      189–190
*Disease Concept of Alcoholism, The*
   (Jellinek), 185, 190, 191
*Disease Concept of Alcoholism
   Today, The* (Blume),
   189–190
disulfiram (Antabuse), 184, 242–
   244, 246

Dowling, Edward, 79
drinking:
  excessive, alcoholism vs.,
    196–197
  heavy, 39, 206, 263
  problem, 16, 255
  stopping of, vs. reason for,
    110–111
  see also alcoholism, alcoholics
Drinking in America (Lender and
    Martin), 187, 188
drug addiction, drugs, 36, 45, 140,
    190, 261
  alcohol abuse compared with,
    156, 208
  alcoholism combined with,
    25–26, 94
drunk driving, 196, 197, 198, 228
drunk tank, 31, 210–225
  A.A. as, 99
  see also rehabilitation centers
Dundy, Elaine, 86

East Dorset, Vt., 38–39, 85
Ebby T. (Bill Wilson's friend), 39,
    44, 60, 65, 139
Egypt, ancient, 186
Eighteenth Amendment, 190
Ellison, Jerome, 105
Employee Assistance Programs
    (EAPs), 196, 221–222
  information sources for, 274
enablers, 156–157
Encyclopedia of Alcoholism, The
    (O'Brien and Chafetz, eds.),
    186, 255
environment, alcoholism and, 199,
    204–207
euphoriants, natural, 198
Euripedes, 185
Evans, Helen, 80

family, 16, 26, 155–182
  alcoholism in, 95, 96, 198–199,
    201–208

see also Adult Children of
    Alcoholics; Al-Anon;
    Alateen; children of
    alcoholics; nonalcoholic
    wives
fetal alcohol syndrome, 198
Firestone, Harvey, Sr., 51
Firestone, Leonard, 223
Firestone, Russell, 51
First American National Assembly,
    60
First Century Christian Fellowship,
    58–59
  see also Oxford Group
First Steps (Al-Anon's official
    history), 160–161
"flushing reaction," 96, 201
Ford, Betty, 25–27, 129, 223
  and Betty Ford Center, 25–26,
    94, 219, 222
Ford, Gerald, 26, 27
Ford, Mike, 26
Ford, Steve, 26
For Sinners Only (Russell), 60
Fosdick, Harry Emerson, 73
Founders' Day weekends, 22,
    146–148
Fox, Ruth, 184–185, 242–246
freestanding rehabilitation centers,
    218, 222–223
Freud, Sigmund, 250

Gallup poll, 156
Gandhi, Mohandas K., 131
Geller, Anne, 126–127
General Service Conference, 103,
    148
General Services Office (GSO),
    101–108
genetic predisposition to alcoholism,
    95–96, 199, 201–208
  adoption and, 204–206
  twin studies and, 199, 204
Germany, Nazi, 67
Gilmore, Margaret, 252

Gitlow, Stanley, 108
Glass, Carol, 150
Golden Anniversary International
    Convention (1985), 87–88,
    93
Goodwin, Donald, 199–200, 202,
    205–207
Gorbachev, Mikhail S., 92
Grapevine, see A.A. Grapevine
Gravitz, Herbert, 177
Great Britain, A.A. in, 92, 247–248
Greeks, ancient, drinking as viewed
    by, 185, 198–199
Griffith, Emily, 39
Grimm, Gordon, 143–145
Guatemala, A.A. in, 92
"guidance," Oxford Group's use
    of, 53
guilt, disease concept and, 195–
    196, 197

Hayward, Susan, 91
Hazelden Educational Materials
    Press, 273
Hazelden rehabilitation center,
    143–145, 148, 218–220
    cost of, 222
    staff-patient ratio at, 223
Health Communications, Inc., 273
health insurance coverage, 196
Heatter, Gabriel, 74–75
heavy drinking, alcoholism vs., 39,
    206, 263
Helena, Mont., A.A. meetings in,
    249
Helen W. (Bill Wilson's mistress),
    84
Helling, Mrs. Ethelred (Sister
    Francis), 28
Herman, Patricia, 241
High Watch Farm, 27–28
Hispanics, in A.A., 18, 24–25, 91–
    92, 96, 104
Hitler, Adolf, 67
Hock, Ruth, 69, 76

homosexuality, 36, 98–99,
    175–176
honesty:
    importance of, 16, 18, 26, 126
    Oxford Group and, 44, 45, 59,
    66
Honor Dealers, 69, 76
Hoover, Herbert, 190
hormones, alcohol and, 198, 203
hospitals:
    alcoholics refused admittance by,
    21, 218
    see also specific hospitals
Hound of Heaven, The
    (Thompson), 240
house parties, of Oxford Group,
    59–60, 65–66
Houston, Tex., A.A. in, 97
Huss, Magnus, 187
Huxley, Aldous, 108

Ignatia, Sister, 107–108
I'll Cry Tomorrow (Roth), 91
I'll Quit Tomorrow (Johnson), 223
Inquiry into the Effects of Ardent
    Spirits on the Human Mind
    and Body, An (Rush), 57,
    187–188
insanity, alcoholism confused with,
    31, 218
insurance:
    health, 196
    life, 221
Intergroups, 22–24
International A.A. Convention
    (1970), 85
"internationalists," in A.A., 107
Intervention (Johnson), 223
intervention technique, 129, 223
"intoxicate," etymology of, 110
Irish Americans, 95, 201
Irvine, University of California at,
    195
Is Alcoholism Hereditary?
    (Goodwin), 199

Islam, 185
"I Was a Drug-Hype Junkie"
    (Weisman), 208

Jackson, Charles R., 91
Jackson, Joan K., 104–105
JACS (Jewish Alcoholics, Chem-
    ically Dependent Persons and
    Significant Others)
    Foundation, 96, 149–150
Jaffrey, N. H., 221
James, William, 60–61, 142–143
Jellinek, Elvin Morton (E. M.), 185,
    190–192, 196–197, 198,
    220
Jews, 200
    in A.A., 96, 98, 149–150, 186
    historical alcohol use among, 186
job rotation, 104
Johnson, Vernon, 129, 223
Johnson Institute, 223, 273
Jolliffe, Norman, 190
Journal of the American Medical
    Association, 73, 77

Katzander, Shirley, 252
Kemper, James S., Jr., 221
Kennedy, Foster, 77
Kennedy, John F., 85
Kent, Conn., A.A. in, 27–28
Kress, Samuel H., 77
Kroc, Joan, 223
Krock, Arthur, 85

labor unions, 222
Landers, Ann, 162–163, 259
Lasker Award, 83, 90–91
Laurie, Piper, 91
leadership, of A.A., 83–85, 100–
    103, 104–105
Lemmon, Jack, 91
Lender, Mark, 187, 188, 189
Levey, Rob, 235
Levey, Stanley, 227, 228, 232, 242,
    250, 252

Liberty, 75–76
life insurance, 221
Lincoln, Abraham, 57–58
Living with an Alcoholic (Al-Anon
    Family Groups), 163, 172
Lois Remembers (Wilson), 157–158
London, A.A. meeting in, 247–248
"loners," in A.A., 107
Loners-Internationalists Meeting,
    107
Long Beach Naval Hospital, 26–27
Lord's Prayer, 148–149
Lost Weekend (Jackson), 91
Lost Weekend (movie), 91
love:
    A.A. and, 37, 131, 143–144
    Adult Children of Alcoholics and,
        177–178
    enablers and, 157
    Oxford Group and, 44, 45, 59,
        66
LSD, Wilson's use of, 36, 45, 140
Lutheranism, 142–143

McElrath, Damian, 126
Manders, Dennis, 84, 100–101
Mann, Marty, 28, 82, 90, 135–137,
    191, 220, 262–265
Mann, William Henry, 135–136
Manual on Alcoholism (AMA), 260,
    267
Marin County, Calif., A.A. meetings
    in, 249
Martin, James Kirby, 187, 188, 189
Maryland, A.A. problems in, 99
Marx, Karl, 67
Massachusetts, alcoholism treatment
    in, 224–225
Mather, Increase, 187
Maxwell, Milton A., 148
    A.A. Experience of, 120–123
medical profession:
    A.A. as viewed by, 73, 77, 91
    alcoholism concealed by, 52

medical training, alcoholism and, 193–195
medication, 212–213
meetings, A.A., 17–27, 87–89, 109–126
author at, 230, 237–239, 245–249
closed, 114, 122–123
collections at, 117
discussion period at, 117–119, 123
diversity of, 246–247
first, 120–123
humor and fun at, 18, 19, 25, 87, 113
"keeping down with the Joneses" attitude at, 124–125
length of, 109–110
open, 122–123
Preamble to, 72, 107, 115
public image of, 221
required number of, 95, 133–134
rewards at, 125
round-robin, 114
shopping around for, 123–124
speaker arrangements for, 116
tapes of, 19–20
typical, described, 114–120
see also specific towns and sites
meetings, Al-Anon, 160–161, 164–171, 175–176
meetings, of Adult Children of Alcoholics, 177–179
Menninger, Karl, 108
mentors, see sponsors
Mesopotamians, alcohol records of, 185
Mexico, A.A. members in, 18, 24–25, 92
Milland, Ray, 91
Miller, J. P., 91
Ministry of High Watch, 28
Montreal, Canada, A.A. International Convention in, 87–88, 93

"Moral and Physical Thermometer, A" (Rush), 187–188
Moral Re-Armament (MRA), 58, 67
see also Oxford Group
Mount Peace Cemetery, 21, 83

Nairobi, Kenya, A.A. meetings in, 248
Nation, 105
National Alcoholism Test, 258
National Association for Children of Alcoholics (NACOA), 176–177, 181, 273
National Association of Addiction Treatment Providers, 274
National Clearinghouse for Alcohol Information, 273
National Council on Alcoholism (formerly National Committee for Education on Alcoholism), 82, 90, 181, 256–258, 273
National Institute on Alcohol Abuse and Alcoholism (NIAAA), 177, 181, 186, 188–189, 273
alcohol abuse statistics of, 208–209
Rand Reports and, 192
rehab study by, 220
National Rubber Machinery Company, 46
Nazi Germany, 67
Neal, Kathleen, 224–225
New Primer on Alcoholism, A (Mann), 135, 262–265
New Republic, 208
New York City:
A.A. headquarters in, 76, 81, 82, 84, 93, 101–107
A.A. meetings in, 89, 113–114, 247, 248–249
Intergroup in, 22–24
Oxford Group in, 59, 65–66

New York Hospital, Payne Whitney
    Psychiatric Clinic of,
    251–252
*New York Times*, 37, 73, 85, 87
*New York World-Telegram*, 66–67
NIAAA, *see* National Institute on
    Alcohol Abuse and Alco-
    holism
Niebuhr, Reinhold, 108, 148
Nocona, Tex., A.A. meetings in,
    20–21
nonalcoholic wives, 70–71, 84, 86,
    88
  A.A. role of, 62–63
  pre–Al-Anon life of, 156–159
  resentment of, 64–65, 216
  surrenders as viewed by, 63
Norris, John, 84
Norwich University, 39

O'Brien, Robert, 186, 222
obsession, as enabler's illness,
    156–157
O'Connor, Sean, 207
Oliver-Diaz, Philip, 182
*One Day at a Time in Al-Anon*
    (ODAT), 171, 172–173
Orientals, drinking and, 96, 200,
    201
"Over Thirty" groups, 94
Oxford Group, 30–32, 44–46,
    51–53, 56–67
  alcoholics' secession from, 66
  Dr. Bob's view of, 51–52
  founding of, 58–59
  "Four Absolutes" of, 45
  "guided" as used by, 53
  house parties of, 59–60, 65–66
  international controversy of,
    66–67
  naming of, 59
  nondenominational character
    of, 59
  other names for, 58
  popular books on, 60

principles of, 44, 45–46, 56, 58,
    59, 66
  publicity sought by, 66–67
  recruitment techniques of, 59–60
  surrenders in, 63

Pandina, Robert J., 193
paraldehyde, 62
Payne Whitney Psychiatric Clinic,
    251–252
Persia, ancient, 185
Peterborough, N.H., 89, 249
pink-cloud experience, 133
Plum, Fred, 231–232, 233
Plutarch, 199
Poland, A.A. in, 93
pregnancy, drinking and, 198
prisons:
  A.A. members in, 106–107
  alcoholics placed in, 224–225
problem drinking, alcoholism vs.,
    16, 255
professions, alcoholism and,
    200–201
Prohibition, 42–43, 49, 67, 136,
    190
psychological problems, alcoholism
    and, 198
psychotherapy:
  A.A. members' views of, 111,
    136–137
  of Wilson, 80
public education, 82, 90, 197–198
publishing operations:
  of A.A., 102
  of Al-Anon, 171–173
  *see also specific books and
    pamphlets*
*Purposes and Suggestions for Al-
    Anon Family Groups*
    (Bingham and Wilson), 160
Pursch, Joseph A., 26, 134

Rabinowitz, Renah, 96, 149–150
Rancho Mirage, Calif., A.A. in, 25–
    27, 94

Rand Corporation of California, 192
Rand Report (1976), 192
Rand Report (1980), 192
recovery:
  disease concept and, 197
  obstacles to, 213
  timetable for, 134
rehabilitation centers, 210–225
  A.A.'s impact on, 220
  case study of, 210–218
  cost of, 222
  freestanding, 218, 222–223
  funding of, 223
  number of, 218
  treatment of alcoholics prior to, 218
  *see also specific centers*
religion:
  A.A. role of, 17, 19, 55, 69–70, 81, 99–100, 138–151
  abstinence and, 189
  agnostics and atheists and, 145–146, 148
  alcohol's role in, 186
  Dr. Bob's views on, 47, 140–141
  Oxford Group and, 30, 44, 45, 51–52, 58–59
  psychology of, 61
  spirituality vs., 143–146
  Twelve Steps and, 69–70, 139, 149–151
  Wilson's experience with, 31, 139–142
  *see also* Roman Catholicism
Remick, Lee, 91
responsibility, disease concept and, 196–197
rewards, 125
Richardson, Willard, 67–68, 77
Ripley, Anne Robinson, *see* Smith, Anne Robinson Ripley
Robards, Jason, 93
Robertson, Cliff, 91
Robertson, Nan (author), 226–253

at A.A. meetings, 230, 237–239, 246–249
Antabuse used by, 242–244
compulsion to drink experienced by, 239, 241–244
depression of, 250–251
drinking of, 226–234
final sobering up of, 15–17, 233–237
in Fox group, 242–247
at Intergroup, 22–24
toxic shock syndrome of, 252–253
Rockefeller, John D., Jr., 67–68, 76–78
Rockefeller, Nelson, 77–78
Roman Catholicism, 45, 79, 80, 126
Rome, ancient, drunkenness as viewed in, 185
Roosevelt, Franklin Delano, 35, 43
Rose, Maureen, 225
Rosenthal, Abe, 233
Roth, Lillian, 91
Rush, Benjamin, 57, 187–188, 189, 191, 198
Rush Medical College, 48
Russell, Arthur James, 60
Rutgers Center of Alcohol Studies, 274
Rutgers University, 192

St. Anthony Hospital, 252–253
St. Johnsbury, Vt., 46–47
St. Johnsbury Academy, 47
St. Thomas's Hospital, 37
*Saturday Evening Post*, 76, 90, 146, 162
Schneider, Max, 193–195
Schuckit, Marc, 202–203, 204
Schwarzlose, John T., 94, 210
Scott, Albert, 68, 77–78
Seiberling, Dorothy, 29, 33, 52–53, 63
Seiberling, Frank A., 32

Seiberling, Henrietta (Henri), 20,
31–34, 51–55
background of, 31–32
in Oxford Group, 31–32, 51–53
Wilson-Smith meeting and, 21,
32–34, 52–53
Seiberling, J. Frederick, 32, 52
Seixas, Judith, 177
self-knowledge, 125–127
Seneca, 185, 198
Serenity Prayer, 93, 119, 148–149,
171, 245
service, A.A. and, 37, 131–132,
143–145
sex, 133, 172
Sheen, Fulton J., 80
Shoemaker, Rev. Samuel, 59
Shoffstall, Veronica A., 168
Silkworth, William Duncan, 43–46,
58, 65
"Doctor's Opinion" by, 71
Smith, Anne Robinson Ripley, 20,
21, 32, 34, 54
alcoholics aided by, 158–159
death of, 83, 159
husband's drinking and, 49–52
Smith, Robert Holbrook (Dr. Bob),
17, 18, 46–55
background of, 46–48
death of, 20, 21, 36, 37, 83
drinking of, 32, 47–54
effectiveness of, 61–63, 66, 68
financial problems of, 52
marriage of, 47, 48
in Oxford Group, 51–53, 58,
61–65
personality of, 36–37
phobias of, 49
physical appearance of, 33, 35,
47–48, 62
religion as viewed by, 47, 140
speeches of, 37
treatment methods of, 62–63
Wilson compared with, 33–35,
49, 50, 66

Wilson's first meeting with, 18,
20, 21, 32–35, 46
Smith, Robert Holbrook (Young
Bob), 20–21, 34, 50, 63–64
on Eddie R., 54–55
on father's effectiveness, 61
Smith, Suzanne, 50, 52–53, 63, 64
Smithers, J. Brinkley, 223
Smithers Alcoholism Center, 16–17,
127, 211–219, 222, 233–
237, 246
sobriety:
as beginning, 173–174
faith and, 140
newcomers' fears about, 132–133
Society of Washington
(Washingtonians), 57–58,
189
Soviet Union, A.A. in, 92–93
spirituality:
Grimm's views on, 143–145
Maxwell's views on, 148
sponsors (mentors), 82, 123, 180–
181, 244–245
Al-Anon, 169
staffers (coordinators), 104–107
Stanford Research group, 222
Stepping Stones, 79–80, 84, 160,
161
Stepping Stones Foundation, 84
stock market crash (1929), 42
stress, reduction of, 134
Strong, Dorothy Wilson, 39, 44
Strong, Leonard, 44, 67, 68
suicide, 54, 66, 110, 250–251
surrenders, 58, 63, 142–143

Tabakoff, Boris, 201–202
"Take-It-Or-Leave-It Club," 61
tape services, 19–20
teenagers:
alcohol abuse by, 209
see also Alateen
telephone therapy, 118

temperance movements, 57–58, 99,
120, 188
ancient, 186
decline of disease concept and,
189–190
Jellinek's views compared with,
191
see also Prohibition
temporal lobe seizures, 140
temptation, avoiding, 117–119
Thompson, Charles, 228–229, 230
Thompson, Francis, 240
Tiebout, Harry, 80, 136–137
tolerance, 112–113
Towns, Charles, 67
Charles B. Towns Hospital, 43–44,
139–140
toxic psychosis, 45
toxic shock syndrome, 252–253
tranquilizers, 213
Tunks, Walter, 31
Twelve Concepts for World Service
(Wilson), 104
Twelve-Stepper, defined, 23
Twelve-Stepping, Twelfth-Step call,
129–133
Twelve Steps, 38, 80, 82, 83, 89,
102, 129–133, 192–193,
245
A.A. Family Groups and Auxiliaries and, 159–160
Al-Anon and, 166, 169
as antiscience, 193
Judaism and, 149–150
religion and, 69–70, 139,
149–151
text of, 69–70
Twelve Traditions, 18, 38, 82–84,
89, 100–102
Twenty-fourth Street Clubhouse,
79, 161
twin studies, 199, 204

Ulpian, 185
unanimity idea, 104

"Understanding Heart, The" (TV
show), 162
Union Club dinner, 77–78
United States, statistics on alcohol
consumption in, 188–189
unselfishness, Oxford Group and,
44, 45–46, 59, 66

Varieties of Religious Experience,
The (James), 60–61,
142–143

Washingtonians, 57–58, 189
Washington University, 202, 205
Watson, Thomas J., 77
Weekes, Frances, 80
Wegscheider-Cruse, Sharon, 177
Weisman, Adam Paul, 208
We the People (radio program),
74–75
Whitman, Joan, 234
Wholey, Dennis, 93
Wilder, Billy, 91
Wilder, Thornton, 89
Williams, Clarace, 21, 63
Williams, T. Henry, 21, 63
Willmar State Hospital, 144, 218,
219
Wilson, Bill, 17, 29–46, 53–55,
57–61, 64–85, 100–101,
191
background of, 35–36, 38–40
Big Book of, see Alcoholics
Anonymous
as businessman, 30, 41–42,
45–46, 67, 69
death of, 38, 40, 85, 104
depressions of, 36, 39, 44, 79, 80
Dr. Bob compared with, 33–35,
49, 50, 66
Dr. Bob's first meeting with, 18,
20, 21, 32–35, 46
drinking of, 29–31, 39–46
evangelism of, 45–46
guilt of, 36, 79, 84

Wilson, Bill *(cont.)*
  hallucinations of, 31–32, 42,
    44–45
  Hank B.'s rupture with, 76
  hard years of (1939–1940),
    75–78
  hypochondria of, 79
  as idea man, 35–36, 104,
    105–106
  marriage of, 36, 40–41
  Oxford Group and, 30–32, 44–
    46, 58, 59–60, 65–66
  personality of, 35–37, 38–39,
    40–41, 42, 43
  physical appearance of, 33, 35,
    39
  psychotherapy of, 80
  rejections suffered by, 76–78
  religious exaltation of, 31, 44–
    45, 139–142
  Roman Catholicism and, 45, 79,
    80
  as saint, 21, 84
  scandalous behavior of, 36, 45,
    84
  Seiberling and, 21, 31–34, 53
  sobering-up attempts of, 29–30,
    43–46, 60–61
  sphere of influence of, 37–38
  on Twelfth-Step call, 128–131
  womanizing of, 36, 40, 84
Wilson, Dorothy, *see* Strong,
    Dorothy Wilson
Wilson, Emily Griffith, 39, 40
Wilson, Gilman, 38–39, 40
Wilson, Lois Burnham, 17–18, 30,
    36, 69, 78–80
  in Akron, 64
  Al-Anon and, 157, 160–162, 176
  autobiography of, 157–158
  control compulsion of, 157
  diary of, 65

  husband's drinking and, 30, 41–
    44, 64–65
  "momism" of, 40, 65, 174
  pregnancies of, 41
  resentment of, 65, 70–71, 158,
    174
  supportiveness and devotion of,
    30, 36, 40, 42, 46, 65
  "To Wives" and, 70–71
  wealth of, 83–84
Wing, Nell, 81
withdrawal, medical supervision of,
    213
Wit's End, 80
wives, nonalcoholic, *see*
    nonalcoholic wives
Woititz, Janet, 177
women:
  in Al-Anon, 156, 160–171,
    174–176
  in alcoholism research studies,
    206, 207–208
  *see also* nonalcoholic wives
women alcoholics:
  in A.A., 72, 81–82, 87, 94,
    135–136
  A.A. admission denied to, 37, 62,
    158
Wood, John, 68
World Service Office, Al-Anon, 163,
    165, 172
World War I, 40, 46
World War II, 67
*Wo [sic] to Drunkards* (Mather),
    187

Yale School of Alcohol Studies, 82,
    90, 190, 191, 220
  transferred to Rutgers, 192
Youcha, Geraldine, 177
Young, Loretta, 162